KIERKEGAARD

THE DIFFICULTY OF BEING CHRISTIAN

Texts Edited and Introduced

by

JACQUES COLETTE, O.P.

ENGLISH VERSION BY

RALPH M. McINERNY

AND

LEO TURCOTTE

KIERKEGAARD

THE DIFFICULTY OF BEING CHRISTIAN

UNIVERSITY OF NOTRE DAME PRESS

NOTRE DAME   LONDON

Copyright © 1968 by
University of Notre Dame Press
Notre Dame, Indiana 46556

Original French title:
Kierkegaard et la Difficulte d'Etre Chretien
First published by Éditions du Cerf, Paris, 1964

Library of Congress Catalog Card Number: 68–17063
Manufactured in the United States of America

PREFACE TO THE ENGLISH EDITION

The invention of printing, it has become clear, is a mixed blessing and the time has surely arrived when one must think twice before taking, however secondary, a hand in visiting yet another book upon the jaded reader. Is there any real need for the present volume which consists of selections from the works and papers of Søren Kierkegaard?

There would seem to be no need to bring Kierkegaard to the attention of the American reader. Not only have most of his works but also his doctoral dissertation, *The Concept of Irony with Constant Reference to Socrates,* found their way into English. A marvelous five-volume English edition of selections from his journals and papers has begun to appear, which will complement, if it does not supplant, earlier one-volume efforts along the same line. Furthermore, and *mirabile dictu,* Kierkegaard scholarship is gaining a dizzying momentum, and the day is not far off when library shelves will groan under the burden of monographs, dissertations, and sweeping summaries devoted to the thought of this remarkable nineteenth-century Danish author. There is even a Søren Kierkegaard Society whose membership is international. Nor is knowledge of Kierkegaard confined to the specialist. It is the unusual liberal arts undergraduate who cannot place Kierkegaard, whether as the father of existentialism or the proponent of some odd notions in the philosophy of religion. In short, Kierkegaard is accessible in English, widely known and ever more increasingly discussed. Why then this book?

It would be simply Kierkegaardian to suggest that Kierkegaard is in danger of being so well understood that he is misunderstood. He has come to be regarded as relevant to so many topics that the single overriding question to which he addressed himself can be forgotten. His affinity with so many recent thinkers—Tillich, Barth, Heidegger, Camus have recently been joined by Wittgenstein—can obscure his peculiarity. It is not simply that we must constantly remind ourselves that Kierkegaard was from first to last a religious author—to forget that is to forfeit historical accuracy and to court misunderstanding of what he wrote—but we must be clear on the kind of religious thinker he was. Just as Kierkegaard cannot properly be called a philosopher, so too it is misleading to describe him as a theologian. He was a religious writer who posed ultimately but one question: what does it mean to be a Christian? It is the merit of Father Colette's presentation of Kierkegaard that we see both the centrality of that question and the mode in which an answer to it was sought.

There are some questions to which the appropriate response is not information, a verbal formulation, but an altered way of life. Kierkegaard wrote for readers who could answer the question, "What does it mean to be a Christian?" with a quick and catechetical reply, and he was not, of course, opposed to clarity and accuracy on the level of information. What troubled him was the misunderstanding which can go hand in hand with the understanding such information is. He did not consider the Christian revelation to be a matter of an alteration of theoretical thinking, of getting the answer straight, of having a sweeping and speculative vision of things—Christian revelation is an existence communication. One does not have to be erudite in order to lead a Christian life; here the natural difference between the intellectually gifted and ungifted is not of much importance, unless perhaps the intellectually gifted are more prone to misunderstanding than are the ungifted. For the gifted can appear to think—though of course they would never say this—that Christ came in order that men might become theologians. Not all of us have the time or talent to be theologians, but every man has time enough to be or to become a Christian—a lifetime, in fact.

Kierkegaard was himself a frighteningly gifted man whose intellectual powers were rivaled by those of his imagination and he had sensed in himself, and not merely by way of possibility, the myriad ways in which man can be deceived about Christianity. One of his recurring themes is the discrepancy between thought and action, between knowing and doing, between understanding and existing. In many cases there is no direct relevance of thought to action, but there are many cases where thought bears on doing or existence and must be considered to have been short-circuited if it does not lead to action. Thoughts about Christian revelation can fail to connect with a mode of existence; when such a failure takes place, correct thought of that revelation can never substitute for existing as a Christian. Kierkegaard became an author when he decided to pose the question, "What does it mean to be a Christian?" in such a way that his reader would find it difficult to misunderstand its import.

Nominal Christians—they who do not exist in Christian categories, though it is to those that they aspire—must exist somehow, whom Kierkegaard is out to catch where they live. Not where they think, abstractly, for he could easily reach agreement there, but where they exist. It is a tricky thing to pose, and without authority, a question which requires more than a thoughtful answer, and Kierkegaard's reflection on his task led him to views on communication as well as to the notion of spheres of existence. These spheres were presentations of how nominal Christians really live when they are not living as Christians. His views here are well known. The nominal Christian may live in aesthetic categories or in merely ethical categories; he may live in religious categories which are short of specifically Christian ones. It would be wrong, I think, to say that Kierkegaard provides a phenomenology of modes of life. That makes it sound as if all he did was offer glosses on the observation, as old as the Greeks and already adapted to Christian purposes, that men mistakenly seek happiness in pleasure or fame or riches or philosophy. It is easy to find compelling arguments that man cannot be made happy, achieve his specifically human perfection, in the pursuit of pleasure or fame or riches; the great difficulty with such arguments is that one can give assent while continuing to pursue pleasure or fame or riches as if these were indeed felicific.

I am not suggesting that Kierkegaard had hit on some device of human engineering which enabled him to achieve a more existential assent to general judgments about what does and what does not render a man happy. He was wary of abstract arguments, true, and wary because they seemed to him to invite misunderstanding. His own technique was such that he claimed only that it made misunderstanding more difficult. What he proposed to do was dramatically and dialectically to contrast aesthetic and ethical personages with the demands of the Christian message. As his authorship begins, it proceeds in two lines, one consisting of works which bear his name as author; the other consisting of works attributed to a variety of pseudonyms. The pseudonymous authors represent the aesthetic or ethical or a less than Christian religiousness; they are played off against *Edifying Discourses* which simultaneously appear under Kierkegaard's name. The result is intended to be, not an intellectual puzzle, a matter of figuring out where Kierkegaard himself really stands, but a Kierkegaardian hope as author and as author of the pseudonymous authors that his nominally Christian reader would come to see that this literature, like Christianity, calls him into question and seeks more than a disengaged response.

One of the disturbing notes in the current spate of studies on Kierkegaard is that his works are regarded as more grist for the scholarly mill as if interest in them were of a piece with interest in the writings of Aristotle, Aquinas, Kant, or Russell. The works are read to understand Kierkegaard's concept of truth or of existence or of faith or of other abstractions. There is no doubt that such studies can be made; there is no doubt that Kierkegaard makes contributions to an understanding of abstract topics. But what must be insisted on is that he does so only in passing, obliquely; that is not where his importance lies. It would be better if Kierkegaard were downgraded as philosopher and theologian, even as creative writer. He is none of those principally, but without risking much he may be considered to be first of all a spiritual writer. He is out to give such aid as one man can give another in living a Christian life. His authorship in its totality speaks in the disturbing way that spiritual writings do, something they share, *salva reverentia,* with the New Testament. Kierkegaard with his parables and personages is quite close to the Gospels but like John of the Cross, Henry Suso, and the Johannes Climacus whose name he borrowed for a pseudonym, he has an eye for the way to go, not to understand Christianity, but to exist as Christians. His notion of stages on life's way or spheres of existence has affinities with those ways of which the mystics speak. These affinities, when recognized, alert us to the fact that in Kierkegaard we are not confronted simply by a philosopher or theologian or an artist but rather with that type of writer whose presence is most felt in his elusive withdrawal when we are left alone before God, faced with the question not of what Christianity means but of what it means to the individual. When this happens it is not error in the sense of falsehood that is of immediate moment, but the consciousness of sin; it is not intellectual doubt but a felt anguish and gripping despair. Christian revelation may then seem to involve not merely difficulties for the philosophically trained mind but absurdity in the sense that all lived history finds it an affront and a threat. On this plane it is not abstract arguments which are decisive, but grace. Nor are anguish and dread, despair and felt absurdity terminal for faith, but love. How can this be shown? *Gustate et videte.* When the task of becoming a Christian is accorded proper place in existence and rescued from thought, whether philosophical or theological, as though by taking thought one could add one cubit to stature, then a truer philosophy and theology, rooted in a mode of life, may perhaps arise. In an older terminology, we might say that Kierkegaard is reminding us that without *fides qua creditur* there is no *fides quae creditur*. No theology or Scripture scholarship can produce what they presuppose. It is a simple point, easy to understand but, alas, far easier to misunderstand. Hence Kierkegaard's single major message: it is difficult to *be* a Christian. It is so easy to misunderstand the task and think that it consists of reconciling faith and science, faith and the muddle of Scripture scholarship, faith and the latest philosophical fad. Is it really surprising to hear that all those efforts are secondary, that none is the one thing needful?

How disconcerting that clarity about such confusion only brings us to the starting point.

RALPH MCINERNY

Notre Dame
March, 1968

EDITOR'S FOREWORD

We have not tried to give an expose of the totality of Kierkegaard's thought in our introduction, but have restricted ourselves to indicating what is meant by "Christian becoming." Thus we have left aside the discussion of properly philosophical and theological questions. In the reader's guide, on page 5 of this book, will be found references useful for passing judgment on Kierkegaard, particularly from the point of view of Catholic theology.

As the title of the present collection suggests, we have endeavored to present, in Kierkegaard, a believer who provides us with an introduction to "Christian becoming," but an introduction "which in effect seeks to make the transition more difficult than we had thought it, but not more difficult than it really is." "Objectively, it is no more difficult to understand what Christianity is than to understand Islamism or any other historical fact, except insofar as Christianity is not simply an historical fact; the difficulty is to become a Christian, because every Christian is one only when nailed to the paradox of having founded his eternal happiness on a relation to an historical fact."

Better than any remarks of ours, the plan of these extracts shows the stages of an existential itinerary following in the steps of Kierkegaard: from ignorance to listening to the Word which saves; from anguish to love. If Kierkegaard, this believer without authority in the Church, has not himself been able to arrive at the goal, we shall not throw the first stone. His merit is not thereby lessened, for he has reminded us that the way is long when one wishes to follow a knight of faith, the venerable father Abraham, to the land of Moriah.

CONTENTS

INTRODUCTION

INTRODUCTION

Occasional theologian, a philosopher despite himself, Kierkegaard was above all a living man involved with the visible and obsessed by concern with his eternal happiness. Unmistakably marked by his epoch and country—the Danish Lutheranism of the first half of the nineteenth century—his message is still of interest today because he poses the insistent question which concerns existence.

His name was unknown beyond the borders of Denmark until a half century after his death. Today his writings are translated into the majority of European languages as well as into Japanese—a belated renown for one conscious of being destined to live "in the provincial hole,"[1] the Copenhagen of his day. Kierkegaard has been read for fifty years by theologians, philosophers, and those who do not think it futile to reflect on the mystery of human destiny. For one with ears to hear, his voice has the resonance of a religious thinker who had no other concern than to apply all the resources of his spirit, all his knowledge of the human heart, to meditation on a single theme: Christian becoming.

If Kierkegaard seems to take the thoughts of philosophers seriously this is because from the outset he was convinced that the Christian answer could manifest the importance of the philosophical *question* concerning being and truth, the importance of that properly human process which poses

[1] *Journal,* X 3 A 4.

3

questions and arrives at the astonishing realization of the inadequacy of all coherent and theoretical answers when set side by side with the enigma which is God's creation of a free being. That enigma erects before man a cross that philosophy cannot bear but on which it can only remain suspended.

It would be convenient to distinguish in Kierkegaard the philosopher from the theologian, seeing in the former the ancestor of existentialism and in the latter the father of dialectical theology. But such a simplification must be rejected if one wants to remain faithful to the historical Kierkegaard whose thought was one with his life.[2]

---

[2] We will not dwell in this introduction on the events of Kierkegaard's life but simply call attention to the chronology, the reader's guide, and to the first grouping of selected texts.

A READER'S GUIDE
TO KIERKEGAARD

The best introduction to Kierkegaard for the English reader is James Collins, *The Mind of Kierkegaard* (Chicago: Henry Regnery, 1953), now in paperback as a Gateway Edition. Other general presentations of great value are Hermann Diem, *An Introduction to Kierkegaard* (Richmond: John Knox Press, 1966); Regis Jolivet, *Introduction to Kierkegaard* (New York: Dutton, 1951); Theodor Haecker, *Søren Kierkegaard* (New York: Oxford University Press, 1937); David Swenson, *Something About Kierkegaard* (Minneapolis: Augsburg, 1949).

Because of the close relationship of Kierkegaard's life and literature, the following biographical materials are important: Walter Lowrie, *Kierkegaard* (New York: Oxford University Press, 1938) and *A Short Life of Kierkegaard* (Princeton, 1942); Johannes Hohlenberg, *Søren Kierkegaard* (New York: Pantheon, 1954); H. J. Blackham, *Søren Kierkegaard* (London: Routledge and Kegan Paul, 1952); M. Channing-Pearce, *Søren Kierkegaard* (New York: Devin-Adair, 1947); Peter Rohde, *Søren Kierkegaard* (New York: Humanities Press, 1963). Recollections of Kierkegaard's contemporaries have been translated by T. H. Croxall, *Glimpses and Impressions of Kierkegaard* (London: James Nisbet, 1959).

Works of particular interest to readers of this selection are Edward Geismar, *Lectures on the Religious Thought*

5

of Kierkegaard (Minneapolis: Augsburg, 1937); Reidar Thomte, *Kierkegaard's Philosophy of Religion* (Princeton, 1948); Louis Dupre, *Kierkegaard as Theologian* (New York: Sheed and Ward, 1963); J. Heywood Thomas, *Subjectivity and Paradox* (New York: Macmillan, 1957); Carl Michalson, *The Witness of Kierkegaard* (New York: Association Press, 1960); Jaroslav Pelikan, *From Luther to Kierkegaard* (St. Louis: Concordia, 1950); H. Roos, *Kierkegaard and Catholicism* (Westminster, Maryland: Newman Press, 1954). Essays by many hands are found in *A Kierkegaard Critique,* edited by Howard Johnson and Nils Thulstrup (New York: Harper, 1962).

A work of great usefulness is J. Himmelstrup, *Søren Kierkegaard: International Bibliografi* (Copenhagen: Arnold Busck, 1962).

THE WORKS OF KIERKEGAARD

Besides his published work, Kierkegaard left a tremendous number of journals and papers. Arranged under three main divisions—journals, sketches of writing projects, and notes on his reading—this material was brought together in twenty volumes, *Søren Kierkegaards Papirer,* edited by Heiberg, Kuhr, and Torsting (Copenhagen, 1909–1948). Alexander Dru published his one volume *Selection from the Journals of Kierkegaard* (London: Oxford University Press, 1938); Ronald Gregor Smith brought out *The Last Years* (London: Collins, 1965). There has now begun to appear a five volume English presentation of materials drawn from the *Papirer,* arranged according to topics with the entries under each topic set down in the chronological order of their composition. Thus far only one volume has appeared: *Søren Kierkegaard's Journals and Papers,* Volume 1, A-E, edited and translated by Howard V. Hong and Edna H. Hong, assisted by Gregor Malantschuk (Bloomington: Indiana

University Press, 1967). It is difficult to overestimate the salutary effect this five volume work will have on Kierkegaard studies. The first volume contains a general bibliography; moreover, in the notes accompanying each section, there are often special bibliographies. As a source of primary material and as a guide to secondary literature, this work will have no parallel in English. Niels Thulstrup has brought together correspondence and documents in *Breve og Aksykker Vedrørende Søren Kierkegaard* (Copenhagen: Munksgaard, 1953–54).

A new Danish edition of the published works of Kierkegaard is *Samlede Vaerker* (edited by Drachman, Heiberg, Lange and, for this new edition, Peter Rohde), 20 volumes (Copenhagen: Glydendal, 1963–64). A new Danish edition of Kierkegaard's papers is being published: *Søren Kierkegaards Papirer,* edited by Niels Thulstrup (Copenhagen: Gyldendal, 1968–). Most of Kierkegaard's works have been translated into English.

The Concept of Irony, trans. by Lee Capel (New York: Harper and Row, 1963). Kierkegaard's dissertation.

Either/Or. The earlier Swenson-Lowrie translation has been improved by Howard Johnson (New York: Doubleday, 1959, 2 volumes, paperback).

Johannes Climacus or De omnibus dubitandum est, translated by T. H. Croxall (London: Black, 1958).

Edifying Discourses, I–IV, translated by David F. Swenson and Lilian Marvin Swenson (Minneapolis: Augsburg, 1943–46).

Fear and Trembling and *The Sickness Unto Death,* translated by Walter Lowrie (New York: Doubleday-Anchor, 1954).

Repetition, translated by Walter Lowrie (Princeton: Princeton University Press, 1941).

Philosophical Fragments, a revision of the David Swenson translation by Howard V. Hong (Princeton: Princeton University Press, 1962).

The Concept of Dread, translated by Walter Lowie, second edition (Princeton: Princeton University Press, 1957).

Thoughts on Crucial Situations in Human Life, translated by David Swenson and Lilian Marvin Swenson (Minneapolis: Augsburg, 1941).

Stages on Life's Way, translated by Walter Lowrie (Princeton: Princeton University Press, 1940).

Concluding Unscientific Postscript, translated by David Swenson and Walter Lowrie (Princeton: Princeton University Press, 1944).

The Present Age (including two treatises by H.H.), translated by Walter Lowrie (New York: Oxford University Press, 1940).

On Authority and Revelation: The Book on Adler, translated by Walter Lowrie (Princeton: Princeton University Press, 1955).

Purity of Heart, translated by Douglas Steere, second edition (New York; Harper Torchbooks, 1948).

The Gospel of Suffering and *The Lilies of the Field,* translated by David Swenson and Lillian Marvin Swenson (Minneapolis: Augsburg, 1948).

Works of Love, translated by Howard and Edna Hong (New York: Harper and Row, 1962).

Christian Discourses, including *The Lilies of the Field and the Birds of the Air* and *Three Discourses at the Communion on Fridays,* translated by Walter Lowrie (New York: Oxford University Press, 1940).

The Crisis in the Life of an Actress, translated by Stephen Crites (New York: Harper and Row, 1966).

The Point of View, translated by Walter Lowrie (New York: Oxford University Press, 1939).

Training in Christianity, translated by Walter Lowrie (New York: Oxford University Press, 1941).

For Self-Examination, translated by Edna and Howard Hong (Minneapolis: Augsburg, 1940).

Judge For Yourselves, including *For Self-Examination,*

Two Discourses at the Communion on Fridays and *The Unchangeableness of God,* translated by Walter Lowrie (Princeton: Princeton University Press, 1944).

Attack Upon Christendom, translated by Walter Lowrie (Princeton: Princeton University Press, 1946).

Meditations from Kierkegaard, translated by T. H. Croxall (Philadelphia: Westminster Press, 1955).

The Prayers of Kierkegaard, translated by Perry D. LeFevre (Chicago: University of Chicago Press, 1956).

I   A Spy in the Service of the Most High

1. A SIMPLE BELIEVER, NEITHER PREACHER NOR TEACHER

One among many ancient texts, the Bible is for the believer endowed with a quality which makes this venerable document of antiquity more than a venerable document: this book has authority. The Word of God announced by the apostle requires from the listener an attitude of receptivity made up of silence and obedience. Its message does not convey a vision of the world or of man but a vision of God: that is why the qualities demanded of one who would listen to the Word of God are qualities of openness and renunciation of every cultural prejudice whether political or social. In its irreducible novelty, the Christian message is radically different from the many conceptions of life (*lebensanschauung*) that men have been and will be able to invent. Silence—not verbal silence, but the absence of all ideological construction—and unconditional obedience, are for Kierkegaard, the fundamental dispositions demanded of him who would be a hearer of the apostolic preaching. It is, moreover, the lesson given us by the lilies of the field and the birds of the air.

Kierkegaard never considered himself to be an apostle or a prophet.[3] The correct expression of his own thought,

---

[3] We analyzed the Kierkegaardian theory of communication and of preaching in our introduction to *Discours édifiants* (Paris: Desclée de Brouwer, 1962), pp. 36–43.

which proposed above all to indicate the need for each man to withdraw into himself in order to decide to act, required him to avoid the direct proclamation of the Word which belongs to the Church. "To preach is to have recourse to authority."[4] Kierkegaard was neither preacher nor pastor. Nothing could better convince us of this than the following wonderful parable taken from *The Instant*.

A DARK CLOUD ON THE HORIZON

Imagine a great ship, larger than any of today's liners, one that can carry a thousand passengers and on which, of course, all is arranged on a vast scale of ease, comfort, and luxury. It is near evening. In the salon there is entertainment. Beneath the sumptuous lighting, a concert is being heard. There is, in a word, nothing but joy, leisure, and enjoyment, and the sounds of care-free gaiety are carried on the evening air.

On the bridge the captain stands. Beside him, the second officer takes his glass from his eye and hands it to the captain who says, "It's not necessary. I can see it well, that little cloud on the horizon. It will be a terrible night."

Then, with the noble and resolute calm of the experienced seaman, he gives his orders. "Everything must be in readiness for tonight. I myself will take command."

He goes into his cabin where there are few books. There is, however, a Bible. He opens it—strange!—at this passage: "This very night your soul will be demanded of you." Strange indeed!

Having collected himself in prayer and meditation, he dresses for the evening service; again, disposed and on the job, he is a seaman of much experience.

But in the salon there is entertainment; one hears music

[4] Cf. "The Genius and the Apostle," included in *The Present Age*.

and songs, conversation, bustle, the sound of tableware, the pop of champagne corks. They drink to the health of the captain. The night will be terrible. Perhaps this very night your soul will be demanded of you.

A terrible scene? Yet I know one more terrible still. The situation is the same, but there is another captain. In the salon there is entertainment and the gayest of all is the captain. A dark cloud on the horizon, the night will be terrible, but no one sees the cloud nor suspects what it portends. No, that would not be most terrible. No, there is someone who sees the cloud and knows what it portends, but he is not in command; he is in charge of nothing. The one thing he can do he does; namely, ask the captain to come up on the bridge, if only for a moment. The latter makes him wait, finally arrives, but is in no mood to listen and quickly returns to the salon to share in the noisy disordered joy of the passengers who in the general heartiness drink to his health while he warmly responds.

In his anxiety the poor passenger decides to disturb the captain once more; but this time the captain is not even polite with him. Nevertheless, the dark cloud is still on the horizon. The night will be terrible.

Isn't that more terrible? It is terrible to think of those thousand carefree passengers, terrible to think the captain alone knows what is coming, and the essential thing is that he knows. But more terrible, the only one to know the imminent peril is—a passenger.

That from a Christian point of view there is a storm cloud on the horizon, portent of an imminent and terrible tempest, I have known. But, alas, I have been, and am, only a passenger.[5]

This passenger was not an apostle. "Between God and man there is an essential and eternal qualitative difference. The paradoxical religious relation, which, properly speak-

---

[5] From the *Journal* of 1855.

ing, is not an object of thought but only of faith, appears when God imposes on a particular man a divine authority . . . He who is thus 'called' is not, in his relation to the other, in a relation of man to man; his relation to the other is not based on a quantitative difference (as is the case with the genius or the exceptionally endowed man). No, his relation is paradoxical because it is marked by a specific quality . . . The man thus 'called' is, because of this specific paradoxical quality (divine authority), different from all other men . . . apostolic designation belongs to the sphere of transcendence, to the sphere of the paradoxically religious."[6]

What objective then does Kierkegaard seek in his numerous publications which treat of Christianity? What was the message of this disquieting Christian, neither apostle nor theologian, who was convinced that the most difficult thing in the world was, not to be, or to think, but to become a Christian?

By means of his pseudonyms, Kierkegaard described the progression, the human development in the direction of Christianity, all the possible existential ramifications, all the possibilities of human life sketched from the Christian point of view. He wrote in the *Journal,* "I hope with my writings to have achieved this much: to have left behind me so exact a description of Christianity and its relation to the world that a young man with enthusiasm and nobility of mind will be able to find in it a map of the conditions, as accurate as any topographical map by one of the well-known institutes. I have not had the help of such an author. The old doctors of the Church lacked one side, they did not know the world."[7]

Thus in *Either/Or* (the aesthetic stage), Kierkegaard lets Don Juan, the hedonist, speak. In *Stages on Life's Way,*

[6] Cf. *On Authority and Revelation* and the texts below in "The Preaching of the Gospel."
[7] *Journal,* IX A 448 (Dru, n. 849); Cf. X 6 B 127.

he presents a husband as the representative of the ethical stage. In the *Postscript,* Johannes Climacus embodies the religious stage in which he has not yet made the leap of faith. Kierkegaard uses pseudonyms when he speaks of stages he has surpassed. However, the case of Climacus, author of the *Philosophical Fragments* and the *Postscript* is special, for Kierkegaard will consider himself as for a long time arrested at "Religiousness A," the threshhold of Christianity. In the *Journal* there is an important series of texts posterior to the two books of the last pseudonym, Anticlimacus, which shows that he is resolutely Christian because he presents a Christianity which includes the acceptance of the martyr. Kierkegaard was not able to sign these works with his own name. For, as he says, "I count myself higher than Johannes Climacus, lower than Anticlimacus."[8] What does this mean? That Kierkegaard, like Simon of Cyrene, considers himself to have borne the cross of Christ only "externally." That he considers it disloyal to publish under his own name Christian works while his own existence is not yet entirely placed under the sign of the imitation of Christ. It will only be so placed when he will have renounced his tranquillity and his fear of the public to move to an attack on the state church which reposes, according to him, only on a phantom of Christian faith and which, by pretending to be Christian, commits the most serious of impostures. Prior to arriving at that point, Kierkegaard will be the *poet of the religious*[9] and a spy in the service of the Most High,[10] coming among men only in disguise. "The undersigned, Johannes Climacus, who wrote this book, does not claim to be a Christian; as everyone knows, he is entirely occupied in thinking that that might be every bit as difficult as becoming one; but still less is he someone

---

[8] *Journal,* X 1 A 517; see X 1 A 316.
[9] Cf. *Sickness Unto Death* (New York: Doubleday-Anchor, 1954), pp. 208–210.
[10] Cf. *Journal,* IX A 142 (Dru, n. 791).

who, after having been a Christian, has ceased to be one by going beyond. He is a humorist: content with the situation in which for the moment he finds himself while all the while hoping that one day it will be given to him to go higher. . . ."[11]

Finally Kierkegaard goes beyond the stage of humor. His *Edifying Discourses* and the satiric attacks of the final invective addressed against the Church are, in very different ways, the deed of a man unmasked. But he was, even then, essentially an ironist in the sense that "irony is a determination of existence" and, in some way, "the cultivation of spirit."[12] Irony characterizes the man who has a sense of the infinite and of the incommensurability of the inner and outer. He was an ironist like Socrates; his existence unrolling on the crestline of the serious, in the unity of ethical passion (which infinitely accentuates interiority) and of culture (which is the passion of the Idea). His purpose was to deliver the individual from his errors by disturbing his naive beliefs, by shocking his unreflective convictions and by plunging into the darkness of regions supposedly conquered. This irony consists in establishing surprising connections between the particularities of finite life and the infinite demands of becoming a Christian. These connections produce a contradiction. Irony is possible only when the infinite enters the scene, making manifest the insufficiency of objective thought.

[11] *Concluding Unscientific Postscript* (Princeton: Princeton University Press, 1944), p. 545. (Although quotations in the text have been translated from French into English, the page references are to the English translation of the *Postscript*.)
[12] *Postscript*, p. 464.

2. THE MESSAGE OF KIERKEGAARD

It is often asked what "the true face of Kierkegaard" was. Even after a long acquaintance with a thinker, as confusing as he is prolix, one can answer the question only with many reservations. Was he an unhappy lover of religion? Did he propose to bewitch those among his contemporaries who believed themselves to be good Christians? Sincere believer, misled by philosophy, did he opt for faith against reason? His commentators reply differently to these questions but that they all feel obliged ultimately to pose them suffices to indicate that there is a problem. To some, Kierkegaard appears to have been a man too ironic, too much of a fantasist, too much of a poet to have been, at the same time, a truly religious man. His irrepressible penchant for existential analysis, for the examination of the perversions and the false psychological motivations of faith—did that not prevent him from being himself a simple Christian?

There is no question here of judging the man, but only of indicating the dominant line of his most personal writings. Without pushing too far the affinity of Kierkegaard and Pascal, we would say he is close to the Pascal who wrote, "it is not only just but useful for us that God was in part hidden and in part revealed because it is equally dangerous for man to know God without knowing his own misery and knowing his own misery without knowing God."[13]

[13] Pascal, *Pensées* (*Oeuvres complètes*. Paris: Le Seuil, 1963), n. 446.

Doubtless it is not superfluous to indicate briefly how this poet-philosopher, who was also a believer, understood his task as a personally engaged writer.

After the death of his father to whom he owed his love of dialectic and his representation of Christianity as the religion of the suffering God, the young Kierkegaard, having broken his engagement, abandoned himself to the introspection which made direct communication with others so difficult for him. Possessed by a taste for the secretive, quite romantic in that respect, he was persuaded that in the world triumph belongs to baseness, mendacity, and injustice. "My only desire, at one time, was to be in the police. It seemed to me a fitting occupation for my sleepless, intriguing mind. I imagined that among criminals there were people worth fighting with, clever, crafty, desperate men. Later on I recognized that it was a good thing that I gave up the idea; for almost everything the police have to deal with is concerned with poverty and misery, not criminals or gangsters. It is usually about a penny and some poor wretched creature. Next it was my desire to become a priest. But is it not just the same in this case? How few men have a really religious need."[14]

From an affective point of view, the young Kierkegaard was melancholic, convinced that suffering, the great educator, would be always his burden, for the divine pedagogy is not without cruelty. Long is the road that leads to acceptance and straight is the gate which opens onto the road. This narrow gate Kierkegaard was slow to enter. Educated, as he often said, by Providence, he came after many crises to penetrate his melancholy with the thought of God, to become conscious of God's designs on him. It was only in 1848, at the age of thirty-five, that he was able to write, "I feel a longing to say nothing more except: Amen. I am overwhelmed by gratitude for all that

[14] *Journal*, VIII A 171 (Dru, n. 679).

Providence has done for me. How is it possible for things to go so well? Poetically speaking, there is nothing which has happened in my life of which I cannot say, that is the very thing which perfectly suits my nature and disposition; I lack nothing. I was unhappy in my life; but I simply cannot imagine myself happy unless I were to become a different person altogether. But in my unhappiness I was happy. Humanly speaking, I am saved by one already dead, by my father; but I simply cannot imagine myself having been saved by someone living. And so I became an author in exactly the way which suited the latent possibilities of my nature; and then I was persecuted—oh, had that been wanting, my life would not have been mine. There is melancholy in everything in my life, but then again an indescribable happiness. But in that way I became myself through God's indescribable grace and support and, as I am almost tempted to say, by his special favor, if that did not mean less to me than the blessed thought, which I believe and which brings me such perfect peace: that he loves all men equally. I have, quite literally, lived with God as one lives with one's father. Amen."[15]

This text, which seems central to us, gives the why of the existential progression from anguish to faith, of the pathetic introversion in the glance directed toward God: "And so I became an author." Everything is there, and the error of too many biographers is to separate Kierkegaard's life from his work. "Providence gave me my education which is reflected in the process of my production." Kierkegaard did not write any *Metaphysical Meditations* or a *Critique* or even an *Introduction to Philosophy,* he quite modestly offered an *existential communication* to whomever might wish to hear it. In this domain progress in discovery is unthinkable apart from the deepening of the interior life; the progress of understanding is linked to the intensification

[15] *Journal,* IX A 65 (Dru, n. 771).

of knowledge of self. His lucidity and his intellectual virtuosity come to counterbalance the narcissism of his beginnings. Rigorous dialectic will order, to the degree that it is possible, the existential tumult. Philosophers will teach him how far the desire for truth can go. He will learn, from contact with them, to bring to the attention of those who are "without God in this world" the presence of God in Jesus Christ in his unforeseeable novelty. Thanks to the resources of dialectic and aesthetics, he will define the limits of the ethical sphere, the illusions of romanticism, the hypocrisies of pastors as organization men, the naive ambitions of philosophers themselves.

His meditation roams most often over biblical figures: Abraham (*Fear and Trembling*), Job (*Repetition*), Christ himself (*Training in Christianity* and *Philosophical Fragments*), the Virgin Mary, the apostles Peter and Paul,[16] and Judas. In these personages he finds the existential attitude free of all theory, something which seems to him more suggestive than long discourses. Kierkegaard always had a pictorial sense, one might say; brief entries in the *Journal* are like sketches for a portrait. One sees the scene, the silent actors, the gesture of one isolated on a great plain where the light beam of irony or of tenderness projects.

Today when his name is most often linked with those of existentialist authors, it is useful to recall the religious and Christian orientation of his work. "It seemed to me that Providence laid its hand on me and said: 'Your task is to call attention to Christianity; you have the qualities to do that and, moreover, you shall have whatever you require.' I have never been able to understand my life otherwise. Christianity has so evaporated from the world that it is necessary to form an exact conception of it. That has also been my task."[17] Unlike so many great philosophers, Kier-

[16] *Journal,* X 3 A 271.
[17] *Journal,* X 3 A 140.

kegaard is inseparable from his work. His *existentialism* is in no wise an affair of mind. His thought surged from his existence and was constantly regulated by it. But we have to do here with a thought which is forever taken up in a *double reflection,* that is, always confronted by the existence of the thinker himself; which existence provokes, judges, and reminds the speaker or writer how silly it would be to abandon the word or the writing which is concerned with existence to a logical development. In his works Kierkegaard lets the pseudonymous authors speak; he conceals himself behind them and they successively proclaim all the possibilities of existence of which man is capable. One can read as watermark in the pseudonymous works both the declaration of the *existing subjective thinker* (as opposed to impersonal objective mind) and all the sudden leaps of a simple human life when it interrogates itself on the possibility for man of relating himself to the Absolute and when it calls in question the naivete with which one commonly admits that thoughts can be communicated directly whatever may be the case with existence.

If Kierkegaard still interests us today, it is because he appears opposed to an atheistic or pantheistic philosophy, appears as a Christian believing in God and the God Man, and not because he needs security, not by habit, not out of fear of the perils of action, nor out of a reflex of passivity when confronted by a God who is a stranger to the world of men. But Kierkegaard confronts his God and his Savior as one existing, a God whose thought is audacious and is action. His youth, his experience in love, his studies, his intellectual and poetic gifts, his unshakeable faith prepared him to reflect on human existence, not in order to deduce it from thought, but in order to explode the philosophy which thinks itself capable of surpassing itself. The religious factor is decisive at this point. That is why Kierkegaard devoted all his efforts to confronting the data of human experience with Christian demands. Does not the greatest test of faith come when it is put in question in a world which has become conscious of the possibilities of thought and the living resources of the human heart? To understand, with Kierkegaard, that faith is neither passivity before the menacing sacred nor the seeking of domestic or individual consolations, *one must sense how dangerous is the temptation to become too easily religious,* how insinuating the illusion of calculating the future at the least cost, as if one could scarcely act otherwise. Kierkegaard enables us to verify the remark of Pascal: "Atheism, a sign of the power of mind, but only to a certain point."[18] He teaches us how difficult it is to become a Christian, what spiritual strength faith requires. Between the knowledge of God and the knowledge of misery—the latter being understood quite seriously—Kierkegaard opts for the knowledge of Jesus Christ, knowledge which "creates the milieu, since we find there both God and our misery."[19]

Faith should not be confused with natural religious need, for faith involves consciousness of the vital demands announced in the evangelical Word. Kierkegaard lived and expressed that. And one might ask, what is so astonishing or marvelous about that? How many saints and doctors of the Church preceded him with as much if not more perfection and heroism. That is true. Kierkegaard is neither saint nor great theologian; he is not a doctor of the Church. He was an obstructive teacher, this Lutheran believer whom the Church of the Danish State (*Folkeskirche*) had many reasons to distrust. If he is still close to us today, it is because he thought and formulated with all desirable rigor the chief stake of Christian life in a world marked by the historical result of the *philosophia perennis;* in the nineteenth century he had mysteriously the presentiment that the sacred disappears from daily life at the moment when man becomes conscious

[18] *Pensées,* n. 157.
[19] *Pensées,* n. 192.

of himself and of his relations with nature and society as measurable phenomena, assessible and wholly penetrated by analytic or dialectical reason. In his epoch marked by philosophical idealism (Schelling, Hegel) and by German romanticism, he denounced the alienation and illusion there where his contemporaries thought they had found liberation: in pure thought and in the aesthetic of extravagant and magic irony. To denounce this absurdity, to stigmatize this error, this was the austere program Kierkegaard could assign himself because he was aware of the aesthetic of Don Juan and Faust, because he was singularly endowed for the speculation with which he twitted those who thought themselves capable of discovering the absolute in every singular juncture and reducing the individual to a pure moment in the total becoming of history.

Certainly the "poet of the religious" effectively mixed jokes and smiles with anguish and despair, as Camus observed; he put into dialectical play impotence and power, the failure of guilt and the triumph of faith. In a text of 1850, he seems to me to have expressed his secret. "What an ardent desire my soul harbored, particularly when I was young, to be a man like others in order to enjoy life. But by terrible sufferings I have been set outside the usual human conditions. I am not in that sense one of the profound religious natures. From childhood I was a man constrained. By way of all the torments caused by what was refused me, my task appeared clearly and then procurred for me an unspeakable satisfaction for which I will never be able to thank God enough."[20] This writer is constrained. If the comparison is permitted, recall that the Apostle Paul did not feel free not to announce the message which had been confided to him. Kierkegaard believed in his mission. To his last breath he was the prisoner of it. His turning on himself, his regrets and nostalgia, made of him a sensitive

[20] *Journal,* X 3 A 140.

man, very human, extremely conscious of the heroism
that the imitation of Christ requires, abandoned by all:
". . . alone almost with human language against me . . .
alone in decisions where one has need of friends and if
possible of the whole of humanity to sustain one; alone in
dialectical tensions which, without the help of God, would
drive a man with my imagination mad; alone in agony unto
death; alone in the absurdity of a life without the ability,
even if I had wished it, to make a single one understand
me." He found nevertheless sufficient strength and energy to
accomplish his task, to produce a work that intrigued the
philosophical minds of his time. His dialectical vigor and
isolation make him a difficult thinker, his craft and disguises, the whole machinery of the pseudonyms, make him
a complicated author. But no doubt is possible that the
main purpose of his work was Christian and that the meaning of his life can only be found in his faith.

3. A LIVING PROTEST

Why did this enterprise isolate its author from the crowd and make of him an exception? Because it was a matter of denouncing an imposture, of pointing a finger at a usurpation in virtue of which modern society at the beginning of the nineteenth century proclaimed itself Christian. Faced with a situation so improbable from the point of view of the New Testament, Kierkegaard prosecuted the case against this self-styled Christian and self-styled enlightened epoch. His adversaries accordingly are intellectuals and churchmen. One must never forget, in reading him, that he wanted to be only a *corrective*. "The corrective makes himself understood, in a certain measure, at the expense of what is corrected. If that is so, an apparently penetrating mind can reproach the corrective by pointing out that he sees only one side of things and he can easily persuade the public that this is so. Good God! What is easier than for one who has first given the corrective to go on and add the complementary aspect?"[21] This shows us how conscious Kierkegaard was of the partial character of his plea. Like Bloy and Bernanos, Kierkegaard is a prophet, a protestor. The strength of such solitaries is not synthesis or positions of delicate balance, but the vigor, even violence, with which they underscore a generally overlooked aspect of the total truth. Concerning

[21] *Journal,* X 1 A 640.

social values, for example, Kierkegaard did not admit that a synthesis was possible between the individual charism and the institution, between prophecy which cries out its indignation and the established rule which requires obedience to tradition. Hence his decisive opposition to the visible Church which he rejects in his disapproval of every form of social idolatry. But one must ask if social organization is essentially opposed to inspiration, if administration is essentially opposed to grace, the institutional to the mystical? It could be, as a matter of fact, that the non-conformism of the prophet involves an unconscious assumption of angelism. Regulated social organization, even in the spiritual domain, is always a support and it could even become an irreplaceable source of strength. It is to men that the revelation and grace of God come to help and men live in society, with all the tediousness that can entail. Like Simone Weil, Kierkegaard recoiled before the totalitarian spirit that he thought he descried in a spiritual and social *institution*. But no doubt he could also have said with her: "I would be more disposed to die for the Church—if she had need one day soon for someone to die for her—than to enter her."[21b] One can understand that the spectacle of an imperfect Church could rebuff spirits too lively, too absolute and, let's say it, too *spiritual*. . . . But all in all the temptation to let oneself be weighted down by the institution, the rule and traditions, is doubtless more common than to give in to impatience and the sometimes anarchic impetuosity of spirit.

The message of such protestors is not generally bathed in the shining light of certitude. It often goes hand in hand with the sense of paradox and scandal. It is the vehicle of provocations rather than explications. Moreover, such violent Christians more often than not have a sense of abandonment, of interior and exterior desolation, and their experience will always disturb those whose meditation ordinarily avoids the abasement of Bethlehem and Golgotha.

[21b] *La Pesanteur et la Grâce,* p. xxiv.

Kierkegaard wrote *Thoughts Which Wound from Behind in Order to Edify;* Bernanos said, "Grace strikes from behind." The Dane professed the militant Christianity which "in Christendom, attacks from the rear." By and large, this attests to an experience dominated by an invisible Partner, present everywhere but whom some better than others see rise unexpectedly, summoning us violently as Paul of Tarsus was once summoned by this God who lies in wait. Without having received an official mission, Kierkegaard came to believe himself charged to recall to his contemporaries their Christian duties; this was something he did with the wounded tone commonly indicating the deception caused by a friend's blindness. After so much had been said of conciliating love, this was perhaps for the Christians of his time and of his country an excessive severity. This simple believer was wary of the preaching of Christian orators who, not living themselves in the Christian spirit, "could no longer help others, by their sermons, to live it." For a long time he preferred, according to himself, "to go see Christ at night, like Nicodemus," for "among Christians" he saw only "habit, torpor and the lack of spirituality."[22] Then he changed into a prosecutor. If the violence of his anathemas is explained by the type of frenzy which impaired him at the end of his life, it remains that his sense of God and of faith in Jesus Christ provided him with unmistakable accents.

Is it not naivete to believe that the Christian experience is reserved to those with untroubled souls?[23] Kierkegaard's great interior dislocation serves only to render more moving the distraught appeal that he ceaselessly addressed to God during the profound final crisis that led to his death. The loud cry of protest that runs through the *Journal* cannot be dissociated from his faith. This does not mean that the protest, like his faith, was wholly supernatural.

[22] *Journal,* X 5 A 127.
[23] Cf. Pierre Mesnard, "Le *Journal* de Kierkegaard a-t-il une valeur philosophique?" in *Etudes philosophiques,* 3 (1963), pp. 299–314.

II An Existential Itinerary

1. ANGUISH AND THE CHRISTIAN

In its origin, existential thought is not without relation to the importance Kierkegaard accorded to the theme of anguish, that anguish which surges forth when modern man becomes conscious of his solitude. At the heart of the most dense social concentrations, surrounded on all sides by the collectivity, constantly surprised by anonymous but all the same human glances, modern man is nonetheless a solitary because he has lost that spontaneous sense of human solidarity that philosophers feel when they speak of reason and liberty. Without being experienced or expressed in a lyric or sentimental fashion, the anguish of our contemporaries is nevertheless real for they have experienced a freedom which has not always coincided with reason. The optimism and serenity of the Greeks and of the philosophers of the seventeenth and eighteenth centuries are not ours. The Christian too can, and doubtless ought, to be in this sense a modern man. To understand, as Christian and as philosopher, the sense of this new experience, it is necessary to go back, beyond Kierkegaard's psychology of the individual, to the intimate link which unites the themes of freedom, grace, and faith, as response to the love of God, with anguish.

The grasp of oneself as a possibility which engenders anguish, the vertigo of freedom, that is the point of departure of the existential adventure. Prior to that there can be only a state of innocence which necessarily includes the condition of the possibility of failure. Prior to the dialectical interplay of good and evil (not from an abstract point of view but in life itself) only one state is possible: ignorance as ignorance. Yet undetermined, man is at this stage without unrest because he is still this side of opposition. All possibilities are still nothing: it is nothing which engenders anguish, which is the very secret of innocence and which characterizes infancy as well as all people who retained it under the form of reverie of spirit.

This reverie Kierkegaard sees as the ultimate condition of anguish which is the vertigo that grips the spirit when there opens before it the bottomless abyss of existential possibilities. It is indeed of those that it is a question, and not notional or symbolic possibilities which are offered to the endless play of a combinatory virtuosity on the intellectual level. In his relation to existence, man—that is, one who exists—sees arise as complement to his thirst for adventure the lure of the mysterious, the unusual, the unexpected. Then the pursuit begins, animated by a sort of unforeseen rhythm which is existence itself as act, as becoming, as eminently active process, that is to say, in constant coming to be.

Anguish is thus linked to existence. It was, for Kierkegaard at any rate, on its way to being discovered to the degree that existence is nothing other than the forever doubtful conquest of spirit, which is infinite, just as the abyss of possibilities open to man is infinite. Only that individual will be said to exist whose spirit dwells on the very coming to be of freedom, the possibility of yes or no which renders man captive of a seduction not exempt from anxiety, of a desire mixed with revulsion and a knowledge which distrusts itself as knowledge because it reposes on possibility alone. It is in this contradiction that the ambiguity of the one who exists resides, for he is both free and constrained, and innocent because he can always become guilty.

The abyss of anguish which prompts this insight enters the soul as a thorn in the flesh, as a mortifying secret which

becomes the very condition of life. The inexplicable conflicts which feed each life, the terrors, victories, defeats, with-
drawals and imaginative anticipations, all that composes
the backdrop of existence on which Kierkegaard would
sketch paradoxes at a time when many of his contemporaries
had undertaken to drive man not toward a consecration to
man but to the idea.

Must we think that the Kierkegaardian discovery of the
existent or, as he liked to say, of the individual, is simply
the sad privilege of a declining romantic age? Is it only the
product of a subjectivism and irrationalism let loose which
are characteristic of a whole hotbed of uprooted bourgeois
intellectuals become parasites? Is it only a reaction undertaken in the name of the principle of activity against the
irrationalism of a Schopenhauer who nobly withdraws from
every practical involvement?

It can indeed seem that Kierkegaard's disaffection with
the social and the generic being of man and his emphasis on
the individual as the living center of all thought and life
derive their sense only from the Christian religious option
which requires the rejection of dialectical conciliations
whether rational or historical. Outside this perspective one
can only misunderstand the direction of Kierkegaardian
thought by explaining it either as a psychic phenomenon of
a pathological sort or as a literary episode in the individual-
istic reaction against the great rationalist utopia or against
the idolatry of science, history or society.

2. EXISTENCE IN THE PRESENCE OF GOD

What then is the nub of his thought and how is the individual's consciousness of his freedom as emanating from anguish to orient us toward a Christian solution of the problem of existence? How is the understanding of oneself in existence to provoke a surpassing of the self-knowledge recommended by Socrates?

Self-consciousness, the basis of the interiority required by every religious life, implies that man is formed by anguish, that is, *that he is capable of measuring the boundlessness of the possible opening before him.* This formation will involve tortures more cruel than any grand inquisitor might inflict, more subtle ruses than a spy who is a past master at his art might devise, an incessant interrogation more slashing than that of the most astute judge. The infinite attack a man leaves himself open to when he takes his own destiny in hand in order to subject it to questioning and free it from the automatic and from every withdrawal outside freedom, this fight with the angel can form man *absolutely* and *infinitely,* that is, by surpassing all individual and social conditioning. But it can do so on one condition: that man has faith. "By faith I understand here . . . the interior certitude which anticipates infinity."[24]

---

[24] *The Concept of Dread* (Princeton: Princeton University Press, 1957), p. 226. As is so often the case with Kierkegaard, the reference to Hegel is imprecise.

Taking Kierkegaard literally here, faith is the one way in which man can rely on Providence, the one way in which the autodidact can become theodidact. In effect, this is the unique way by which the individual can achieve the unmasking "in the anticipation of faith" of all the false idealizations of the finite and all the idolatries of the temporal. Such a faith takes guilt quite seriously into consideration, that is, fault itself which has nothing to do with the shame a police arrest might give or with the disgrace attendant on disapproval by public opinion and still less with the humiliated self-esteem of the guilty one. The believer is thus a man who has not defrauded the possible, has not inveigled anguish, but has run the risk of assuming his own existence with the lucidity of insight of the mature man who no longer deludes himself. This entails the demystification of false gods and renunciation of magic solutions and the confused belief in a deus ex machina who will appear to save everything, the renunciation of the absurd trust in time which solves everything. A lucidity which refuses as well to think that everything is written on high, that everything has been settled elsewhere unbeknown to us, our fate sealed above from the moment nature made us.

Self-awareness in existence differs from Socratic self-knowledge and that is why Christian existentialism differs from Greek interiority which would find in the depths of the human soul a divine, in the neuter, but not a Person endowed with the Word. An abyss separates the discovery of an immanent truth inscribed in the very foundation of the spirit and the self-awareness of an individual who is at the same moment conscious of living in the presence of God. There can be here, consequently, as rendered possible by anguish, an anticipation in virtue of which the appearance of God as Total Otherness involves in itself the correlative meaning of an existential structure. The God who thus manifests himself will respond to an expectation which is not pure passivity and which makes possible the very historicity of subjective Christian becoming. This expectation possesses sight: the prophets were visionaries. The eye is the organ of the future. This anticipative look, the reflexive presentiment which opens the eyes, makes possible the autopsies of faith. Sight weakens with age and the elder is the man of memories. Whereas reminiscence connotes a relation to an immemorial past—it finds the mark of an absence indicated in immanence—anticipation is oriented toward the future. By means of it, the subject is projected toward infinity in virtue of the movement of transcendence.

It is not superfluous to reflect on the meaning of such a movement. One might in effect think that it is the key to the whole Kierkegaardian edifice. The vigor with which Kierkegaard undertakes the refutation of any pantheistic tendency is well known. He intends to replace a logic which is thoroughly rational with a dialectic of ruptures. The category of faith is central here; it is neither transitory nor purely instrumental, for the religious relation, with respect to what is essentially paradoxical in it, is characterized by the relation to authority which plays no role in the speculative dialectic of the Greeks or of Hegel. Kierkegaard has much insisted on the dialectic of authority[25] which introduces a specific quality and new value in the bosom of human language. The play of absolute authority recognized as such introduces true infinity into existence. "Every system, just because of its finite character, must be pantheistic."[26] The pantheistic system is the system par excellence, that is, the one which is well-rounded and operates in absolute continuity—that continuity which binds the thinker to the immemorial capital accumulated by the human spirit. Kierkegaard, on the other hand, sees the individual man as the permanent possibility of a relation to a unique truth, as the

[25] See VII, 2 B 235 (*On Authority and Revelation: The Book on Adler* [Princeton: Princeton University Press, 1955]).
[26] *Postscript*, p. 111.

passionate anticipation of the eternal, and not as recollection, anamnesis of eternity. Such an anamnesis could only be an excursion outside existence, an elegant disappearing of the man who deserts existence and is sheltered from existential decisions now seen as meaningless shadowplay concealing what has become essential: the kingdom of ideas.

3. LOVE AND SUFFERING

Have we been asked to enjoy the benefits of a consoling religion? Did Kierkegaard live his faith as that which definitely stops all disquiet? Was the Christian solution sought and lived by Kierkegaard as a remedy for anguish? Why is the relation to self with which Kierkegaard defines the ego as spirit conceived as desired by God?

In order to reply to these questions, it is important not to think of passivity and activity as absolutely exclusive of one another. My existence is willed by God because I receive it from God and this means that it is *simultaneously* constructed by me and received as a gift. Kierkegaard's numerous prayers to the Heavenly Father and Creator attest to the capital importance of the recognition. Everything stems from this initial gift; the whole history of our acquiescences to it which are contradicted by our lapses and refusals are continuous with it. The relation of the self to itself is at the same time a relation to the Other, to a Third who has constituted the relation. The relation is transparent to the Absolute who constitutes it.

All this is indissociable from the religious faith that Kierkegaard regards in a way that owes much to Luther.[27] The discovery of divine love is not something the believer

[27] Cf. L. Bouyer, *Du Protestantisme à l'Eglise* (Paris, 1954), pp. 105–110.

can separate from the discovery of his own unworthiness nor is it separable from the *Works of Love* where God takes the initiative. The total giving over of the self to God in faith is possible because Jesus Christ manifests the benevolence and "love of God which has been diffused in our hearts by the Holy Spirit who has been given to us." (Romans 5, 5) A fundamental passivity, therefore, gives rise to the activity par excellence: that of love which confronts the love of the Other who gives himself by revealing himself through grace. Grace which heals at the same time underlines need and potentializes the passion for existing. If it consoles the Christian it does so only to prepare him for action.

The individualism of the believer is quite the opposite of egoism since it can arise only from the justification by faith and grace that Kierkegaard sees as a unique existential event. The grace that gives and the faith that receives Christ as gift and Christ as model are the two poles of the dialectic of anticipation which unfolds essentially as a progress completely directed to the future since hope is constitutive, with love, of the faith that saves.

It is evident that this conception is demanded by reflexion on Christian becoming. The believer is not that humorist, of which the *Postscript* speaks, who constantly withdraws because he is persuaded that the explication is always in arrears. The Christian believes that the ultimate explanation cannot be found by the regressive method of reflexion, but that reflexion is only the condition of the possibility of the essential movement which consists in starting from what lies ahead: *Respice finem.*[28] Yet this movement cannot be conceived as the sure and optimistic conquest of self. It is at the very heart of faith as victory over anguish that there returns that negativity Kierkegaard never renounces. That is why Christianity can never in any fashion be reduced to

[28] *Postscript,* p. 402.

a religion of consolation, the opium of the people. The anticipation of infinity is never such that the discord between the finite and infinite is totally overcome. That is the significance of the Kierkegaardian position on the permanence of the suffering essential to the religious life. As opposed to the ethical and the aesthetic, Christianity is not the locus of peaceful acquisitions. An absolute relation to God while based on love involves suffering. So anguish returns: the adventure of life does not exclude (quite the contrary) the possibility and the infinite range of choices in the life of the existent. That life is as negative as it is positive and when one is a believer his faith does not impose on his life the mark of necessity, setting him apart from other men, by dispensing him from enjoying the play of freedom. No doubt this is a matter which confuses many. Unbelievers caricaturing the life of the believer see it as a life without risks and surprises, without passion because the die is cast in advance, certitude given at the outset and the price of admission correctly announced. Too many believers give a partial justification to such an estimate by their conformist attitude, lack of reflection and interiority, and their herd spirit.

The suffering Kierkegaard says is the sign of the religious stage points up the negative aspect various dogmatisms too easily conceal when they expatiate on the truth and the justice. The precision of ancient or rationalist wisdom because of its formal beauty often prepares us to overlook sudden leaps of flesh and spirit, psychological and historical contingencies, the reality of appearances. To all the fanatics of truth, Kierkegaard recalls the necessity not of a kind of relativism, as is sometimes said, but of this certitude of the believer: we live in the state of fallen nature (*in statu corruptionis*) and, in this state, things are not so clear as some naive people, including philosophers, think. Disquiet, hesitations, anguish, presentiments, and equivocal perceptions are as real as ideas; velleities no less important in life than real desires. The delicate perceptions of the unbeliever and of the believer who suffers are as pregnant with reality as the more or less finely made dialectical grills on which are inscribed what is usually called thought, and as the collection of noble motives on which the resolutions and decisions shimmering with virtue depend. The existent is as negative as he is positive. God is not the transcendence lacking to man, his truth is not the solution we have not yet found and on which we call in limit cases: God is at the center of what we positively and negatively are, animating within our being the being of the possible and therefore of anguish. "To have an absolute representation of God does not mean: to have the absolute representation in passing, but to have it at every moment. This is the cessation of immediacy and the condemation to death of nihilization."[29] *If God does not occupy every nook, he is absent.* This does not mean, however, that every preoccupation with the finite must disappear. On the contrary. The believer has not withdrawn from this world, it is in the world that he sustains his absolute relation to the Absolute and his relative relation to the relative. The knight of faith lives incognito, his outward appearance is quite common and ordinary; ". . . he is not a genius, for in vain have I tried to surprise in him the incommensurable mark of the genius. At night he smokes his pipe; content in a finite day, one would swear he was a butcher."[30] *His suffering results precisely from the fact that he has no adequate means to express his faith.* There is a radical incommensurability between the inner and the outer. Every expression of religious happiness is essentially finite and it runs the risk of being provoking and involving a sort of "arrogance toward other men"[31] who do not have this happiness. Doubtless it is better to be silent at the feet of Jesus, like the sinful woman, than full of verbose assurance

[29] *Ibid.*, p. 432.
[30] *Fear and Trembling* (New York: Doubleday-Anchor, 1954), p. 56.
[31] *Postscript*, p. 434.

like the pharisee. Kierkegaard feels that part of the suffering of the religious man arises from the silence to which he is condemned. The silence of the knight of faith unable to reveal himself corresponds to the demoniac silence of the possessed who has been rendered mute. Neither Sarah nor Eliezer, not even Isaac himself, can understand Abraham's test when he is profoundly marked by his relation to God. This silence—which is that of Jesus interrogated by Pilate on the subject of truth—makes the religious man a suffering servant who can know the anguish of the agony.

But, according to Kierkegaard, silence in religious matters is particularly important in the nineteenth century, for the modern epoch has strangely abused language which has become in many ways devalued. "Just as an old man who has lost his teeth chews now only with his gums, so modern Christian discourses on Christianity have lost the bite of an energetic terminology—there is babbling but no chewing."[32]

If anguish is the mark of authentic existence, if its overcoming by faith means no definitive victory over suffering, the reason must doubtless be sought in the fact that Jesus Christ himself took on suffering and the negative. He took it on in its lacerating positivity, which does not mean that he suppressed it. Joy itself, as a sentiment of the real, does not exclude the sense of the vulnerability of man and of his instability. Freedom is lived only at this price and the dialectic of existence reveals that the individual experiences fear and trembling in the restraint of isolation; his relation to God as a subjective history rebels in its thousand configurations against every conceptual analysis.

[32] *Ibid.*

4. FAITH AND PARADOX

One should not think, for all that, that this Kierkegaardian perspective wholly centered on subjectivity ignores the
objectivity of doctrine and grace. It must not be forgotten
that all the existential constructions of this "positive individualism, of which the Lutheran 'justification by faith'
was the vehicle, thrive, with all their subjectivity, on the
objectivism of *sola gratia* and would be void of sense if one
cut them from the stem that bears them and the sap that
sustains them."[33]

From the theological point of view first of all: the Kierkegaardian Christology has often been suspected of heresy.
But the objections contradict one another, as can be seen.
Christ, according to Kierkegaard,[34] would have only the
appearance of humanity, a theology of Docetist tendancy;
on the other hand, Kierkegaard wanted to avoid the dangers
of docetism and, unlike Luther, fell into a reverse monophysitism, as it were; Christ's divinity would be in some
way 'absorbed' by his humanity.[35] Historians of dogma

---

[33] L. Bouyer, *op.* cit., p. 110.

[34] "Dans l'esprit de Kierkegaard, la phrase, 'Christ est Dieu,' s'est
fixée inaltérablement, mais il lui répugne d'admettre qu'il soit en
même temps homme." M. Grimault, *Kierkegaard par lui-même,*
p. 11.

[35] This is the view of H. Roos, "Søren Kierkegaard und die Kenosis-
Lehre," in *Kierkegaardiana,* II (Copenhagen, 1957), pp. 54–60.

know how prudently theological categories must be employed, particularly in the matter of monophysitism where it is difficult for one without solid historical information to distinguish heresy from orthodoxy. As for Kierkegaard, his faith in Christ, the God Man, seems to us to conform to the Chalcedean formula: "One and the same Christ, Son, Lord, Only Son, two natures without mixture, transformation, division or separation." This stands out in texts from the *Journal* where it is said that Christ commands the attention of men by his miracles and his divine authority.[36] The Incarnation has indeed the value of a theophany but the kenosis, the humility of a servant (Ph. 2, 7), is not, for all that, lost sight of. "The *forma servi* is not borrowed but real, it is not a parastatic body but a real body."[37]

The Christian life which according to Kierkegaard is centered in Christ as a model proposed for imitation and as a gift, grace, is characterized above all by faith. It results from a new point of departure, a new birth, and that is why it is sometimes designated as a new or second immediacy. It is a break with philosophical immanence. By contrast with rationalist speculation, it results from a leap; *it is a risk because it surges forth from the heart of a paradox* (absurd for the Greek or the German idealist) *which manifests itself in the coexistence of time and eternity.* Christian faith is an affair of existence and not of ideology. That is why it is essentially a becoming, having a new history in each Christian, a history in which every believer becomes contemporary with Christ. The stumbling stone and sign of scandal, Christ Jesus is the object of faith because, humbled even unto death, he is in his hidden power and glory Savior and Redeemer of humanity.[38]

[36] Cf. *Journal,* IV A 108 and *Training in Christianity.*
[37] *Philosophical Fragments* (Princeton: Princeton University Press, 1962), p. 68.
[38] *Training in Christianity* (New York: Oxford University Press, 1941), pp. 11–15.

"Faith rests on a free decision which answers to a new and paradoxical situation: the existence of the God Man in time. Thus it can only be a gift of God. This gift coincides with the revelation of sin. From sin to faith, that is the passage of primordial importance, the decisive temporal instant and, at the same time, 'full of eternity'[39] which makes man a contemporary with Christ. Kierkegaard's interest for the problem of the relation of faith and history is not fortuitous; one can say that it is both religious and philosophical. Better, that the origin as well as the consequences of his reflection on this point are linked with the philosophical problems of his time as well as with the difficulties he experienced in practicing his Christianity in a world where Christian values were systematically perverted and Christian exigencies methodically softened. Even when he poses apparently theoretical questions, Kierkegaard always pursues a practical end, placing himself on the level of fact where decision (*Beschluss*) and not the conclusion (*Schluss*) comes into play. This is particularly evident when the pseudonym Climacus studies, around 1844, the problem said to be Lessing's: "Contingent historical truths can never be the proof of rational necessary truths." That is a formulation quite characteristic of the *Aufklärung*. Kierkegaard will surreptitiously substitute for universal, rational and necessary truth, an eternal happiness, and concerning it he asks what relation it can have to a contingent and particular historical event. This substitution of the existential for the rational is revealing and permits us to see how continuous progressive transition finds itself replaced by the leap which is the mark of the discontinuous. This leap can only be effected in the constraint of isolation. Some will admit that this perilous jump must be made.[40] Others will stop in their tracks because they are not animated by "the will to discover

---

[39] *Fragments,* p. 22.
[40] The famous *Salto mortale* discussed by Lessing and Jacobi.

the paradox."[41] This free decision is a factor of discontinuity, but we know that existence, unlike thought, is made of ruptures and perpetual beginning anew.

For Kierkegaard, the substitution of impassioned decision for objective knowledge typifies the privileged and decisive moment of human life which gives rise to a transcending of the historical. In this sense, for him as for Kant, "only real action enables us to attain transcendence."[42] It is by action that man lays hold of his own being. The real existence of the total man is crystalized in those mediating moments which are not susceptible, in their turn, of being mediated. In *The Concept of Dread,* Kierkegaard spoke of the moment which aquires its full weight of decision only in Christianity where eternity becomes essential. Contrary to the moment of demonstration, which is without influence on its internal structure, the moment of decision is precisely decisive because its influence is determining for the future, even for eternity. The sense of free action which frustrates the timeless manouevres of abstraction has its reality in time; or, more exactly time has its reality in it. That is why "time is assigned no place in pure thought."[43] It is decision, the bold strike, choice, that gives rise to time. The time in which the individual marked by sin is called to live is the "time of decision," that which man lives strained toward paradox, conscious of the present existence of the God Man.[44]

[41] On all this, cf. *Postscript,* pp. 86–96, and our study, "La dialectique kierkegaardienne de l'existence," *Revue de Philosophie et de Théologie,* IV (Lausanne, 1963), p. 320.

[42] Karl Jaspers, "Le mal radical chez Kant," *Bilan et Perspectives,* p. 210.

[43] *Postscript,* p. 271.

[44] The relation to Jesus Christ appears, therefore, as the integrating element of the free act in its very finitude, since it is existentially inscribed in subjectivity's process of auto-mediation.

5. A COMBATIVE CERTITUDE

Christ's real existence does not exclude time. Likewise, human life wholly oriented toward eternity assumes the positivity of an historical datum. Concretely stated, the problem is one of the conciliation of the irreducible originality of each thought, of each human destiny tending toward God, and the psycho-social constellations in which they take place. Paradoxical by its very object (the God Man, eternal and temporal) faith is also paradoxical because it is not the product of progressive transitions brought about by a mindless sliding from faint and fugitive appearance to certitude, from conditioning to choice. *Faith is the moment in which is decided, with all the solemnity of serious existence, either the orientation toward truth, or the regression to the regions of the interesting.* This orientation toward truth is not only an objective step, it is the engagement of all our being and when it is taken seriously it can cause the most crucial unrest. Perhaps this was the case of Pilate's wife who, unlike her husband, was troubled by nightmares[45] when her husband objectively washed his hands.

"Socratic incertitude is like a mere pleasantry in comparison with the seriousness of the absurd and socratic existential interiority is like Greek insouciance in comparison

---

[45] *Postscript,* p. 206.

with the tension of faith."[46] Folly for the Greeks, a scandal to the Jews, faith is not for all that conceived as a purely voluntarist tension, because its object is effectively the truth. But Kierkegaard wants above all to put into relief the existential aspect of faith, its subjective assimilation as existential message, that is, the existence of the believer is his becoming a Christian, something completely dominated by the reality of God in existence. As relation to oneself before God, faith is the exact contrary of the pathos of aesthetic immediacy and of the ethical relation governed only by the "ideal."[47] In the aesthetic sphere of art closed to any pursuit of the absolute or in the bedeviled chase after pleasure as well as, strangely, in the world of moral rigor, it is always the self that is at the center of the debate, point of departure and destination. It is, respectively, the self of enjoyment or the self of duty that commands everything since they are the exclusive points of reference. In faith it is the reality of the other that confronts the reality of the self.

Certainly one can wonder if in this case Kierkegaard has managed to integrate harmoniously the "values of life" and the "values of thought" or, put otherwise, wonder if his problematic is not excessively marked by this dualism. We must note here that if one takes into account not only his pseudonymous polemical writings but also his *Journal* and *Discourses,* it must be recognized that Kierkegaard lived and preached an integral Christianity and, in the final analysis, one with more equilibrium than is usually thought. His polemical passion against the rationalization of dogma, his desire to shock, have led him to employ formulas which are daring but which retain a partial truth. If faith is for

[46] *Ibid.,* p. 188.

[47] The constitution of free subjectivity as subject of existence is foreign to the concern to posit a "supreme principle" of morality. The inevitable choice between God and the world represents the mediation between the self with freedom and the self-oriented by the decisive choice of itself.

him a risk, it is also certitude: "It is foolish here below to believe in a wisdom that will grant a certitude greater than that of faith."[48] Unlike the aesthetic libertine and the speculative professor, the believer remains in existence and there he must "content himself with a combative certitude."[49] Called forth by the gift of God, faith always remains a restless tension, for here below it is impossible to think it in terms of union, since God is the totally other with whom one cannot fraternize. Kierkegaard always shows a certain mistrust of the mystic whom he regards as a gourmand a trifle too exotic in his relation to God.

It would be inexact, however, to consider Kierkegaard as a thinker for whom the religious life always takes the form of unhappy consciousness. As many texts of his *Journal* attest, he had known the joy of living with God. If he never acquired the serenity of those whose vocation is spiritual union, this is not because he misunderstood the ultimate meaning of Christian destiny, which is to attain to unity, in a single breath, of faith, love and understanding. He saw this possibility as the term of the odyssey of conscience, as the possibility of possibilities of which, in the tumult of existence, we can have only fleeting, ephemeral but indispensable, presentiments.

One should make these views explicit and the best way to do it would be to discuss *ex professo* the many interpretations and the no less numerous criticisms of the Kierkegaardian thesis of the paradox. This is not the place for such a discussion. We shall only suggest that the Kierkegaardian paradox is not located at the purely intellectual level: it concerns existence. As Professor N. V. Søe has well remarked,[50] it does not arise from reason; it is given with revelation and not as a question posed by man, but against all expectation.

---

[48] *Postscript,* p. 209.
[49] *Ibid.,* p. 201.
[50] N. V. Søe, "Søren Kierkegaards laere om paradokset," *Nordisk Teologi* (Lund, 1955), pp. 102–121.

It transcends therefore both rationality and irrationality which, the one as well as the other, are always measured intellectually. The paradox concerns the total situation of the man who has heard the word of God, and not the man in the clutches of the abstract thought of the mystery of the Incarnation. One might spontaneously think that by paradox is meant an obscure representation, a contradictory theological structure. To make of paradox a representation or a structure is to speak of what cannot be in the existential climate. To see in Kierkegaard the very type of the fideist or irrational attitude, is to refuse to place oneself on the level where the Danish thinker chose to reflect. It is certain that he admits Christian dogma and its specific intelligibility in terms of truth. The paradox is not constitutive of dogmatic truth; it is the emblem of the existential style that such a truth, when recognized, conditions. One cannot lay hold of the Kierkegaardian paradox by enclosing it in the dilemma, for or against reason. The unlikely is not devoid of reasonableness. It requires the use of reason as the faculty of the perception of continuity; it even assumes it. It attests simply to the experience of a permanent surprise before the irreducible inadequation of knowledge and existence, even when that knowledge is revelation and that existence is the apprentice-Christian's. In no way is it a matter of excluding reason, of combatting it, of reducing it to servitude. It is not a matter of deciding, for or against, continuity between God the Savior and man the sinner. For the Christian it is a matter of living in full consciousness of being determined, in his very existence, by revelation, of comprehending his life in this light and of willing to live while certain both of his sin and his salvation. The relation of the particular individual to the Absolute is paradoxical, therefore, and paradoxical as well the relation of the historical existent to eternal truth, the fact that the eternal has come to be in time, that God has been made man, that the sinner is called to be a believer: in each case, one can see, the paradox concerns human existence.

This appears still more clearly when one notices the following proportions that Kierkegaard insists on in the *Postscript* and that we set down schematically in order that their systematic character be made clear.[51]

I. $\quad \dfrac{(a)}{(b)} = \dfrac{\text{true religiosity}}{\text{hidden inwardness}} = \dfrac{\text{omnipresence of God[52]}}{\text{invisibility}}$

II. $\quad \dfrac{(a)}{(b)} = \dfrac{\text{omnipresence of God}}{\text{invisibility}} = \dfrac{\text{revelation[53]}}{\text{secret}}$

III. $\quad \dfrac{(a)}{(b)} = \dfrac{\text{the religious paradigm}}{\text{irregularity}} = \dfrac{\text{omnipresence of God}}{\text{invisibility}}$

$$= \dfrac{\text{revelation[54]}}{\text{secret}}$$

The most complete formula[55] takes the three terms of Formula III and puts them in proportion with

IV. $\quad \dfrac{(a)}{(b)} = \dfrac{\text{the highest seriousness of the religious life}}{\text{facetiousness}}$

Formula III puts into relation the irregularity evoked by the figure of Abraham obliged to suspend the ethical and, by that very fact, to serve as example to all the believers of whom he is the father because he must make an exception by withdrawing himself from the universality of moral

---

[51] The relation of term (a) to term (b) is evidently paradoxical. That is, in each case, (b) passing for what is not directly knowable, becomes, for Kierkegaard, the index of (a). Thus, *hidden inwardness* and the *invisibility of the secret* attest the presence of true religiosity and of God himself, a presence men naively believe they can directly verify without risk of error. Kierkegaard wants to contest that pretense. We give a rigorously faithful translation of the Kierkegaardian terms.

[52] *Postscript*, pp. 423–424.

[53] *Ibid.*, pp. 220–221.

[54] *Ibid.*, p. 231.

[55] *Ibid.*, p. 233.

law.[56] Formula IV adds the theme of the incognito of the truly religious man which is not expressed in the form of the pontifically serious or extremely devout. The central paradox which makes of God's presence in his creation a dissimulation which alone can unmask one who has posed in inwardness his relation to God, recalls the contrast of a Revelation which is a mystery or secret (*Hemmelighed*) and a disclosure which is a concealment.

This table makes it clear that the dogmatic paradoxes, if one can put it that way, are surrounded by existential paradoxes. The first relation of formula I and that of IV concern the existence of man insofar as religiosity is one of his possibilities; one might say insofar as he is capable of entering into relation with God (*capax Dei*). Thus Kierkegaard intends to speak of a God hidden and manifest both in the world and in the Word, always with reference to the very ambiguity of all religious existence. If the signs of God —his glory that the heavens tell (*Coeli enarrant gloriam Dei*), his love that the Scriptures manifest—do not act magically, if they have to be decoded; this is because man is not, definitively and by nature, connaturalized to mystery. The reading of these signs will require therefore a generalized hermeneutic which is obliged to remain in touch with the *existence* of the subject. Mysterious and secret, the presence of God is not for things or beasts but for man alone, or rather for those among men who present in this world a presence which is not of this world.

It is a false perspective consequently that would place Kierkegaard in the framework of fideism vs. rationalism. The old thesis of Torsten Bohlin[57] which opposed the line of experience to that of paradox by attributing the latter to a sort of decay of intellectualism is no longer acceptable.

---

[56] This is the theme of *Fear and Trembling*.

[57] Torsten Bohlin, *Kierkegaards dogmatische Anschauung im ihren geschichtlichen Zusammenhange* (translated from the Swedish), (Gutersloh, 1927).

The origin of the thought of paradox is by no means speculation in the sense that it results from thought's exasperation with its proper limits—it is existential. "If . . . one reached the point where . . . one understood Christianity speculatively, one would have attained the maximum of misunderstanding . . . I have preferred to call Christianity an existential message precisely to mark its difference from speculation."[58]

[58] *Postscript*, p. 339, note.

6. THE FULLNESS OF TIME
AND CONTEMPORANEITY

The category of the *Moment* asserts itself when one wishes to make precise the aspect under which the mystery of the Incarnation and our relation to that mystery appeared to the eyes of Kierkegaard.

The notion of the moment is susceptible of a double use, as anthropological category and as theological category. These two uses are not strangers to one another; they manifest a similarity of structure between two essential moments of history, the privileged moment of the collective becoming of humanity which is the instant of the Incarnation and the privileged moment of every individual history which is the instant of free choice. In each of these instants there is an encounter of two heterogeneous and incommensurable energies. By his free act, man affirms himself and inscribes himself in a temporality consciously and therefore humanly lived. By the Incarnation, human history acquires a direction, for with it real time appears; this permits an avoidance of the reef of Greek eternity, Platonic recollection; in short, every form of abstract timelessness. It is insofar as the instant of the Incarnation is the encounter of the eternal and temporal in the unique person of the God Man that this instant becomes decisive for every man in whatever epoch he might live. One might say that this contact of time and eternity vivifies time; thanks to the instant, time is full of eternity. Taking the expression of Paul to the Galatians Kierkegaard writes, "Such an instant ought truly to have its own name: let us call it *the fullness of time*."[59] At once an anthropological and a theological category, the instant expresses the valorization of history and the valorization of individual existence.

The answer to Lessing's question, therefore, is as follows: not only is the point of departure of eternal happiness historical (the existence of Christ is the unique point of reference, limited yet universally valid), but it is in time that man is led toward that beatitude. In other words, the historical realism of the existence of the God Man is such that it accentuates historical existence to the point of giving it preeminence over every form of timelessness. To say that the instant is decisive and that the instance of free choice posits real temporality is to use equivalent expressions. The Greeks did not know real temporality because they lacked the category of spirit. Christianity alone posits spirit truly because it confers on human existence the possibility of being able to make authentic decisions and thus of becoming involved with the seriousness of existence—in short, of constructing internal happiness.

The instant of the Incarnation fundamentally modifies man's situation, for by the fact that "the eternal truth has appeared in time . . . (it) is no longer behind but before because it exists or has existed itself; so it is that if the individual does not come into possession of the truth in existing, in existence, he will never possess it."[60]

The instant of the Incarnation thus causes the infinite and eternal to become in some way commensurable to the finite and to time. "The instant is that ambiguity in which

[59] *Fragments,* p. 22.
[60] *Postscript,* p. 187.

time and eternity are in contact and thereby is posited the concept of temporality in which time constantly rejects time."[61] The Incarnation as instant is a point of departure which signifies that, for man, the past is finished and that eternal truth ought not be sought there as systems do. Time vivified by eternity becomes the Archimedean point which allows the individual to orient his whole existence toward the future by referring it not to the past by memory, but to this eternal present, this fullness of time which appears only with Christianity. The point of insertion of eternity in time is the instant par excellence which makes possible other human instants, not those of Platonic contemplation or of aesthetic experience, but those of decisions made in virtue of the desire to imitate Christ in renunciation and suffering.

THE INSTANT OF REVELATION OR THE GRANTING OF THE CONDITION

The present of all believers is linked to a unique and irrevocable past: the irruption into history of the eternal truth. This fact gives a sense to history by ceaselessly demanding of the man who reflects on it and risks being absorbed by it an effort which enables him to escape from the mirage of the eternal return. But his modification of the relations of being and time, of human thought and temporality, cannot be a result of man's initiative; it results from the appearance of the paradoxical instant of the Incarnation. To the two meanings of instant distinguished above —anthropological category of the act of free choice and theological category, the existence of the God Man—it is important that we add a third: the instant of the gift of faith by the God Man to the free individual. *The instant is that point of time when the revelation of Christ takes place*

---

[61] *The Concept of Dread*, p. 130.

in history; it is also the moment when faith is given to a particular man.

One can see in the theme of the condition given to the disciple by God, a condition permitting a man to escape from immanence, the most exact expression of what the revelation in Jesus Christ represents for Kierkegaard. The revelation in the person of Jesus is a reality for all men no matter to what epoch they belong because it is a bridge thrown up by God himself over the great abyss opened between man and God by sin. Sin has darkened man's spirit and weighed down his heart. Revelation illumines the spirit by relieving the heart. It is not therefore a pure notification, simply a conceptual arrangement or enrichment of the mind. It is an event constituitive of the history of men insofar as their most personal life is marked by it. The Christian is a man conscious that his existence would be completely different if God had not spoken, if the Gospel did not provoke that potentialization of the passion to exist. But sin, as separation from God, is what renders impossible the perception of man's new possibilities. The sinner is a man who can no longer see far; he stares myopically at what is closest. He lacks the condition *sine qua non* for seeing beyond the large gap that separates him from God. Revelation is this condition because in its concrete historical form it manifests, in existence, the eminently existential objectivity of transcendence.

In what, more precisely, does this revelation consist? "The object of faith is the reality of another, its attitude an infinite interest. The object of faith is not a doctrine. . . . The object of faith is not a professor who has a doctrine, for when a professor has a doctrine, the doctrine is *eo ipso* more important than the professor, and the relationship is intellectual. . . . But the object of faith is the reality of the one who teaches, that he really exists. That is why the response of faith is announced in an absolute fashion: yes or no. . . . The object of faith therefore is the reality of

God in the sense of existence. But to exist means above all to be an individual. . . . The object of faith is thus the reality of God in existence: that is to say, as an individual: that is to say, that God existed as an individual man."[62] Above all else, therefore, revelation is the very person of Christ as God and as Man, and revelation itself is the gift God gives to man of everything he lacks in order to encounter Christ. It is the condition of faith, the condition of contemporaneity, in short, the condition of the whole coming-to-be-a-Christian.

THE CHRISTIAN IS CONFRONTED BY THE ABSOLUTE FACT

What for Kierkegaard is the proper function of that divine aid so necessary that without it no relevant movement of Christian religiosity would be possible? The instant of the appearance of the God Man is the paradoxical instant; as such it represents that reality, that fact that human thought cannot contain: it is the very limit of understanding. But we must say even more: this fact cannot be recognized *as a fact* if the Master (God) does not give the condition. In effect, this fact is not an ordinary historical fact, embedded and relativized like all others in the historical flow; no more is it a purely eternal fact, with regard to which all men are by nature in the same situation. It is the case of a fact that Kierkegaard qualifies as absolute,[63] an absolute fact which is at the same time historical. With respect to such a fact, immediate and direct encounter, such as contemporaries had, as well as the historical information which the disciples at second hand receive, constitute only the occasion. "But, just as this historical event is for the contemporary the occasion of becoming a disciple by receiving, be it well noted, the condition from God himself

[62] *Postscript*, p. 290.
[63] *Fragments*, p. 125.

(for otherwise we speak the Socratic language), so too the testimony of contemporaries will be for every man of later generations the occasion for becoming a disciple, provided . . . that he receives the condition from God himself."[64] The condition constitutes, one might say, the very core of Christ's manifestation as revealer; it is present in the historical fact itself (called "absolute") as the force permitting man, summoned to choose faith or scandal, to commit himself to the way of faith. The gift of the condition is thus intimately linked to the instant so that the latter might be considered as the absolute paradox or as the act of free choice of a man making the most important decision in his pursuit of eternal happiness. That is why it is permissible to consider the condition of the gift of faith as one aspect of the instant.

In fact, this third aspect of the instant is what both unites and distinguishes the first two: Kierkegaard's theological reflection is centered essentially on the Christian mystery as the mystery of salvation. If we must distinguish the instant as anthropological category (the act of free choice) from the instant as theological category (the moment of the Incarnation), this is because all things must be seen in function of the man who is to be saved: the individual existing today who "has heard talk" that one day God was born of a woman. Kierkegaard uses but one term to express these three events: the Incarnation, God's gift of faith to man, the free choice of the believer. The instant is the global category and the instant, as the gift of the condition to a man confronted by the absolute historical fact, is "revelation."

Revelation as the giving of the condition by God to men has a double function. First, the condition makes understanding possible. What must be understood? Above all, the global fact of the truth revealed by God of which man has been deprived by sin. Further, it must be understood that this truth concerns and conditions man in that which

[64] *Ibid.*, pp. 125–126.

most passionately involves him: his striving for an eternal happiness. The instant is really the decision of eternity. The condition must be received in order that faith become that happy passion which is that of the believer who knows that he owes everything to his master. It is the master who gives to the disciple the power of sustaining with him personal relations, relations "of existence to existence, where the master sustains and nourishes from his own substance, so to speak, the consciousness of the disciple." It is necessary to receive the condition in order not to be scandalized, to break with immanence and emerge from Socratism. The reception of the condition is the point of departure of Christian becoming. Evidently there is no question of receiving this condition passively; one does not become a Christian despite oneself. To be authentic, revelation must encounter an awakened spirit, an infinite interest, a subjectivity already transformed by the surpassing of the aesthetic and by consciousness of guilt.

Secondly, the condition is given to remedy the inadequacy of historical knowledge which is always subject to error since it is essentially approximative. The contradiction involved in wishing to ground one's happiness on an approximation can be surmounted only if God himself gives to man the power lacking him. The paradoxical accenting of existence and faith as a happy passion go hand in hand because the existence of the believer proceeds under the immediate protection of God. In short, the whole of Christian becoming rests on this gift of God which transforms man and makes him a new creature.

THE FULLNESS OF TIME AND THE HUMBLING OF THE SERVANT

The faith of Kierkegaard bears essentially on Christ as Savior whom he sees rather in his humiliation, his state of the offered victim, than in the glory of Tabor. This does not mean that his whole Christological conception must be reduced to the doctrine of humiliation, kenosis. The humiliation of Christ is one of the chosen themes of the *Edifying Discourses* and the *Journal,* but rather than considering it the fundamental theme which explains and justifies the categories of paradox, faith, and the instant, we would simply say that it is for Kierkegaard part of the whole given furnished by the New Testament. The humiliation of Christ was not such that his divinity became unknowable, for in that case the paradox would be impossible. In his very abasement, the God Man was recognizable; were that not so, Kierkegaard observes in his *Journal* of 1843, God would have been the supreme ironist. This text of the *Journal* deserves to be quoted for it shows a theological balance in Kierkegaard that few commentators notice: "The divine paradox is to be seen, in Christ, in default of other things, in his crucifixion at least, and in the working of miracles. This implies, however, that he is recognizable in his divine authority, although faith is needed to solve its own paradox."[65]

The theme of Christ's incognito is intimately linked to that of kenosis. Kierkegaard himself wanted to live his Christianity incognito and his meditation on the mystery of Christ is inseparable from his reflection on the demands of the imitation of Christ. Such a process runs through the *Journal* but one finds it as well in several other works and in the *Discourses.*[66] Particularly with respect to the incog-

[65] *Journal,* IV A 103.

[66] On this point one might consult G. Malantschuk, *Søren Kierke-gaard's Modifikationer af det kristelige* (Kierkegaard's Modifications of Christianity) in *Dansk Theologisk Tidsskrift,* XX (1957), pp. 224–241. The author shows that the theory of Stages underlies the analysis of 'intermediary determinations (*'Mellembestemmelserne'*—the term is Kierkegaard's own: X 5 B 107) which lie between the perfect realization of the ideal in Christ our model and ordinary human existence. In his description of these intermediary degrees, Kierkegaard frequently uses texts from Scripture to illustrate the different degrees of realization of the ideal. "On

nito of Christ it is clear from the *Training in Christianity* that the utilization of biblical texts and the presentation of the thought are based on the personal experience of the author: the suffering of one who wanted to pass incognito, the misunderstanding of which he was the object. This idea is proper to Anticlimacus, the pseudonymous author of *Training in Christianity,* because, as has been seen above, this pseudonym is presented as an advanced Christian: at that moment, in effect, Kierkegaard begins to be misunderstood because of the intransigeance with which he affirmed his Christian faith against the deforming of faith perpetrated by the official theologians of the Danish Church.

One might also say that the theme of the incognito is useful for Kierkegaard in his desire to maintain his faith in the real and complete humanity of Jesus Christ. "He has become a man like all the others . . . ." ". . . the humblest is, as we know, the one who must serve others, the God ought then to show himself in the form of a servant. But this is not a borrowed form."

Despite his abasement, the Servant will not be unperceived; he will attract the attention of the masses. The divine paradox will allow the divine nature to be apparent in the human nature of Christ to which it is conjoined. Such is the law of revelation. A personal revelation made to a person, to the individual who encounters God, to the disciple who encounters the Master.

Christ, true God and true man, voluntarily humbled by love, manifests his divinity by signs. *Training in Christianity* takes up the subject of miracles several times: "Assuredly he pays taxes, but he earns money by a miracle, that is to

the subject of the three discourses on Lilies of the Field and Birds of the Air, the first is aesthetic, the second ethical and the third religious." (VIII 1 A 1) "Biblical texts are very often employed to illustrate the itinerary of the individual in his effort at progressive interiorization." (Malantschuk, *op. cit.,* p. 238) say he shows himself to be the God Man."[67] A miracle certainly never constitutes a direct proof of the divinity of Christ, but it renders one attentive; that is why it is necessary to watch that "they not be taken in vain."[68] The possibility of the scandal of faith attaches to this indirect manifestation of divinity.

For Kierkegaard, the paradox is precisely that "this man here, this determined figure, with an exterior like other men, with their language, uses and customs, is the Son of God."[69] Kierkegaard likes to emphasize the realistic character of the Incarnation; from his birth to his death, Jesus acts like a man, but he also acts like God by feeding five thousand men with five loaves of bread and two fish.

The doctrine of kenosis is essential to the Incarnation as the paradoxical instant of the manifestation of Christ, as revelation. The historical revelation is effected by the deeds of Christ, including the crucifixion, death, and resurrection. Faith—and thus the possibility of scandal—is possible because man is placed before the historical fact in which two heterogeneous dimensions are manifested simultaneously. The fact experienced by contemporaries is not to be considered purely historically or speculatively, which is what Hegel did in his philosophy of history or of religion; it must be vitally encountered in faith. The task of Christianity is not to expose the whole situation from "a strictly historical point of view,"[70] but to be referred to this unique historical situation that is the absolute fact, to live it here and now in a history become, since then, the locus of the manifestation of God.

Commenting on John 13,32, Kierkegaard writes, "Moreover, Christ is the same in his abasement and in his elevation, and the choice will not be correct if one thinks he must

[67] *Training in Christianity,* p. 94.
[68] *Ibid.,* p. 135.
[69] *Journal,* IV A 47.
[70] *Training in Christianity,* p. 109.

choose between the Christ of the abasement and the Christ of the elevation; for Christ is not divided, he is one and the same person . . . He is a composite and still one single same person in his abasement and in his elevation . . . Being lifted up, he desires to attract *all men* to himself. . . ."[71] It is of this attraction that we must now speak.

THE CONTEMPORANEITY OF THE DISCIPLE

Much has been written on contemporaneity. Some Protestant theologians have taken up the notion, transformed it and integrated it into their thought;[72] others have categorically rejected it.[73] It is an extremely complex notion; essentially religious, it nevertheless includes a whole series of traits belonging to the Kierkegaardian conception of the multiple configurations possible to a temporal existence. But above all it was conceived by Kierkegaard the theologian meditating on the situation of the Christian in the present time, the time of so-called Christendom, and feeling the need to express the temporal characteristics of becoming a Christian. We could not hope to make an exhaustive study of contemporaneity here. We shall only single out the essential elements of this category which denotes the concrete existential situation of the adult and fervent Christian—one

---

[71] *Ibid.*, pp. 154–155.

[72] Cf. "the importance given by Karl Barth to the concept of 'contemporaneity" which he borrows from Kierkegaard. The Word of God can never be considered and treated as a past fact, delivered over to the historian or to any attempted human exploitation of a divine gift." L. Bouyer, *op. cit.*, p. 135.

[73] ". . . the vaunted 'contemporaneity' that faith should establish with Jesus incarnate has no basis in the New Testament. Kierkegaard who more than anyone insists on contemporaneity by that very fact implicitly destroys the line of salvation by excluding from it, properly speaking, the present period." O. Cullmann, *Christ et le Temps*, p. 119.

impassioned, even in his life of faith, to the degree that it takes into account that the object of faith (the God Man in his abasement) obliges him to find in the limits of history and his own temporally limited experience the supreme eternal truth which, as such, transcends history.

Contemporaneity is a characteristic of Christian existence insofar as this is concerned with the history of salvation: the God Man inhabits the world, he has pitched his tent among us. The mystery of Christmas is the primordial sacrament. Contemporaneity is never attributed to Christ. Contemporaneity is a part of the Kierkegaardian analysis of the act of faith, it is a subjective category: *to become a believer is to make oneself contemporary with Christ, of his presence as Savior by His grace and by the infinite demand that he makes as Model for sinful man.* The Kierkegaardian theory of contemporaneity is unduly transposed when it is referred essentially to the thought of the divinity of Christ. In this fashion, one represents contemporaneity as being the property of each generation: all are before God in the same situation, none is privileged. This comes down to considering contemporaneity as centered on Christ as God, when for Kierkegaard it is entirely oriented by Christ as paradox, that is, as God Man. If all generations are equidistant from the historical fact of Christ, this is not because Christ is God and as such transcends temporality and suppresses distances. Certainly there would be no contemporaneity if the Servant was not God; moreover contemporaneity does not express the direct relation to the Absolute but on the contrary an indirect, mediate relation to a fact which permits no immediate encounter. This follows from the paradoxical structure of the instant.

One could say that contemporaneity is not conceived by Kierkegaard for purposes of transcending history by a vertical recourse to God. Rather, it is elaborated to express the fundamental equality of all generations before an historical fact which can only be attained by faith. "The absolute fact is an historical fact and, as such, an object of faith."[74] The immediate contemporary must attain this fact by faith in the same way as later generations because "God cannot be known immediately."[75] But to the disciple, no matter of what epoch, God "has given the Condition that he might see and has opened for him the eyes of faith."[76] The Condition, necessary "lest we revert to Socratism,"[77] is received in the instant, which is the point of reference of contemporaneity because it is just that paradox "which rightly conciliates the opposition since it is the eternalization of the historical and the historicalisation of eternity."[78] "As long as the eternal and historical remain external one to another the historical is only an occasion."[79] It is not necessary, therefore, to dissociate the horizontal relation to the historical Christ from the vertical relation to God, for it is in the instant that the condition is given. This means that "contemporaneity is the condition of faith and, to be precise, is faith."[80] Contemporaneity is not an expression of the divine presence at all times and in all places; it is a characteristic of the situation of the Christian to the degree that he is modified by the obligatory and essential relation of understanding and will to a determinate historical fact.

The believer become contemporary with Christ has acquired the second immediacy in which God, naturally *intimior intimo meo,* becomes external to me as is every particular man: God becomes temporal and this transforms man. This transformation, actively and consciously lived in faith always active, elicits contemporaneity. The contemporary escapes from the objectivity of historical knowledge

[74] *Fragments,* p. 125.
[75] *Ibid.,* p. 78.
[76] *Ibid.,* p. 80.
[77] *Ibid.,* p. 76.
[78] *Ibid.*
[79] *Ibid.,* p. 75.
[80] *Ibid.,* p. 77.

for contemporaneity puts the whole of existence with all its risks in play. By submitting himself to the Christ event, the Christian describes a profound movement which surpasses the detachment of the scholar or the strength of the pagan hero; he renders himself vulnerable by putting his strongest hope in time, something that will perhaps require of him sacrifices and renunciations terrible because they are terribly concrete.

In affirming the necessity of contemporaneity, Kierkegaard expresses the essence of the message he wants to convey, for he was convinced that a very precise mission had been assigned him in the Danish Protestant Christianity of the nineteenth century: the object worthy both of the meditation of the philosopher and of every believer is not Christianity as an ensemble of concepts, it is the fact of being a Christian. "For the idea of the *religious cosmos* where every creature has his place, every question its answer, every anguish its reason and which tends to its perfection by its essential determination, Kierkegaard substituted the idea of *religious becoming.* . . . The confrontation of the individual with the object of his belief demands a ceaselessly renewed contact with the world of fact, of becoming, of history."[81]

THE REJECTION OF THE ETERNAL RETURN

Kierkegaard rejects any cyclic movement, every species of eternal return, but he accepts the reversibility of each individual becoming; the individual in effect ought not to be seduced by any progressive and immanent evolution. In Christianity, he finds himself obliged, in order to continue to become, to refer himself to an instant given in time. An instant particular like all others but an instant unique

[81] R. Bespaloff, "Etudes kierkegaardiennes," *Revue philosophique,* 127 (1939), p. 306.

of its kind. In effect, far from presenting itself as pure past, it has on the contrary all the power of eternity. Moreover, this instant is such that it demands a movement of thought that can be described as reversing, because it brings into play the will which in some fashion prohibits the understanding from pursuing and prolonging its natural movement: reason must desist from admitting no criterion other than itself; it must agree to submit to the control of an exterior objectivity, not simply of empirically perceptible reality, but of the "fact." A contingent fact which is the reality with which the Christian occupies himself and which, as fact, concerns man in that which is most intimate and essential to him: his dynamism toward the Good.

Immediate or direct contemporaneity, that of the eye witness, is in no way an advantage in the case of Christianity. True contemporaneity, that of faith and not of fact, is, in the subject, a consequence of the instant, for it consists essentially of the reception of the condition. "Man receives the condition in the instant, a condition which, being a condition for the comprehension of eternal truth, is *eo ipso* the eternal condition."[82] This condition lifts man above himself, above the socratic, and that is why God alone can provide it by a direct intervention escaping the normal course of human history. That is why the understanding ought to be dismissed.[83] That is why the gift of the eternal condition in time is a sort of miracle.[84] Chapter IV of the *Philosophical Fragments* is extremely clear and exploits the tradition on the Incarnation.[85] ". . . in order that the Master might give the condition, it is necessary that he be the god

---

[82] *Fragments,* p. 77.

[83] *Ibid.,* p. 73 ("set aside").

[84] *Ibid.,* p. 81.

[85] Cf. St. Anselm in *Cur Deus Homo,* I, 2, cap. 6: ". . . satisfactio, quam nec potest facere nisi Deus, nec debet nisi homo; necesse est ut eam faciat Deus homo." (Migne PL 158, col. 404)

and if the disciple is to be put in possession of it, he must be man."[86]

Contemporaneity therefore is the state of the believer who, thanks to the condition, is in contact with the instant. Clearly it is the state of one who has received grace. "It must be recalled that, in contemporaneity the paradox being beyond human capacities as the object of faith, for that very reason the apostles were rightly endowed with superhuman powers that they might be made able to endure believing. For us it is a little easier, besides we have Grace as the fruit of Christ's death. But one should never forget this point: if one could fully prove by the consequences that Christ is what he said he was, he would not then be the object of faith."[87] "Christ died . . . and his death is redemption: that is grace. The Holy Spirit whom Christ will send, henceforth it is he who is at bottom the dispenser of grace, the grace acquired by Christ."[88] To become a Christian is to become a contemporary of Christ and this is only possible because Christ died and redeemed us once and for all. This event is the obligatory point of reference in Christianity for every believer. To be before God is to be before Christ. "Each time that someone truly becomes a Christian one can say: today a Savior is born to you."[89] Man cannot give the contemporaneity to himself; it is a gift.

The second immediacy signifies indeed that man is radically modified in his very existence. It is of this modification of the self that Anticlimacus speaks in *Sickness unto Death:* "The potentialization of self-consciousness is here a knowledge concerning Christ, a self placed before Christ . . . A self placed before Christ is a self potentialized by the ineffable concession made by God, potentialized by the ineffable intensity that invests him from the fact that God willed,

[86] *Fragments,* p. 77.
[87] *Journal,* X 2 A 447.
[88] *Ibid.,* X 2 A 451.
[89] *Ibid.,* X 2 A 283.

because of the guilt of the self, to be born, to become a man, to suffer and die. The more one augments the idea of God the more one augments the self; that has been said earlier and it applies, as well here; the more the idea of Christ is intensified, the more the self is intensified. Qualitatively, a self is that which is its own measure. From the fact that Christ is the measure, the expression come from God becomes extremely vigorous and witnesses to the prodigious reality the self enjoys; in effect, it is primordially and par excellence in Christ that God is the end and measure of man, his measure and his end."[90] To encounter Christ in contemporaneity is to encounter him as Grace, as Reconciler, as Savior, as Liberator.

From this it can be seen that O. Culmann's critique of contemporaneity is not well taken. His problematic of an essentially cosmological time is not situated at the same level as that of Kierkegaard for whom contemporaneity is a category of faith lived essentially on the basis of a condition immediately given by Christ the Savior. This gift is the constant work of the Spirit in the existing man who has attained the maximum of subjective passion. Contemporaneity thus appears as what renders possible the passage of existence to its greatest intensity because it furnishes man with the possibility of expressing his relation to an eternal happiness and thus of acquiring eternal validity; this is brought about by the encounter with the historical Christ as point of departure of man's eternal consciousness. Kierkegaard has all this in mind when he speaks of contemporaneity, grace and faith.

Become contemporary with Christ, the Christian sees himself confronted by new demands. This new man is not set up as a judge of others as if he were the possessor of a new vision of the world. He is held to see himself in the mirror of the Word of God to be constantly measured by the model it presents. "Living indeed is the Word of God,

---

[90] *Sickness Unto Death,* p. 185.

efficacious and more incisive than a two-edged sword . . .
it can judge the sentiments and thoughts of the heart."
(Heb. 4,12)

The notion of contemporaneity adds to the idea of sovereign and universally operative grace, the condition, the note of a demand addressed to man on the level of free action: the imitation of Christ. This rigorous demand which cannot be avoided corresponds to the gift of all powerful grace. Numerous entries in the *Journal* illustrate this thought: Christ is the Model—then he dies and is transformed and becomes eternally Grace for our own imperfect effort to imitate the Model.[91] The matter is clear: it is Christ as model who must now be advanced from a dialectical point of view, precisely because the dialectic put into play by Luther—Christ as gift—has ended by being taken completely in vain, so much so that the imitator resembles in nothing at all the model and is completely alien from it while grace is seen only from time to time. It must be recalled, as I have noted elsewhere, that when contemporaneity with Christ is the rule, the death of Christ is the redemption whence, in a sense, grace properly dates.[92] "While the Apostle [Paul] preaches this doctrine [the redemptive death], his life expresses imitation."[93] Contemporaneity with Christ includes dying to this world: one must continually die to oneself.[94] To imitate Christ in his life, in his proper mode of existing, is to be conformed to him, it is to respond to an infinite demand. This response causes existence to fly into pieces; the absoluteness of the demand makes existence explode.[95] Faith brings new determinations to human existence which concern not the necessary essence of man but free human becoming.

The idea of imitation will provide Kierkegaard an occa-

[91] *Journal,* X 2 A 451.
[92] *Ibid.,* X 2 A 361.
[93] *Ibid.,* X 3 A 409.
[94] *Ibid.,* X 3 A 171 and 294.
[95] See *Journal,* X 3 A 712 and 409.

sion to develop at length the theme of the suffering of
Christ. It is the Christ of the abasement with whom we
must become contemporary. The reality of Christ's suffering
is not that of pure appearance, so neither must that of the
Christian be. Before Christ, as before his task in existence,
man is tempted by scandal. Christ was, one night, an occasion of scandal for all his disciples; it is in that situation
that they encountered him truly for the first time. "The possibility of scandal is linked with faith . . . the disciples who
believed in his divinity and leapt over the possibility of
scandal in becoming believers, stumble at his abasement,
at that other possibility of scandal given when the God Man
drains the chalice of human suffering."[96] "It is thus that
Christ serves as example in the situation of the contemporary."[97] The decisive element of Christian suffering is in its
"voluntary acceptance and the possibility of scandal that
it brings in for him who suffers."[98] "Only the man whose
being has received a shaking so that he becomes spirit . . .
has had contact with God."[99] Only the man thus shaken can
pray to God, can try to imitate Christ by proceeding toward
the interiorization of the evangelical Law in the contemporaneity of love. Kierkegaard teaches us "that spirit cannot
be defined in terms of a category but only recognized in
terms of existence itself . . . For him it is a matter of *im-
posing* spirit on things and that perhaps is the profound
meaning of the idea of contemporaneity which attacks the
irreversibility of time . . . in the contemporaneity of the
guilty self with the Mediator, man tends toward a God
with a human face."[100]

Contemporaneity is the central notion of the Kierke-

---

[96] *Training in Christianity*, p. 107.
[97] *Ibid.*, p. 110.
[98] *Ibid.*, p. 111.
[99] *Sickness Unto Death*, p. 45.
[100] R. Bespaloff, *art. cit.*, p. 320.

gaardian analysis of the dialectic of Christian existence.[101] It introduces temporality into the world of spirit in the relation of the subject to the truth. Founded on an intrinsic modification of existence, faith makes man contemporary with a concrete history in which is given the condition of the possibility of the Christian experience. Human life is fundamentally unified not by the objective time of external actions nor by the timelessness of spirit but by the permanence of God's gift in the depths of the human heart. Movements of human intelligence and will echo this gift to the degree that the existent is impassioned not with the mythical dream of lost paradise, not by the facile certitudes of a verbal knowledge or by the immediacy of an unforeseen obligation, but by the interest which makes his subjective existence a spiritual adventure contemporary with the central event of history: the existence of the God Man.

THE IMITATION OF JESUS CHRIST IS NOT AN ABSTRACT IDEAL

"Insensibly the individual becomes aware of the seriousness of life conceived as an examination, the ultimate question of which is to know if one wishes to be a Christian or not."[102] "That is the test: to become a Christian is to persist in being one."[103] Kierkegaard has expressed his experience of practical Christian life in typically Protestant terms. The astonishing thing is that in such an atmosphere he arrived at a conception of the Christian attitude toward the world quite close to the Catholic attitude as it is expressed by mystics,[104] spiritual writers and the reflections,

[101] Contemporaneity is that toward "which my whole effort as a writer has tended." (IX A 95)

[102] *Training in Christianity*, p. 184.

[103] *Ibid.*, p. 196.

[104] On this subject, cf. M. Mikoluva Thulstrup, "Lidelsens problematik hos Kierkegaard og mystikerne" (The Problem of Suffer-

to whatever age they belong, on the religious life and the states of perfection.

A typical example is the problem of the relation of nature and grace. Kierkegaard does not hesitate to say: "Recall that the New Testament with divine perspicacity is fashioned to wound natural man on the widest possible scale."[105] Christianity is often presented by Kierkegaard as the most radical enemy of human nature. By that he means that Christianity demands a very great ascesis of detachment, renunciation of self-will, in an affective solitude and an effective poverty. The way of expressing these demands was, particularly toward the end of his life, often violent and hard; one senses there a sort of rigidity suggesting their author is misogynous and misanthropic, even that he is possessed by a semi-masochistic fury. One certainly ought not seek in Kierkegaard, on this matter, the marks of human balance one finds in Christians of the St. Francis de Sales sort. But it should be noted that the verbal virulence of Kierkegaard on the subject of his coreligionists, especially the clergy, in part results from the necessity he felt to express a demand of practical Christian life with the aid of theological categories ill-fitted to the task, notably those defining the Protestant anthropology of liberty depraved by sin and rendered absolutely heterogenous to grace.

Besides, Kierkegaard is situated between two schematic representations of Catholicism and Protestantism, the former characterized by that mad temerity which consists in imagining that man can come effectively to resemble Christ, to imitate perfectly the Model of perfection, abasement and suffering, the latter marked by temerarious humility which despairs of ever attaining that admirable ideal, which sees in this effort the very type of human hubris, the sign of the

ing in Kierkegaard and the Mystics), *Kierkegaardiana*, III (Copenhagen, 1959), pp. 48–72.
[105] *Journal*, XI 1 A 157.

lack of faith[106] and for this reason renounces every effort at imitation. Kierkegaard was right to seek a mean between these two extremes caricatured for purposes of polemics.

This is further intensified in him by the presence in Denmark of a theoretical Christianity which represented rather an evolved cultural atmosphere than a milieu of social life based on evangelical values. One understands how, on the basis of a Lutheran anthropology, he could write: "Only a man of will can become a Christian. Indeed he alone has one that can be broken. But a man of will whose will is broken by the absolute or by God, that is a Christian. The more natural power a will has the more profound will the fracture be and the better the Christian. This is what has been characterised by the significant phrase, 'the new obedience;' a Christian is a man of will who . . . wills the will of an Other . . . A man of reason can never become a Christian, at the most he will be led by the imagination to puzzle over Christian problems." But he added, "However, Providence in its mercy can, of course, do much with a man of reason, to change him into a man of will, so that he might become a Christian."[107]

To grasp the historical sense and meaning of such a position requires discernment. The Catholic reader instinctively feels the excesses and, at the same time, the partial truth it contains because his conception of man and of the world is such that the evangelical spirit is adapted to it without entailing the terrible demand of self-hatred. That it should be necessary to renounce his reason to arrive at a renunciation of his will, that is a way, perhaps, of stating the dimensions of the new birth, on condition that this death to self be lived as a dying to sin which is only the negative aspect of the interior justification of the regenerated soul.

The objective pursued by the ardent Kierkegaard appears

[106] *Ibid.*, X 5 A 139.
[107] *Ibid.*, XI 2 A 436.

more clearly when one confines himself to the precise problem of the imitation of Christ and the psychological conditions of the pursuit of such an ideal. Thus is discovered a Kierkegaard close to experience and more subtle than when he is engaged in polemic with the aid of abstract concepts and categories which sometimes betray his profoundly religious sense of the one thing necessary and his rich comprehension of the heart of a man engaged on the arduous way of becoming a Christian.[108]

Emerging from adolescence, the young man and woman who have received a Christian education find themselves charged with a heavy heritage: the image of the ideal of sublime perfection both religious and moral. This image does not leave them. Being given only in imagination, this image is infinitely distant from reality and Kierkegaard in 1850 regards with sympathetic commiseration the young man he had been. Consider this young man started on the road of life, enthusiastic and equipped with a pure imagination: that famous ideal of which many have spoken to him and which seems inseparable from his youthful soul. In some ways that ideal is his own perfect and ideal self, seemingly near, so nearly victorious over him; that victory always so nearly in hand seems only accidentally distant by a fraction of time so small it is pointless to speak of it.

All that is too abstract because time, which is always in effect limitation and suffering, does not yet play any role. Indifferent to difficulties in its imaginative permanence, that ideal is unreality itself, something that will be made unequivocally clear when time makes its appearance. Consciousness of terrestrial temporality is the sad privilege of the adult. Perfection is "to be tested day after day by the real suffering of reality."[109] The contrast between this experience and the facile and attractive *image* of perfection is

---

[108] What follows reproduces the movement of the fourth meditation of Part Three of *Training in Christianity*.

[109] *Training in Christianity*, p. 186.

the expression of the contrast which oppose the reality of life to easy and idealizing representations. The young man has only a faint idea of reality and that is why his effort is never a pure effort like that of the adult; he has always some consolation.

What then is experience if not this progressive discovery of the reality of suffering, of the suffering that is the reality of life and of which no imaginative anticipation can give the presentiment? "Of what good are seventy years of experience if one could have lived everything by his twenty-second year?"[110] But the young man is unaware of that, even if an adviser, who wishes him well, puts him on guard. Engrossed by the care of his picture, his ideal, he goes on with head held high and does not see what surrounds him. Though awake, he walks like a dreamer, as the ardent gleam in his eye reveals."[111] In his ardent desire to resemble the image he makes progress and is only a few feet from his goal when suddenly he discovers the environing reality. The great danger is that he will then say, "Let's be realistic, let's renounce what was only imagination."

It is essential that at this point of Christian becoming the young man not allow himself to be seized by consternation before this new situation, that he not renounce his image, but rather that he take account of the fact that his image of perfection lacks an essential element: suffering. Now he knows his love is going to cost him much in suffering and renunciation. At that moment his youth is over. It is to be hoped that his ideal will not disappear together with the optimism of his juvenile imagination. But it is much more difficult "to become again a child" than simply to be young in years.

If Christian becoming is not a religion for children only, this is because the proposed ideal is not an abstract *image,*

110 *Ibid.*
111 *Ibid.*, p. 187.

but a living *model* who appears from the outset in abasement. Christ's suffering will not often detain the adolescent's imagination for he has need to see in Jesus Christ love, sweetness, infinite elevation; in this sense, the young man cannot renounce his image, even in a Christian context. But when progressively he senses that the world is the place of adversity and that the more the ideal is elevated the more intense the suffering in this world he will have always before his eyes not an ideal, but a model who says to him. "Have patience, I have vanquished the world; in but a short while you will have run your course."

This patience which takes time seriously in this world will be, thanks to the power of hope, the privilege of the young man as well as the old, for the model is not an image, it is he who, having been lifted up, draws us all to himself.

The theology of the imitation of Christ by good works has no other foundation than grace.

CONCLUSION

Perhaps better today than in the nineteenth century, the thought of Kierkegaard can be of help to a believer who reflects in order to live his faith in a world whose intellectual climate and moral sensibility are a-religious. The progressive extension of the domains that man conquers, the autonomy of knowledge, technology and art, in a word the very modernity of the dominant mentality of today, all contribute to detach the religious universe from sociological and cultural contexts which, up until now, provided its veneer.

The existential approach to faith obliged Kierkegaard to locate Christian experience as one existential possibility among others: the aesthetic, the ironic, the ethical, the humorous, natural religiosity and pure thought. His existential propaedeutic to dogma forces one who follows to avoid the misunderstanding which consists in reducing faith to an ensemble of rituals or a cult of consoling thoughts. The torture of Abraham, which is in no wise reducible to the tragedy of Agamemnon, the suffering of Job, which is not some masochistic tendency toward pain, the invincible solitude of the believer before God confronted with a world sufficient unto itself, these are expressions of the inevitable rupture between the human and the Christian. Taking existence seriously reveals the ground of existential possibilities and the possibilities of thought this side of the leap, this side of the quite new decision which transfigures a man's life by placing it under the sign of faith in Jesus Christ. We have not analyzed all these possibilities here because within the design of this collection it sufficed to indicate in what way this Danish Lutheran is a Christian for all times. He is that because he puts us on guard against the danger of being too facilely Christian: that is to do it badly for the difficulty is an integral part of the adventure. To avoid this danger is to reject the smugness of one who considers himself unlike the rest of men, not a sinner marked by evil, error, the accommodations of the aesthetic and the generalities of the ethical. To avoid this danger is to resign oneself to being a simple existant, and not a pure spirit, always tempted to slip into that natural religiosity which nobly assumes itself face to face with God, but all too often a man made God.

It is beneficial always to be put in question, to be engaged in a movement of conversion which is never effected once and for all. Is it not after all a kind of spiritual youthfulness that obliges us constantly to be reborn as contemporaries of Jesus Christ? Kierkegaard was engaged in that task. And that is why, unlike Monsieur Teste, his thoughts concern something other than "the very intimate forms of faith reconstituted by artifice and marvelously articulated by a spirit of incomparable boldness and profundity."[112] He has not "coldly explored the ardent soul" for his thought experience always conditioned his immediate future.

Unlike the believer of today, living in a naturally a-religious world, Kierkegaard thought and lived in an officially Christian world. But in that condition of Christianity which he combatted so much, he fought for the rediscovery of the specificity of Christian becoming. His effort is still ours since, for him as for us, it is no longer a matter of exalting values universally recognized as sublime. It is a matter of

[112] Paul Valery, *Monsieur Teste,* nouvelle édition augmentée de fragments inedits (Paris: N.R.F., 1946), p. 52.

rediscovering the true sense of the hope which is as different from despair as from that faith in progress by which so many of our contemporaries are instinctively animated.

To retain as field of reference the scalpel strokes of Valery, we might say that some will be tempted to liken Kierkegaard to Madame Teste who wrote, "My soul has more of a thirst to be astonished than for any other thing. Waiting, risking, a little doubting, exalt and enliven it far more than certain possessing could. I don't think this is good but so it is I am, despite the reproaches I have received. More than once I confessed having thought that I would prefer to believe in God than to see him in all his glory and I have been chided. My confessor told me that was silliness rather than sin."[113] Any likening of Kierkegaard and Madame Teste is illusory for Kierkegaard at bottom would, I believe, share the view of the confessor. Besides, this penitent represents God as the impenetrable and thus admirable order of thought. For Kierkegaard God is not a house of ideas, a supreme thing in some way the prisoner of itself. God is the invisible yet present Person whose very invisibility attests to the reality, however seductive, of the world. Faith in this God—the God of Jesus Christ who has not abandoned us to the world—does not impede a man's attending to the concrete life of his contemporaries who are on the way with him (*Mitmenschen*). His belief in revelation is not belief in a pure positivity (the *bloss-statuta-risch* of Kant), for it manifests itself in the approximations, miscarriages and defeats of existence. The central question is one of appropriation. Official religion, the Christian state, Christian culture always entail the possibility of a subtle temptation, that namely which induces the Christian to believe he can afford the investment of a modest apprenticeship to life, together with whatever humility before another this apprenticeship may require.

[113] *Ibid.*, p. 40.

Kierkegaard did not relish risk for its own sake. He is not the father of that somewhat bitter taste for the absurd some romantically entertain to give the impression of living truly. He encountered the seriousness of existence because on a first class ship "where everyone amuses himself" he found an old copy of the Bible and, having opened it, could not raise his eyes yet kept on hearing the music and conversation coming from the salon. For the ship sails on and the believer too is a passenger.

CHRONOLOGY *

The events of Kierkegaard's personal life became so interwoven with his writings that the following chronology is necessarily a bio-bibliography. It may seem odd that a man who championed existence over thought and warned about dehumanizing effects of speculation and scholarship should have expended himself in the writing of books. The oddness dissolves when we consider Kierkegaard's distinction between primitivity and the traditional. "Nowadays one becomes an author by reading, not by his primitivity; just as one becomes a man by mimicking others, not by his primitivity." (*Journal,* VIII 2 B 82; cf. *Philosophical Fragments,* rev. trans., Vol. 1, p. 277) Kierkegaard's life was not sacrificed to an ideal of objectivity; his writings in various ways take their rise from his personal life and constitute in their entirety an existence communication in which *cor ad cor loquitur.*

The Point of View of My Work as an Author should be consulted for Kierkegaard's most concentrated effort to show the relationship between his mode of life, his pseudonymous works and the works he published under his own name. From the appearance of *Either/Or,* Kierkegaard writes simply and solely as a religious author; pseudony-

---

* Father Colette's presentation of the events in Kierkegaard's personal life and of the various streams of his writings has been altered somewhat in form. Translator.

mous works do not express his own views, certainly not without many qualifications, and the books published under his own name, particularly the various *Discourses,* make clear the ultimate drive of the authorship as well as establishing a dialectical tension between their viewpoint and that of the pseudonyms. *The Works of Love* is the true point of fusion of the earlier personal and pseudonymous works. The later pseudonym, Anti-Climacus, represents a Christian attitude beyond what Kierkegaard considered his personal one. At the end of his career, Kierkegaard launched an increasingly sharper attack on the Danish State Church.

1813

May 5   Søren Aabye Kierkegaard born in Copenhagen.
June 3   Baptized in Holy Ghost Church, Copenhagen.

1821

               Enters Borgerdydskolen in Copenhagen.

1830

October 30   Begins studies at the University of Copenhagen.

1834

April 15   Begins *Journal.*

1837

May   Meets Regina Olsen.

1838

               "The Great Earthquake" (Cf. II A 805)
May 19   10:30 A.M. Writes in his *Journal* of an "indescribable joy." (II A 228)
August 8/9   Kierkegaard's father dies.
September 7   *From the Papers of One Still Living* published.

1840

June 2   Requests examination in theology.
July 3   Passes examination *magna cum laude.*
July/August   Journey to Jutland.
September 10   Engaged to Regina Olsen.

1841

July 10   *The Concept of Irony with Constant Reference to Socrates*, dissertation for Master of Arts degree (equivalent of doctoral degree).

September 29   Defense of his dissertation.

October 11   Breaks engagement with Regina.

October 25   Leaves for Berlin where he hears Schelling.

1842

March 6   Returns to Copenhagen.

1843

February 20   *Either/Or*, edited by Victor Eremita, published.

May 8   Short trip to Berlin.

May 16   *Two Edifying Discourses*, by S. Kierkegaard.

October 16   *Repetition*, by Constantine Constantius.
     Fear and Trembling, by Johannes de Silentio.
     Three Edifying Discourses, by S. Kierkegaard.

December 6   *Four Edifying Discourses*, by S. Kierkegaard.

1844

March 5   *Two Edifying Discourses*, by S. Kierkegaard.

June 8   *Three Edifying Discourses*, by S. Kierkegaard.

June 13   *Philosophical Fragments*, by Johannes Climacus.

June 17   *The Concept of Dread*, by Vigilius Haufniensis.
     Prefaces, by Nicholaus Notabene.

August 31   *Four Edifying Discourses*, by S. Kierkegaard.

1845

April 29   *Three Discourses on Imagined Occasions*, by S. Kierkegaard.

April 30   *Stages on Life's Way*, edited by Hilarius Bookbinder.

May 13–24   Trip to Berlin.

May 29   *Eighteen Edifying Discourses*, by S. Kierkegaard.

1846

January 2   Kierkegaard attacked in *The Corsair*.

January 10	Replies in *The Fatherland* as Frater Taciturnus.
February 27	*Concluding Unscientific Postscript to the Philosophical Fragments*, by Johannes Climacus.
March 30	*A Literary Review*, by S. Kierkegaard.
May 2–16	Trip to Berlin.

1847

March 13	*Edifying Discourses in Various Spirits*, by S. Kierkegaard
September 29	*Works of Love*, by S. Kierkegaard.
November 3	Regina marries F. Schlegel.

1848

April 26	*Christian Discourses*, by S. Kierkegaard.
July 24/27	*The Crisis and the Crisis in a Life of an Actress*, by Inter et Inter.
November	*The Point of View of My Work as an Author*, published posthumously, 1859.

1849

May 14	Second edition of *Either/Or*.
	The Lilies of the Field and the Birds of the Air, by S. Kierkegaard.
May 19	*Two Minor Ethico-Religious Treatises*, by H. H.
July 30	*The Sickness Unto Death*, by Anti-Climacus.
November 13	*Three Discourses at the Communion on Friday*, by S. Kierkegaard.

1850

September 27	*Training in Christianity*, by Anti-Climacus.
December 20	*An Edifying Discourse*, by S. Kierkegaard.

1851

August 7	*On My Work as an Author*, by S. Kierkegaard.
	Two Discourses at the Communion on Fridays, by S. Kierkegaard.
September 10	*For Self-Examination*, by S. Kierkegaard.

1851/2

> *Judge for Yourselves.* Published posthumously in 1876.

1854

January 30   Bishop Mynster dies.

April 15   Martensen appointed bishop.

December 18   Kierkegaard begins attack on Martensen in *The Fatherland.*

1855

May 24   *This Must Be Said; Let It Then Be Said,* by S. Kierkegaard.

> The beginning of *The Moment,* of which nine issues appear during the next four months.

June 16   *Christ's Judgment on Official Christianity,* by S. Kierkegaard.

September 3   *The Unchangeableness of God,* by S. Kierkegaard.

September 25   Ninth issue of *The Moment;* the tenth was published posthumously.

October 2   Kierkegaard collapses on street and is taken to hospital.

November 11   Death of Kierkegaard.

November 18   Burial and commotion at graveside.

SELECTIONS FROM
KIERKEGAARD

I Autobiographical

1. CHILDHOOD AND RELATION TO HIS FATHER

There was once a father and a son. A son is like a mirror in which the father beholds himself, and for the son the father too is like a mirror in which he beholds himself in the time to come. However, they rarely regarded one another in this way, for their daily intercourse was characterized by the cheerfulness of gay and lively conversation. It happened only a few times that the father came to a stop, stood before the son with a sorrowful countenance, looked at him steadily and said: "Poor child, thou art going into a quiet despair." True as this saying was, nothing was ever said to indicate how it was to be understood. And the father believed that he was to blame for the son's melancholy, and the son believed that he was the occasion of the father's sorrow—but they never exhanged a word on this subject.

Then the father died, and the son saw much, experienced much, and was tried in manifold temptations; but infinitely inventive as love is, longing and the sense of loss taught him, not indeed to wrest from the silence of eternity a communication, but to imitate the father's voice so perfectly that he was content with the likeness. So he did not look at himself in a mirror like the aged Swift, for the mirror was no longer there; but in loneliness he comforted himself by hearing the father's voice: "Poor child, thou art going into a quiet despair." For the father was the only one who had understood him, and yet he did not know in fact whether he

95

had understood him; and the father was the only confidant he had had, but the confidence was of such a sort that it remained the same whether the father lived or died.

(Stages, p. 192)

SOLOMON'S DREAM

Solomon's judgment is well enough known, it availed to discriminate between truth and deceit and to make the judge famous as a wise prince. His dream is not so well known.

If there is any pang of sympathy, it is that of having to be ashamed of one's father, of him whom one loves above all and to whom one is most indebted, to have to approach him backwards, with averted face, in order not to behold his dishonor. But what greater bliss of sympathy can be imagined than to dare to love as the son's wish prompts, and in addition to dare to be proud of him because he is the only elect, the singularly distinguished man, a nation's strength, a country's pride, God's friend, a promise for the future, extolled in his lifetime, held by memory in the highest praise! Happy Solomon, this was thy lot! Among the chosen people (how glorious even to belong to them!) he was the King's son (enviable lot!), son of that king who was the elect among kings!

Thus Solomon lived happily with the prophet Nathan. The father's strength and the father's achievement did not inspire him to deeds of valor, for in fact no occasion was left for that, but it inspired him to admiration, and admiration made him a poet. But if the poet was almost jealous of his hero, the son was blissful in his devotion to the father.

Then the son one day made a visit to his royal father. In the night he awoke at hearing movement where the father slept. Horror seizes him, he fears it is a villain who would murder David. He steals nearer—he beholds David with a crushed and contrite heart, he hears a cry of despair from the soul of the penitent.

Faint at the sight he returns to his couch, he falls asleep, but he does not rest, he dreams, he dreams that David is an ungodly man, rejected by God, that the royal majesty is the sign of God's wrath upon him, that he must wear the purple as a punishment, that he is condemned to rule, condemned to hear the people's benediction, whereas the Lord's righteousness secretly and hiddenly pronounces judgment upon the guilty one; and the dream suggests the surmise that God is not the God of the pious but of the ungodly, and that one must be an ungodly man to be God's elect—and the horror of the dream is this contradiction.

While David lay upon the ground with crushed and contrite heart, Solomon arose from his couch, but his understanding was crushed. Horror seized him when he thought of what it is to be God's elect. He surmised that holy intimacy with God, the sincerity of the pure man before the Lord, was not the explanation, but that a private guilt was the secret which explained everything.

And Solomon became wise, but he did not become a hero; and he became a thinker, but he did not become a man of prayer; and he became a preacher, but he did not become a believer; and he was able to help many, but he was not able to help himself; and he became sensual, but not repentant; and he became contrite and cast down, but not again erect, for the power of the will had been strained by that which surpassed the strength of the youth. And he tossed through life, tossed about by life—strong, supernaturally strong, that is, womanishly weak in the stirring infatuations and marvellous inventions of imagination, ingenious in expounding thoughts. But there was a rift in his nature, and Solomon was like the paralytic who is unable to support his own body. In his harem he sat like a disillusioned old man, until desire for pleasure awoke and he shouted, "Strike

the timbrels, dance before me, ye women." But when the
Queen of the South [*sic*] came to visit him, attracted by
his wisdom, then was his soul rich, and the wise answer
flowed from his lips like the precious myrrh which flows
from the trees in Arabia.

(Stages, pp. 236–237)

THE IDEA FOR MY LIFE

Gilleleie, August 1, 1835

What I really lack is to be clear in my mind *what I am
to do,** not what I am to know, except in so far as a certain
understanding must precede every action. The thing is to
understand myself, to see what God really wishes *me* to do;
the thing is to find a truth which is true *for me,* to find *the
idea for which I can live and die.* What would be the use of
discovering so-called objective truth, of working through
all the systems of philosophy and of being able, if required,
to review them all and show up the inconsistencies within
each system;—what good would it do me to be able to
develop a theory of the state and combine all the details into
a single whole, and so construct a world in which I did not
live, but only held up to the view of others;—what good
would it do me to be able to explain the meaning of Christianity if it had *no* deeper significance *for me and for my life,*
—what good would it do me if truth stood before me, cold
and naked, not caring whether I recognised her or not,
and producing in me a shudder of fear rather than a trusting
devotion? I certainly do not deny that I still recognise an
imperative of understanding and that through it one can
work upon men, *but it must be taken up into my life,* and
that is what I now recognise as the most important thing.

---

* How often, when one believes one has understood oneself best of
all, one finds that one has caught the cloud instead of Juno.

That is what my soul longs after, as the African desert thirsts for water.

(Journals, n. 22)

THE GREAT EARTHQUAKE (1838)

Then it was that the great earthquake occurred, the terrible revolution which suddenly forced upon me a new and infallible law of interpretation of all the facts. Then I suspected that my father's great age was not a divine blessing but rather a curse; that the outstanding intellectual gifts of our family were only given to us in order that we should rend each other to pieces: then I felt the stillness of death grow around me when I saw in my father, an unhappy man who was to outlive us all, a cross on the tomb of all his hopes. There must be a guilt upon the whole family, the punishment of God must be on it; it was to disappear, wiped out by the powerful hand of God, obliterated like an unsuccessful attempt, and only at times did I find a little alleviation in the thought that my father had been allotted the heavy task of calming us with the consolation of religion, of ministering to us so that a better world should be open to us even though we lost everything in this world, even though we were overtaken by the punishment which the Jews always called down upon their enemies: that all recollection of us should be utterly wiped out, that we should no longer be found.

(Journals, n. 243)

INDESCRIBABLE JOY

May 19. Half-past ten in the morning. There is an indescribable joy which enkindles us as inexplicably as the apostle's outburst comes gratuitously: 'Rejoice I say unto you, and again I say unto you rejoice'.—Not a joy over this or that but the soul's mighty song 'with tongue and mouth, from the bottom of the heart': 'I rejoice through my joy, in, at, with, over, by, and with my joy'—a heavenly refrain, as it were, suddenly breaks off our other song; a joy which cools and refreshes us like a breath of wind, a wave of air, from the trade wind which blows from the plains of Mamre to the everlasting habitations.

(*Journals*, n. 207)

Aug. 11. My father died on Wednesday (the 9th) at 2 a.m. I had so very much wished that he might live a few years longer, and I look upon his death as the last sacrifice which he made to his love for me; for he did not die from me but *died for me* in order that if possible I might still turn into something. Of all that I have inherited from him, the recollection of him, his transfigured portrait, not transfigured by the poetry of my imagination (for it did not require that) but explained by many an individual trait which I can now take account of—is dearest to me, and I will be careful to preserve it safely hidden from the world; for I feel clearly that at this moment there is only one (E. Boesen) to whom I can in truth talk about him. He was a 'faithful friend'.

(*Journals*, n. 215)

FATHERLY LOVE

I sit here quite alone (I have often been just as much alone but I have never felt so conscious of it) counting the hours until I see Saeding. I can never remember any change in my father and I shall now see the places where as a poor child he watched the flocks and for which, as a result of his descriptions, I have felt such homesickness. What if I were to fall ill and be buried in the churchyard of Saeding! Extraordinary thought. His last wish is fulfilled—is that to be the whole meaning of my earthly life? Great heavens! The task cannot be so small when compared to all that I owe him. I learnt from him the meaning of fatherly love and so was given some idea of divine fatherly love, the one unshakable thing in life, the true archimedean point.

(Journals, n. 335)

FROM MELANCHOLY TO HOPE

For I now see so clearly (once again in renewed joy to God, a new occasion of thanks) that my life is so arranged. My life began without immediateness, with a terrible melancholy, in its earliest youth deranged in its very deepest foundations, a melancholy which threw me for a time into sin and debauchery and yet (humanly speaking) almost more insane than guilty. Thus my father's death really pulled me up. I dared not believe that the fundamental misfortune of my being could be resolved: and so I grasped eternity with the blessed assurance that God is love, even though I was to suffer thus all my life; yes, with that blessed assurance. That is how I looked upon my life. Then once again and sympathetically, I was flung down into the abyss of melancholy by having to break off my engagement and why, simply because I dared not believe that God would resolve the fundamental misfortune of my being, take away my almost insane melancholy, which I now desired, for her sake and then again for mine, with all the passion of my soul. It was as difficult as possible to have to reproduce my own misery. Once again I was resigned. Thinking only of working to free her I went to meet a life of this kind but, God be praised, always certain and with the blessed assurance that God is love, nothing has been more certain to me.

And now, now that in many ways I have been brought to the last extremity, now (since last Easter, though with intervals) a hope has awakened in my soul that God may desire to resolve the fundamental misery of my being. That is to say, now I am in faith in the profoundest sense. Faith is immediacy after reflection. As poet and thinker I have represented all things in the medium of the imagination, myself living in resignation. Now life comes closer to me, or I am closer to myself, coming to myself.—To God all things are possible, that thought is now, in the deepest sense, my watch-word, has acquired a significance in my eyes which I had never imagined it could have. That I must never, at any moment, presume to say that there is no way out for God because I cannot see any. For it is despair and presumption to confuse one's pittance of imagination with the possibility over which God disposes.

(Journals, n. 754)

2. THE THORN IN THE FLESH

As has been said already, the decisions of the finite require constraint. It is liberty's own desire to run the risk of decisions of the infinite, and it is only through liberty that one can reach a decision of the infinite. Most people do not understand this at all, since they are forced to throw themselves into decisions of the finite; as to those of the infinite, most people are completely unaware of them. For myself, it is just the opposite. From the start, I threw myself into life like a ship with leaking bilges; and it is to the very effort of manning the pumps to stay afloat that I owe the development of a peerless spiritual existence. I have succeeded. I interpreted this suffering as a splinter in my flesh, and I recognized the peerless character of my existence by the sting of the splinter and the sting of the splinter by the peerlessness. Thus did I understand myself. Otherwise I would have had to try to fix the leak a bit. . . .

Paul speaks of being an *aphorismenos,* well, I have been one since my earliest childhood. In the first place, my torture was the very suffering that I felt, and then it was the fact that what was but suffering and affliction had to be taken for pride by those around me. It is like the English lord envied by a laborer, until the day the laborer saw that the lord was a legless cripple.

People admired my talents, which is precisely why they wanted me to go along with others. And as I did not want to, they thought it was pride, and that is why they think that everything is merited. Alas! And the reason was a suffering and torture that ordinarily would have made a man lose his senses within six months. They believed it to be pride, and that is why, I am eager to say, they hope and wait for me to go mad. Alas! What saves me once again is that it is not pride, but suffering.

(*Pap.*, VIII A 185)

The danger for the religious man who participates in the religiousness of the absolute is naturally the meritorious, the risk, instead of piety, of falling into insolence, of thinking himself better than others or of giving himself merit before God, or at the very least, to have his conscience satisfied with itself for having done his duty.

For that reason, this type of religious man ordinarily has a secret sign, like Paul's "sliver in the flesh," which gives him the heart to hold out, precisely because this sign teaches him his own nothingness, and really makes of it a truth within him. This is to say that absolute religiousness is something which no man can venture into on his own; it has to begin, in a very special sense, with God. If not, what is dialectically cruelty in absolute religiousness becomes pure and simple cruelty, sin, fault.

(*Pap.*, X 1 A 72)

These are in short the two fundamental deviations of Christianity:

1. Christianity is not a doctrine but an existential message (otherwise, the problem is to bring forward all the abuses of orthodox theologians, with their quarrels over such and such a point, while existence remains perfectly unchanged, so that they argue about what Christianity is in the same way that they argue about the nature of Platonic philosophy). That is why we begin again *da capo* in each generation: all this knowledge about preceding generations is essentially superfluous, but not to be scorned when it

manages to understand itself with its limitations, while in the opposite case it is very dangerous.

2. As a result, since Christianity is not a doctrine, the person who sets forth Christianity, provided he speaks the truth objectively, cannot be distinguished from Christianity, as he would be in the case of a doctrine. No, Christ did not institute *Dozent,* but imitators. If Christianity, by the very fact of its not being a doctrine, is not re-presented in him who sets it forth, then this man does not set forth Christianity; for Christianity is an existential message, and it is your existence that sets it forth. In short, to exist in it, to express it by existing, [etc.,] is to re-present it.

(Pap., IX A 207)

Reduplication means to be what one says: Mankind is therefore infinitely better served by one who does not speak in too lofty a tone but is what he says. I have never presumed to say that the world is bad. I make a distinction: I say, Christianity teaches that the world is bad. I dare not say so myself because I am far from pure enough. But I have said that the world is mediocre, and that exactly expresses my life. Oh would that there was truth in the intercourse between men! One man defends Christianity, another attacks it and in the end, if one examines their lives, neither of them bothers very much about it; perhaps it is their livelihood. . . .

As far as I am concerned, I have had a thorn in the flesh from my earliest years. Were that not so I should have been very worldly. But that I cannot be however much I might wish it. It is therefore no merit of mine, for where is the merit when a man goes along the right path if, he is in a go-cart, or when a horse follows the track if it has a sharp bit.

(Journals, n. 804)

With all the favors I have received in my life, if I had been free from the splinter in my flesh, it is not unthinkable that I would have tried my hand at a bit of asceticism: for then I would have seen without difficulty that, to really control others, one must have complete control, or as much as possible, over one's own body. I am not praising this theme to the skies, I am simply saying that I believe things would have happened this way.

Now I, in the most profound sense, had had my wings irrevocably clipped, and then I had become used to much comfort and pleasure, always to enable me to produce more.

Now it is hardly easy for me to touch on this point because all my existence is an artificial existence.

The hard part, with my capacity for work and my talents, is to have been born in such a small country. For in a large country, I would not have had any difficulties, there would have been enough to be earned as an author. Yet in another sense, I'm content with my small country, for this has repercussions on my development and on my mission in religion.

(*Pap.*, X 3 A 343)

A CHILDHOOD MARKED BY SUFFERING

May 11. The majority of men (if they find that from their earliest years it is their lot to bear one suffering or another, one cross or another, one of those sad limitations of the soul) begin by hoping, or as they say, believing that things will go better, that God will make things all right etc., and then at length, when no change occurs they come little by little to rely upon the help of eternity *i.e.* they resign themselves and find strength in contenting themselves with the eternal.—The deeper nature, or he whom God has fashioned on a more eternal plan begins at once by understanding that this is a thing he must bear as long as he lives, he dares not require of God such an extraordinary paradoxical help. But God is perfect love just the same, nothing is more certain to him. So he is resigned and inasmuch as the eternal lies close to him he thus finds repose, blessedly assured all the while that God is love. But he must put up with suffering. Then in the course of time, when he becomes more concrete in the actuality of life, comes more and more to himself as a temporal being, when time and its succession exercises its power over him, when in spite of all his effort it becomes so difficult to live on with the assistance of only the eternal, when he becomes a human being in a humbler sense or learns what it means to be human (for in his resignation he is still too ideal or too abstract, for which reason also there is something of despair in such resignation):—then the possibility of faith presents itself to him in this form: whether he will believe by virtue of the absurd that God will help him temporally. (Here lie all the paradoxes.) So the forgiveness of sin also means to be helped temporally, otherwise it is mere resignation, which can endure to bear the punishment, though still convinced that God is love. But belief in the forgiveness of sins means to believe that here in time the sin is forgotten by God, that it is really true that God forgets.

That means to say, that most people never attain to faith. For a long time they live on in immediateness and finally they attain to a certain amount of reflection, and so they die. The exceptions begin the other way round, from childhood up dialectical *i.e.* without immediateness, they begin with dialectics, with reflection and in that way live on year after year (just about as long as others live merely in the immediate) and then, at a ripe age, the possibility of faith shows itself to them. For faith is immediateness after reflection.

The exceptions, naturally, have a very unhappy childhood and youth; for to be essentially reflective at an age which is naturally immediate, is the depths of melancholy. But it comes back again; for most people do not succeed in

becoming spirit, and all the fortunate years of their immediateness are, where spirit is concerned, a loss and therefore
they never attain to spirit. But the unhappy childhood and
youth of the exception is transfigured into spirit.

(Journals, n. 753)

3. THE ENGAGEMENT

I asked to speak with Regina, the date was set for the afternoon of September tenth. At that time, I did not say a single word to charm her. . . . I got her promise.

From that moment began a relationship with the entire family. My virtuosity was applied especially to the father, whom moreover I have always liked!

But as to what was going on inside of me, the next day I saw that I had made a mistake. A penitent like me, my *vita ante acta,* my melancholy, now right there was something!

I suffered indescribably all this time!

(Pap., X 5 A 149)

My love story is of a particular kind. The usual tactics of the student for Holy Orders is to begin by being the teacher and little by little the spiritual director of the girl of his choice and end by being her lover and her husband. I began by being a lover and ended by being a parson. One may as well be hung for a sheep as for a lamb, so my behaviour is far better; I have not lowered what is sacred to the service of my love, I submit just as much as I try to get others to submit to religion.

(Journals, n. 428)

But I see more and more clearly as to the things that concern me. Providence has used her to lay its hand on me. The possibility of marrying her, that is what was to make me grow, and so also my responsibility in my relationship to God.

I had to have been captured. And it had to have been by joining battle, in the most profound sense, with myself. That is why my opponent had to be someone who, in a certain sense, was no one, an object and yet no, not an object; something inexplicable, which by succumbing would bring me to struggle with myself. That is why a woman was useful, a woman who fights as a woman with weakness for her weapon. And she had to be charming so that she might strike more deeply . . . and my struggle with myself simply became more deadly. And she had to be so young that, in its turn, her youth itself handed me all responsibility and called me to care for her . . . and I struggled with myself all the more. And she had to be so young that her father, who almost thought her still a child, felt himself all the more bound to hand me all responsibility.

So I was caught or had to capture myself in the relationship to God. And once this was done, it was as if Providence were saying: "You see, as to her, she will be well taken care of and she will manage quite well; but you, you are caught. She can neither free you nor hold you, none of this can change, for here you are, caught in responsibility, and caught for me!"

(Pap., X 2 A 3)

All true love consists in loving one another in a third party; yes, even from the lowest level where, for example, two people love one another in a third person, up to the Christian doctrine wherein the brethren must love one another in Jesus Christ.

(Pap., II A 24)

4. THE TASK AND
THE LITERATURE

The movement of the times, or if you will, the conflict
between the two conceptions of my literary effort, is between
the interesting and simplicity. That is why I was eminently
endowed with what was called for by the period, the interesting. It would be hard to find an author—there is not
a one in Denmark—who can in any way challenge me as
an author for the title of—and I mean the only one of its
kind—"the Interesting One."

By falsifying my task, I would have become the hero and
idol of the moment; in that case, I would have given up
the movement towards simplicity and would have turned
away from it, would have concentrated all my strength on
the interesting and the instant. But having held forever fast
to my task, I have been the martyr of the instant, precisely
the proof that I have remained faithful.

Praise be to God, I owe everything to him. . . .

(Pap., X 1 A 322)

THE POET OF THE RELIGIOUS

From a Christian standpoint such an existence (in spite
of all aesthetic) is sin, it is the sin of poetizing instead of
being, of standing in relation to the Good and the True
through imagination instead of being that, or rather existen-

111

tially striving to be it. The poet-existence here in question is distinguished from despair by the fact that it includes the conception of God or is before God; but it is prodigiously dialectical, and is in an impenetrable dialectical confusion as to how far it is conscious of being sin. Such a poet may have a very deep religious need, and the conception of God is included in his despair. He loves God above everything, God is for him the only comfort in his secret torment, and yet he loves the torment, he will not let it go. He would so gladly be himself before God, but not with respect to this fixed point where the self suffers, there despairingly he will not be himself; he hopes that eternity will remove it, and here in the temporal, however much he suffers under it, he cannot will to accept it, cannot humble himself under it in faith. And yet he continues to hold to God, and this is his only happiness, for him it would be the greatest horror to have to do without God, "it would be enough to drive one to despair"; and yet he permits himself commonly, but perhaps unconsciously, to poetize God, making him a little bit other than He is, a little bit more like a loving father who all too much indulges the child's "only wish." He who became unhappy in love, and therefore became a poet, blissfully extolls the happiness of love—so he became a poet of religiousness, he understands obscurely that it is required of him to let this torment go, that is, to humble himself under it in faith and to accept it as belonging to the self— for he would hold it aloof from him, and thereby precisely he holds it fast, although doubtless he thinks (and this, like every other word of despair, is correct in the opposite sense and therefore must be understood inversely) that this must mean separating himself from it as far as possible, letting it go as far as it is possible for a man to do so. But to accept it in faith, that he cannot do, or rather in the last resort he will not, or here is where the self ends in obscurity. But like that poet's description of love, so this poet's description of the religious possesses an enchantment, a lyrical flight, such as no married man's description has, nor that of his Reverence. What he says is not untrue, by no means, his representation reflects his happier, his better *ego*. With respect to the religious he is an unhappy lover, that is, he is not in a strict sense a believer, he has only the first prerequisite of faith, and with that an ardent longing for the religious. His collision is essentially this: is he the elect, is the thorn in the flesh the expression for the fact that he is to be employed as the extraordinary, is it before God quite as it should be with respect to the extraordinary figure he has become? or is the thorn in the flesh the experience he must humble himself under in order to attain the universal human? But enough of this. I can say with the emphasis of truth, "To whom am I talking?" Who will bother about such psychological investigations carried to the *nth* power? The Nüremburg Picture Books painted by priests are easily understood; one and all, they resemble, deceptively, people as they generally are, and, spiritually understood, nothing.

(Sickness, pp. 208–210)

I cannot repeat too often what I have so often said: I am a poet, but of a quite particular kind; for dialectic is the essential qualification of my nature and normally dialectic is foreign to poets. From an early age destined to an agonising life which few could ever imagine, hurled into the darkest melancholy, and by that melancholy once more into despair, I came to understand myself in writing. The source of the enthusiasm was the ethical—alas, I was agonisingly prevented from realising perfection because I was unhappily shut off from the universally human. Had I been able to achieve it I should probably have been inordinately proud. In that too lay my relation to Christianity. It was my intention, as soon as *Either-Or* was published, to look for a country living and repent my sins. I could not force back my work, it followed its course—naturally it entered the field of religion. There I understood my duty to be to serve truth in such a way that truth became a burden to me, humanly speaking a thankless task involving the sacrifice of everything. That is how I serve Christianity—in all my wretchedness happy only in the thought of the indescribable good which God has worked for me, so much more than I ever expected.

And so I live with the assurance that God will stamp my work with the impress of Providence—as soon as I am dead, not before, that fact belongs to repentance and to the greatness of the plan.

(*Journals,* n. 806)

A SPY IN THE SERVICE OF THE MOST HIGH

It is a true word I said about myself to myself: I am, as it were, a spy in the service of the highest. The police also use spies. They do not always pick out men whose lives have been the purest and best, quite the contrary; they are cunning, crafty offenders, whose cunning the police use, while they coerce them through the consciousness of their *vita ante acta*. Alas, thus does God use sinners. The police do not think of improving their spies, but God does so. He makes use of such people out of compassion and at the same time he educates and improves them. But here again the consciousness of a *vita ante acta* helps to produce absolute obedience because a man like that, humbled and contrite, is compelled to recognise that even though it were possible for a man to make demands of God, he, unquestionably, could make none, and has simply to submit to everything and nevertheless thank God for the grace of punishment.

(*Journals,* n. 791)

Besides, I admit that I, too, as an ironist and melancholic, was a devotee of the interior life, and it is just as certain that I had such a life, and that I applied much effort in trying to cover it up. And there is also some truth in the modesty that hides one's inner life. But as far as I was concerned, on the contrary, I tried to make my actions conform to the requirements of an aspiration towards Christianity. I did not make sure that I was Christian in my inner life, while trying hard in all other aspects to be comfortable in the world. On the contrary, I disguised my inner life, appeared selfish to others, and frivolous, [or], and meanwhile acted in such a way as to undergo Christian conflicts in my existence.

Yet there is still the delicate question of finding out if this is permitted, since Christianity's characteristic is to attract sarcasm and persecution once it is definitely professed. Acting on the level of Christianity, I do in fact attract such treatment to myself. But who knows if the aggravation would not be greater if people knew that it was in order to profess Christ. For in the last resort, people do lean more towards dealing gently with a bit of inspired oddness than towards tolerating Christianity.

Besides, in my case, let us remember that my stages have already marked my relationship to Christianity on a completely different level than that of the ordinary working man or civil servant; but it is a question of doing more, and here I cannot stop recalling that I understood my task to be that of working as a spy.

(Pap., X 3 A 334)

Ideally speaking, what I accomplished should have taken place as follows. It would have required someone who, from the start, was fully convinced, within himself and before God, of being a Christian, and whose existence also respected Christian ethics and then who began with an indirect message. And he would also stick to that line till the end. He would truly be God's spy, whereas for me, it is at one and the same time my own education.

It is also possible that a man like this might one day come

along. In any case, what I keep thinking about more and more is to know if Christianity now is not going to begin inside out by leaving aside imaginary Christians so that, after countless centuries, it finds itself reduced to as small a handful of believers as at its beginning. Christ says: "But when the Son of Man comes, will he find any faith on earth?" (Luke 18:8)

(Pap., X 5 A 60)

However, it is in a way unwillingly and with some uneasiness that I reveal in this manner how all my efforts are connected. For one reason especially: it is that, in spite of the humanly enormous amount of reflection and planning that I put into it, there is always a third power that intervenes, Providence; and while my reflections range over many things, Providence always keeps me in its power and directs me so that afterwards, I always understand better exactly how this or that of my actions has served the cause.

(Pap., IX A 173)

ABOUT MYSELF

I think I should have the courage to depart this life in order to make room for the exception—but to be looked upon as the exception myself, no, that I cannot do; to me that would be to besmirch all that has been granted me. If the worst came to the worst I would rather look about, and seize upon a man who had not perhaps progressed so far out as I have, get him proclaimed the exception and then perhaps risk everything in order to put him across. But I must always be able to say of myself: it is not I who am the exception, I only bow down before him. Only then am I happy, and feel the desire to live and to fight.

Incognito is my very element; that too is the incommensurable sphere which gives me enthusiasm, and where I can move freely. To me it is paralysing, as cramping as tight shoes, quite deadly, not to be more than one is taken for. To be looked upon as more than they are is, to most people perhaps, and encouraging bait, then they make a real effort. For me it is the very reverse; to be looked upon as less than I am is my *working*-capital driving me on. But then too I am a fundamentally polemical nature.

(Journals, n. 1191)

Quite simply, what I want is sincerity. I am not the man that certain orthodox persons have wanted to make me seem; I am not Christian severity in the face of a certain Christian half-heartedness.

Not at all, I am neither halfheartedness nor severity. I am a human sincerity.

This relaxed Christianity, which is the common Christianity in this country, I want to put [it] up against the New Testament to be able to establish their mutual relationships.

If it seems, or if some other man can make it seem that this Christianity can withstand a comparison with the Christianity of the New Testament, then I will very happily defend it.

But if there is one thing that I do not want, at any price whatever, what I don't want, by remaining silent or by some sort of skillful manipulation, is to cooperate in creating the illusion that this country's common Christianity is the Christianity of the New Testament. That's what I do not want.

I want sincerity. If it is this that the people around me and my contemporaries want, they will sincerely, loyally, openly, frankly, and without reservation want to revolt against Christianity, to say to God: "We cannot, we do not want to bend before this power." But notice carefully, this is done loyally, openly, frankly, without reservation, and now, strange as it may seem, I go along with it; for I want sincerity. And wherever there is sincerity, I can go along with it.

(*Samlede Vaerker*, XIV 55 57)

IN THE SERVICE OF TRUTH

Humanly speaking I could of course have made my life much easier and by that very fact have been loved and much respected. But have I the right to do so over against God? And after all it is God with whom I have most to do. That is what no one realises. Alas, and that is why my life is so arduous. When God, as it were, withdraws himself a little from me I have no other confidant to whom I can turn, and so I am constantly accused of doing—the very thing which I am doing, because the most important thing to me is God. Everyone who really has some conception of what it means to have God as one's company will understand me.

Had I lived in the Middle Ages I should probably have gone into a monastery and done penance. As it is I have understood that particular impulse differently. All self-torture in a monastery only leads to conceit; but I have chosen something else. I have chosen to serve the truth, and that at one of the points where it is the most thankless of tasks. Here I have at one and the same time penance and work. If such a work is to result in anything it is simply sacrifice, trouble, and the reward is nothing but thankless-ness, want of appreciation and contumely. But in another sense that satisfies me as a penitent. It is clear enough that I really make myself useful and I am certain that it will always become more clear, particularly after my death, for that belongs to my conception of penance as to my concep-tion of work: the work is such that it can only really be understood after my death, but that coincides with my idea of penance.

I know perfectly well that God does not desire man to martyr himself in order to please Him, that of all things is not pleasing to God; but God will allow, or forgive my doing penance in that way so long as I do not attribute any merit to it, but only do it because I can do no other.

(*Journals,* n. 660)

What burning desires did my soul entertain, especially in my youth, to be a man like others, so that I could enjoy life; but through terrible sufferings, I was placed beyond the general condition of man. I am not, in this sense, one of those profoundly religious natures. Since my childhood, I have been a constrained man.

Throughout all these tortures caused by what was denied me, my task appeared clearly to me, and then it gave me an unmentionable satisfaction for which I can never stop thanking God.

There is a story that I have often used to portray my own life to myself. Somewhere, I suppose, there lives a powerful prince, and elsewhere an artist who can produce what interests the great lord. He has the artist arrested and locked up. Then he tells him: "You will be comfortable here, but you will have to do some work every day until you are finished." Thus it has seemed to me that Providence laid its hand upon me and said to me: "Your task is to make people attentive to Christianity; you have the qualifications required for this, and besides, you will have everything you need. First of all, you will have the leisure to enjoy life as best you can, to have several hours of relaxation every day, and even time to amuse yourself and make a few jokes; but you will be working at your task every day. Your work will also give you an unbelievable satisfaction, but you are no less a prisoner, and in countless moments of weakness it will seem to you that you prefer freedom. All in vain, you must. So be careful. If you act sincerely, if you are grateful for the grace that is given you, happiness will make you

forget all the suffering which is the tie by which I bind you.
But if you do not want to, then you must."

I have never been able to understand my life in any other
way. If I had been one of the blessed, freely choosing
Christianity, then my situation would have been completely
different.

That is why I am always saying that I have no authority.

Christianity has evaporated so much from the world that
we must first of all get an exact idea of it. Such has always
been my task.

(Pap., X 3 A 140)

CHRISTIANITY
MY PROFOUNDEST DOUBT, WHICH IS NOW LIFTED

Oh, I heard these millions upon millions talk of the
gentleness of Chrisitanity—to me that was inconceivable.

That is how things stood. I thought at bottom—however
humbled I may have been before my Lord and Saviour—
that I should come out better if I only had to do with God
the Father, that it was the "mediator" who made things so
hard. For if I only have to do with God the Father, then
no imitation is demanded of me. And so the position was:
if, suffering and as wretched as the most wretched, I turn
to Christ, and he helps me, what then? Then he will say,
But then you must follow me, mortify yourself, suffer for
the doctrine, be hated by all men, briefly, agony such as has
never been suffered except by a Christian. But good God,
to be helped in that way!

Now I understand that the imitation must not be put
forward in that way, that it exists in order to hold the balance of justice, in order to teach humility and the desire for
grace, in order to put an end to doubt.

Then there is consolation and happiness, and then it was
not impossible that a man should be so moved by all that

love and feel himself so happy that mortification became for him love's joy.

If that moment does not come for a man—well, then there is grace, and the imitation must not, as Luther so admirably says, either hurl him into despair or presumption. If that moment comes, then in spite of all the suffering it brings, the imitation is a thing of love, and so blessed.

(*Journals,* n. 1230)

THE SERVICE OF THE ABSOLUTE

All who have served the absolute have first of all felt that pressure which, so to speak, crushed them without killing them, that pressure which in return elevated them infinitely, but still under which their whole existence remained and which has made their entire lives what they were. Thus Paul when he was thrown to the ground (Acts 9:3), thus Pascal when the horses bolted. [or]

This pressure is like a beam of sunlight directly on the head. It is the infinite intensely concentrated to a unique pressure and in a unique moment.

The nearness of the absolute, we cannot, we others, bear it. That is why we always push it away from us a bit, as we would cover our heads to prevent sunstroke. That is why our relationship to the absolute will always be but a reflective relationship, or one which never goes beyond the reflective.

Besides, on his own, who can approach the absolute to this extent? We cannot, nor would anyone dare, for this pressure, this beam of sunlight, is like the most mortal danger. It is that before which all men ought to shudder and draw back, as if it were more terrible than death.

Thus it is Providence itself that brings us so close to the absolute or that strikes the blow. And for all that, it is, on the other hand, the greatest benefit that can befall us.

We no doubt also have forms of this pressure of the absolute through our awareness of sin; one or several faults from a past life can concentrate themselves into a single factor which presses on us and so come to our awareness. Therein lies another form of the absolute capable of supplying the impetus, beside which all movement in reflection is but a moment marking time from which one never gets away.

(*Pap.,* X 5 A 17)

WITH AN EYE TO INTERIORITY

It is one thing to bring a new doctrine into the world, and another to interiorize a doctrine already given.

In the first place, it is necessary to gather disciples, to found a party; otherwise it could happen that the doctrine, when the master has died, does not penetrate into the world.

It is different when it is a matter of interiorizing an already given doctrine. It is precisely here that one must not gather disciples nor found a party, for this is to weaken its power of interiorization. No, it is a matter here of working in isolation, of living in isolation, of being sacrificed in isolation.

In Christendom, there can only be question of the task of interiorization, for the doctrine is known to everyone.

. . . This business of the isolated individual is the pivotal point in the conception of Christianity. The factual situation is Christendom; the doctrine has been sufficiently preached, interiorization is the task, through the isolated, sacrificed individual. As soon as things become party business, after a short time everything falls back into machine-like repetition.

Oh, but it is so hard to hold on by being alone! Nevertheless, that is the task. Think of Luther, that magnificent man, and yet what confusion did he not cause because he did not refrain from founding a party. He was an isolated man, an extraordinary man. His task was interiorization for he did not have to introduce a new doctrine, Christianity indeed existed, but there was a need for interiority. And then, instead of ending up a martyr himself, he founds a party, and in very little time Lutheranism turns into exteriority and machine-like repetition, at least as much if not more than Catholicism.

(*Pap.,* X 5 A 121)

5. MY SECRET

After my death no one will find among my papers a single explanation as to what really filled my life—that is my consolation; no one will find the words which explain everything and which often made what the world would call a bagatelle into an event of tremendous importance to me, and what I look upon as something insignificant when I take away the secret gloss which explains all.

(Journals, n. 431)

From my earliest childhood the arrow of sorrow was embedded in my heart. So long as it remains embedded I am ironical; if it were withdrawn I should die.

(Journals, n. 685)

July 3, 1855

Imagine a large, well-trained hunting dog. He accompanies his master on a visit to a family where, as is often the case nowdays, there is a whole gang of poorly brought up brats. They start mistreating the dog as soon as they lay eyes on it. The animal, who has what the boys do not have, an education, looks immediately to its master to find out what his orders are. And it understands through his look that it must tolerate all these brutalities, and even take them for kindnesses being showered upon it; naturally the boys get even wilder, and finally come to the conclusion that this dog must be quite an idiot to allow all this to be done to it.

However the dog never stops worrying about one thing: what the eyes of its master command it to do. And now, this suddenly different look—and the dog at once understands: use your strength. Right away and with one leap it grabs hold of the nearest brat and throws him down. Now nothing stops it, except a look from its master, and at that moment, the dog is back as it was.

So it is with me. As the dog followed its master, worrying only about the master's eyes, so I, like a dog, follow the omnipotent Majesty of heaven and earth, worrying only about the eyes of him to whose personal service I was early attached.

Then I began to write. As far as I was concerned, it was a matter of complete involvement, and I fixed my eyes only on His, as the dog on its master's.

It did not take me long to notice that I had not fallen into particularly good company, and that a petty mediocrity, thoughtless and concerned only with the temporal, was trying to harm me in every way.

My gaze, locked only on that of the divine Majesty, taught me how He understood my situation: this, you have to undergo, and not merely tolerate it, but take it so lightly as to seem like a man whom everyone showers with kindness.

Through this, the mediocre element became all the more insolent and finally began thinking that I was completely helpless and could be taken in by almost anyone.

(*Pap.*, XI 2 A 423)

LAST WORDS (TO E. BOESEN)

He was very weak, his head hung down on his chest and his hands trembled. He fell into a doze; coughing woke him; he sometimes dozed during the day, particularly after he had eaten. 'Now I have eaten and everything is ready to receive you, and I do so with open arms.' I asked him whether he could collect his thoughts or whether they were confused. Most of the time they were clear, but sometimes at night they wandered. Whether he could pray in peace to God. 'Yes, that I can.' Whether he still had anything to say. 'No; yes, remember me to everyone, I was much attached to them all, and tell them that my life is a great, and to others unknown and unintelligible suffering. It all looked like pride and vanity, but it was not. I am no better than others, I said that and never anything else; I had my thorn in the flesh and so I did not marry and could take no office; for I am a theological student and had a public right and was well sponsored, so I could have had anything I wanted, but instead I became the exception. The day passed in work and effort, and in the evening I was set aside, that was the exception.' When I asked him whether he could pray in peace: 'Yes, that I can; first of all I pray that my sins may be forgiven me, that everything may be forgiven; then I pray that I may be free from despair in death, and the words often occur to me where it is said that death should be pleasing to God; and so I pray for what I so much desire, which is that I may know a little beforehand when death is to come.'

II An Existential Itinerary
From Ignorance to Revelation

1. INNOCENCE AND IGNORANCE: ANGUISH

Innocence is ignorance. In his innocence man is not determined as spirit but is soulishly determined in immediate unity with his natural condition. Spirit is dreaming in man. This view is in perfect accord with that of the Bible, and by refusing to ascribe to man in the state of innocence a knowledge of the difference between good and evil it condemns all the notions of merit Catholicism has imagined.

In this state there is peace and repose; but at the same time there is something different, which is not dissension and strife, for there is nothing to strive with. What is it then? Nothing. But what effect does nothing produce? It begets dread. This is the profound secret of innocence, that at the same time it is dread. Dreamingly the spirit projects its own reality, but this reality is nothing, but this nothing constantly sees innocence outside of it.

Dread is a qualification of the dreaming spirit, and as such it has its place in psychology. When awake, the difference between myself and my other is posited; sleeping, it is suspended; dreaming, it is a nothing vaguely hinted at. The reality of the spirit constantly shows itself in a form which entices its possibility, but it is away as soon as one grasps after it, and it is a nothing which is able only to alarm. More it cannot do so long as it only shows itself. One almost never sees the concept dread dealt with in psychology, and I must therefore call attention to the fact that it is different from fear and similar concepts which refer to something definite, whereas dread is freedom's reality as possibility for possibility. One does not therefore find dread in the beast, precisely for the reason that by nature the beast is not qualified by spirit.

When we consider the dialectical determinants in dread, it appears that they have precisely the characteristic ambiguity of psychology. Dread is a *sympathetic antipathy and an antipathetic sympathy*. One easily sees, I think, that this is much more truly a psychological subject than is the concupiscence of which we have spoken. Language confirms this completely. One speaks of a sweet dread, a sweet feeling of apprehension, one speaks of a strange dread, a shrinking dread. [etc.]

The dread which is posited in innocence is, in the first place, not guilt; in the second place, it is not a heavy burden, not a suffering which cannot be brought into harmony with the felicity of innocence. If we observe children, we find this dread more definitely indicated as a seeking after adventure, a thirst for the prodigious, the mysterious. The fact that there are children in whom this is not found proves nothing, for neither in the beast does it exist, and the less spirit, the less dread. This dread belongs to the child so essentially that it cannot do without it; even though it alarms him, it captivates him nevertheless by its sweet feeling of apprehension. In all nations in which the childish character is preserved as the dreaming of the spirit this dread is found, and the deeper it is, the more profound is the nation. It is only a prosaic stupidity which thinks that this is a disorganization. Dread has here the same significance melancholy has at a far later point where freedom, after having passed through imperfect forms of its history, has to come to itself in a deeper sense.

Just as the relation of dread to its object, to something which is nothing (language in this instance also is pregnant: it speaks of being in dread of nothing), is altogether ambiguous, so will the transition here from innocence to guilt be correspondingly so dialectical that the explanation is and must be psychological. The qualitative leap is outside of ambiguity, but he who through dread becomes guilty is innocent, for it was not he himself but dread, an alien power, which laid hold of him, a power he did not love but dreaded—and yet he is guilty, for he sank in the dread which he loved even while he feared it. There is nothing in the world more ambiguous, and therefore this is the only psychological explanation, although (to repeat what I have said) it never occurs to it to want to be the explanation which explains the qualitative leap. Every theory about the prohibition tempting Adam or the seducer deceiving him has only for a superficial observation sufficient ambiguity, while it perverts ethics, introduces a quantitative determination, and would by the help of psychology pay man a compliment from which everyone who is ethically developed would beg to be excused, regarding it as a new and deeper seduction.

Everything turns upon dread coming into view. Man is a synthesis of the soulish and the bodily. But a synthesis is unthinkable if the two are not united in a third factor. This third factor is the spirit. In the state of innocence man is not merely an animal, for if at any time of his life he was merely an animal, he never would become a man. So then the spirit is present, but in a state of immediacy, a dreaming state. Forasmuch as it is present, it is in one way a hostile power, for it constantly disturbs the relation between soul and body, a relation which endures, and yet does not endure, inasmuch as it has endurance only by means of the spirit. On the other hand, it is a friendly power which has precisely the function of constituting the relationship. What then is man's relation to this ambiguous power? How is spirit related to itself and to its situation? It is related as dread. The spirit cannot do away with itself; nor can it grasp itself so long as it has itself outside of itself. Neither can man sink down into the vegetative life, for he is determined as spirit. He cannot flee from dread, for he loves it; really he does not love it, for he flees from it. Innocence has now reached its apex. It is ignorance, but not an animal brutality, but an ignorance which is qualified by spirit, but which precisely is dread, because its ignorance is about nothing. Here there is no knowledge of good and evil, etc., but the whole reality of knowledge is projected in dread as the immense nothing of ignorance.

Innocence still *is,* but one word suffices, and with that ignorance is concentrated. Innocence of course cannot understand this word; but dread has as it were obtained its first prey; instead of nothing, innocence gets an enigmatic word. So when it is related in Genesis that God said to Adam, "Only of the tree of the knowledge of good and evil thou shalt not eat," it is a matter of course that Adam did not really understand this word. For how could he have understood the difference between good and evil, seeing that this distinction was in fact consequent upon the enjoyment of the fruit?

When one assumes that the prohibition awakens the desire, one posits a knowledge instead of ignorance; for Adam would have had to have a knowledge of freedom, since his desire was to use it. The explanation therefore anticipates what was subsequent. The prohibition alarms Adam [induces a state of dread] because the prohibition awakens in him the possibility of freedom. That which passed innocence by as the nothing of dread has now entered into him, and here again it is a nothing, the alarming possibility of *being able.* What it is he is able to do, of that he has no conception; to suppose that he had some conception is to presuppose, as commonly is done, what came later, the distinction between good and evil. There is only the possibility of being able, as a higher form of ignorance, as a heightened expression of dread, because this in a more profound sense is and is not, because in a more profound sense he loves it and flees from it.

After the word of prohibition follows the word of judgment: "Thou shalt surely die." What it means to die, Adam of course cannot conceive; but if one assumes that these words were said to him, there is nothing to prevent his having a notion of the terrible. Indeed even the beast is able to understand the mimic expression and movement in the speaker's voice, without understanding the word. In case one lets the prohibition awaken desire, one may also let the word about punishment awaken a deterring conception. However, this confuses things. The terrible becomes in this instance merely dread; for Adam has not understood what was said, and here again we have only the ambiguity of dread. The infinite possibility of being able (awakened by the prohibition) draws closer for the fact that this possibility indicates a possibility as its consequence.

Thus innocence is brought to its last extremity. It is in dread in relation to the prohibition and the punishment. It is not guilty, and yet it is in dread, as though it were lost.

Further than this psychology cannot go, but so far it can reach, and moreover it can verify this point again and again in its observation of human life.

(*Concept of Dread,* pp. 37–41)

2. THE DEMONIAC IS HERMITISM

The demoniacal becomes thoroughly evident only when it is touched by the good, which now comes to its confines from the outside. It is noteworthy therefore that in the New Testament the demoniacal shows itself only with Christ's coming in contact with it. Whether the demon is legion (cf. Matthew 8:28–34; Mark 5:1–20; Luke 8:26–39) or is dumb (cf. Luke 11: 14) the phenomenon is the same, it is dread of the good; for dread can quite as well express itself by muteness as by loud cries. The good of course signifies to it the reintegration of freedom, redemption, salvation or whatever name one would give it.

In earlier times there often was question about the demoniacal. It is of no importance here to make studies, or to have made studies, which would enable one to patter or quote from learned and curious books. One can easily sketch the various views which are possible and at various times have also been actual. This may have some importance, since the diversity of the views may lead to a definition of the concept.

(Concept of Dread, p. 106)

The demoniacal is dread of the good. In the state of innocence freedom was not posited as freedom, its possibility appears in the dread of the individuality. In the demoniacal the situation is reversed. Freedom is posited as unfreedom, for freedom is lost. The possibility of freedom is in turn dread. The difference is absolute; for the possibility of freedom manifests itself here in relation to unfreedom, which is exactly the opposite of innocence, which is a determinant oriented towards freedom.

The demoniacal is unfreedom which would shut itself off. This, however, is an impossibility; it always maintains a relationship, and even when this has apparently disappeared it is nevertheless there, and dread manifests itself at once in the instant of contact with the good (cf. what was said above about the accounts in the New Testament).

The demoniacal is *shut-upness* [*det Indesluttede,* or *Indesluttedhed*] *unfreely revealed.* These two traits denote, as they should, the same thing; for the shut-up is precisely the mute and if it has to express itself, this must come about against its will when the freedom lying prone in unfreedom revolts upon coming into communication with freedom outside and now betrays unfreedom in such a way that it is the individual who betrays himself against his will in dread. The word "shut-up" must therefore be taken here in a perfectly definite sense, for in the sense of reserve, in which it is commonly used, it may denote the highest freedom. Brutus, Henry V of England as Prince of Wales, [etc.,] were in this sense shut-up until the time came when it was evident that their shut-upness was a pact with the good. Such a shut-upness was therefore identical with expansion, and never is there an individuality which in the finer and nobler sense of the word is more expanded than he who is shut-up within the womb of a great idea. Freedom is precisely the expansive. It is in opposition to this I would employ the word "shut-up," $\kappa\alpha\tau'$ $\dot{\epsilon}\xi o\chi\dot{\eta}\nu$, for "unfreedom." Commonly a more metaphysical term is used for the evil. It is called "negating." The ethical term precisely corresponding to that, when one contemplates the effect thereof upon the individual, is shut-upness. The demoniacal does not shut itself up *with* something, but shuts *itself* up; and in this lies the mystery of existence, the fact that unfreedom makes a prisoner precisely of itself. Freedom is constantly communicating (it will do no harm to take into account even the religious significance of this word); unfreedom becomes more and more shut-up and wants no communication. This can be observed in all spheres.

(*Concept of Dread*, pp. 109–110)

3. BOREDOM AS DEMONIAC
PANTHEISM

THE ROTATION METHOD

Starting from a principle is affirmed by people of experience to be a very reasonable procedure; I am willing to humor them, and so begin with the principle that all men are bores. Surely no one will prove himself so great a bore as to contradict me in this. This principle possesses the quality of being in the highest degree repellent, an essential requirement in the case of negative principles, which are in the last analysis the principles of all motion. It is not merely repellent, but infinitely forbidding; and whoever has this principle back of him cannot but receive an infinite impetus forward, to help him make new discoveries. For if my principle is true, one need only consider how ruinous boredom is for humanity, and by properly adjusting the intensity of one's concentration upon this fundamental truth, attain any desired degree of momentum. Should one wish to attain the maximum momentum, even to the point of almost endangering the driving power, one need only say to oneself: Boredom is the root of all evil. Strange that boredom, in itself so staid and stolid, should have such power to set in motion. The influence it exerts is altogether magical, except that it is not the influence of attraction, but of repulsion.

In the case of children, the ruinous character of boredom

137

is universally acknowledged. Children are always well-behaved as long as they are enjoying themselves. This is true in the strictest sense; for if they sometimes become unruly in their play, it is because they are already beginning to be bored—boredom is already approaching, though from a different direction. In choosing a governess one, therefore, takes into account not only her sobriety, her faithfulness, and her competence, but also her aesthetic qualifications for amusing the children; and there would be no hesitancy in dismissing a governess who was lacking in this respect, even if she had all the other desirable virtues. Here, then, the principle is clearly acknowledged; but so strange is the way of the world, so pervasive the influence of habit and boredom, that this is practically the only case in which the science of aesthetics receives its just dues. If one were to ask for a divorce because his wife was tiresome, or demand the abdication of a king because he was boring to look at, or the banishment of a preacher because he was tiresome to listen to, or the dismissal of a prime minister, or the execution of a journalist, because he was terribly tiresome, one would find it impossible to force it through. What wonder, then, that the world goes from bad to worse, and that its evils increase more and more, as boredom increases, and boredom is the root of all evil.

The history of this can be traced from the very beginning of the world. The gods were bored, and so they created man. Adam was bored because he was alone, and so Eve was created. Thus boredom entered the world, and increased in proportion to the increase of population. Adam was bored alone; then Adam and Eve were bored together; then Adam and Eve and Cain and Abel were bored *enfamille;* then the population of the world increased, and the peoples were bored *en masse*. To divert themselves they conceived the idea of constructing a tower high enough to reach the heavens. This idea is itself as boring as the tower was high, and constitutes a terrible proof of how boredom gained the upper hand. The nations were scattered over the earth, just as people now travel abroad, but they continued to be bored. Consider the consequences of this boredom. Humanity fell from its lofty height, first because of Eve, and then from the Tower of Babel. What was it, on the other hand, that delayed the fall of Rome, was it not *panis* and *circenses?* And is anything being done now? Is anyone concerned about planning some means of diversion? Quite the contrary, the impending ruin is being accelerated. It is proposed to call a constitutional assembly. Can anything more tiresome be imagined, both for the participants themselves, and for those who have to hear and read about it? It is proposed to improve the financial condition of the state by practicing economy. What could be more tiresome? Instead of increasing the national debt, it is proposed to pay it off. As I understand the political situation, it would be an easy matter for Denmark to negotiate a loan of fifteen million dollars. Why not consider this plan? Every once in a while we hear of a man who is a genius, and therefore neglects to pay his debts—why should not a nation do the same, if we were all agreed? Let us then borrow fifteen millions, and let us use the proceeds, not to pay our debts, but for public entertainment. Let us celebrate the millennium in a riot of merriment. Let us place boxes everywhere, not, as at present, for the deposit of money, but for the free distribution of money. Everything would become gratis; theaters gratis, women of easy virtue gratis, one would drive to the park gratis, be buried gratis, one's eulogy would be gratis; I say gratis, for when one always has money at hand, everything is in a certain sense free. No one should be permitted to own any property. Only in my own case would there be an exception. I reserve to myself securities in the Bank of London to the value of one hundred dollars a day, partly because I cannot do with less, partly because the idea is mine, and finally because I may not be able to hit upon a new idea when the fifteen millions are gone.

What would be the consequences of all this prosperity? Everything great would gravitate toward Copenhagen, the greatest artists, the greatest dancers, the greatest actors. Copenhagen would become a second Athens. What then? All rich men would establish their homes in this city. Among others would come the Shah of Persia, and the King of England would also come. Here is my second idea. Let us kidnap the Shah of Persia. Perhaps you say an insurrection might take place in Persia and a new ruler be placed on the throne, as has often happened before, the consequence being a fall in price for the old Shah. Very well then, I propose that we sell him to the Turks; they will doubtless know how to turn him into money. Then there is another circumstance which our politicians seem entirely to have overlooked. Denmark holds the balance of power in Europe. It is impossible to imagine a more fortunate lot. I know that from my own experience; I once held the balance of power in a family and could do as I pleased; the blame never fell on me, but always on the others. O that my words might reach your ears, all you who sit in high places to advise and rule, you king's men and men of the people, wise and understanding citizens of all classes! Consider the crisis! Old Denmark is on the brink of ruin; what a calamity! It will be destroyed by boredom. Of all calamities the most calamitous! In ancient times they made him king who extolled most beautifully the praises of the deceased king;[3] in our times we ought to make him king who utters the best witticism, and make him crown prince who gives occasion for the utterance of the best witticism.

O beautiful, emotional sentimentality, how you carry me away! Should I trouble to speak to my contemporaries, to initiate them into my wisdom? By no means. My wisdom is not exactly *zum Gebrauch für Jedermann,* and it is always more prudent to keep one's maxims of prudence to oneself. I desire no disciples; but if there happened to be someone present at my deathbed, and I was sure that the end had come, then I might in an attack of philanthropic delirium, whisper my theory in his ear, uncertain whether I had done him a service or not. People talk so much about man being a social animal; at bottom, he is a beast of prey, and the evidence for this is not confined to the shape of his teeth. All this talk about society and the social is partly inherited hypocrisy, partly calculated cunning.

All men are bores. The word itself suggests the possibility of a subdivision. It may just as well indicate a man who bores others as one who bores himself. Those who bore others are the mob, the crowd, the infinite multitude of men in general. Those who bore themselves are the elect, the aristocracy; and it is a curious fact that those who do not bore themselves usually bore others, while those who bore themselves entertain others. Those who do not bore themselves are generally people who, in one way or another, keep themselves extremely busy; these people are precisely on this account the most tiresome, the most utterly unendurable. This species of animal life is surely not the fruit of man's desire and woman's lust. Like all lower forms of life, it is marked by a high degree of fertility, and multiplies endlessly. It is inconceivable that nature should require nine months to produce such beings; they ought rather to be turned out by the score. The second class, the aristocrats, are those who bore themselves. As noted above, they generally entertain others—in a certain external sense sometimes the mob, in a deeper sense only their fellow initiates. The more profoundly they bore themselves, the more powerfully do they serve to divert these latter, even when their boredom reaches its zenith, as when they either die of boredom (the passive form) or shoot themselves out of curiosity (the active form).

It is usual to say that idleness is a root of all evil. To prevent this evil one is advised to work. However, it is easy to see, both from the nature of the evil that is feared and the remedy proposed, that this entire view is of a very plebeian extraction. Idleness is by no means as such a root of evil; on the contrary, it is a truly divine life, provided one is not himself bored. Idleness may indeed cause the loss of one's fortune, and so on, but the high-minded man does not fear such dangers; he fears only boredom. The Olympian gods were not bored, they lived happily in happy idleness. A beautiful woman, who neither sews nor spins nor bakes nor reads nor plays the piano, is happy in her idleness, for she is not bored. So far from idleness being the root of all evil, it is rather the only true good. Boredom is the root of all evil, and it is this which must be kept at a distance. Idleness is not an evil; indeed one may say that every human being who lacks a sense for idleness proves that his consciousness has not yet been elevated to the level of the humane. There is a restless activity which excludes a man from the world of the spirit, setting him in a class with the brutes, whose instincts impel them always to be on the move. There are men who have an extraordinary talent for transforming everything into a matter of business, whose whole life is business, who fall in love, marry, listen to a joke, and admire a picture with the same industrious zeal with which they labor during business hours. The Latin proverb, *otium est pulvinar diaboli,* is true enough, but the devil gets no time to lay his head on this pillow when one is not bored. But since some people believe that the end and aim of life is work, the disjunction, idleness-work, is quite correct. I assume that it is the end and aim of every man to enjoy himself, and hence my disjunction is no less correct.

Boredom is the daemonic side of pantheism. If we remain in boredom as such, it becomes the evil principle; if we annul it, we posit it in its truth; but we can only annul boredom by enjoying ourselves—*ergo,* it is our duty to enjoy ourselves. To say that boredom is annulled by work betrays a confusion of thought; for idleness can certainly be annulled by work, since it is its opposite, but not boredom,

and experience shows that the busiest workers, whose constant buzzing most resembles an insect's hum, are the most
tiresome of creatures; if they do not bore themselves, it is
because they have no true conception of what boredom is;
but then it can scarcely be said that they have overcome
boredom.

Boredom is partly an inborn talent, partly an acquired
immediacy. The English are in a general the paradigmatic
nation. A true talent for indolence is very rare; it is never
met with in nature, but belongs to the world of the spirit.
Occasionally, however, you meet a traveling Englishman
who is, as it were, the incarnation of this talent—a heavy,
immovable animal, whose entire language exhausts its riches
in a single word of one syllable, an interjection by which he
signifies his deepest admiration and his supreme indifference, admiration and indifference having been neutralized
in the unity of boredom. No other nation produces such
miracles of nature; every other national will always show
himself a little more vivacious, not so absolutely stillborn.
The only analogy I know of is the apostle of the empty
enthusiasm, who also makes his way through life on an
interjection. This is the man who everywhere makes a pro-
fession of enthusiasm, who cries Ah! or Oh! whether the
event be significant or insignificant, the difference having
been lost for him in the emptiness of a blind and noisy
enthusiasm. The second form of boredom is usually the
result of a mistaken effort to find diversion. The fact that
the remedy against boredom may also serve to produce
boredom, might appear to be a suspicious circumstance; but
it has this effect only in so far as it is incorrectly employed.
A misdirected search for diversion, one which is eccentric
in its direction, conceals boredom within its own depths and
gradually works it out toward the surface, thus revealing
itself as that which it immediately is. In the case of horses,
we distinguish between blind staggers and sleepy staggers,
but call both staggers; and so we can also make a distinction

between two kinds of boredom, though uniting both under the common designation of being tiresome.

Pantheism is, in general, characterized by fullness; in the case of boredom we find the precise opposite, since it is characterized by emptiness; but it is just this which makes boredom a pantheistic conception. Boredom depends on the nothingness which pervades reality; it cause a dizziness like that produced by looking down into a yawning chasm, and this dizziness is infinite. The eccentric form of diversion noted above sounds forth without producing an echo, which proves it to be based on boredom; for in nothingness not even an echo can be produced.

Now since boredom as shown above is the root of all evil, what can be more natural than the effort to overcome it? Here, as everywhere, however, it is necessary to give the problem calm consideration; otherwise one may find oneself driven by the daemonic spirit of boredom deeper and deeper into the mire in the very effort to escape. Everyone who feels bored cries out for change. With this demand I am in complete sympathy, but it is necessary to act in accordance with some settled principle.

My own dissent from the ordinary view is sufficiently expressed in the use I make of the word, "rotation." This word might seem to conceal an ambiguity, and if I wished to use it so as to find room in it for the ordinary method, I should have to define it as a change of field. But the farmer does not use the word in this sense. I shall, however, adopt this meaning for a moment, in order to speak of the rotation which depends on change in its boundless infinity, its extensive dimension, so to speak.

This is the vulgar and inartistic method, and needs to be supported by illusion. One tires of living in the country, and moves to the city; one tires of one's native land, and travels abroad; one is *europamüde,* and goes to America, and so on; finally one indulges in a sentimental hope of endless journeyings from star to star. Or the movement is different but still extensive. One tires of porcelain dishes and eats on silver; one tires of silver and turns to gold; one burns half of Rome to get an idea of the burning of Troy. This method defeats itself; it is plain endlessness. And what did Nero gain by it? Antonine was wiser; he says: "It is in your power to review your life, to look at things you saw before, from another point of view."

My method does not consist in change of field, but resembles the true rotation method in changing the crop and the mode of cultivation. Here we have at once the principle of limitation, the only saving principle in the world. The more you limit yourself, the more fertile you become in invention. A prisoner in solitary confinement for life becomes very inventive, and a spider may furnish him with much entertainment. One need only hark back to one's schooldays. We were at an age when aesthetic considerations were ignored in the choice of one's instructors, most of whom were for that reason very tiresome; how fertile in invention one then proved to be! How entertaining to catch a fly and hold it imprisoned under a nut shell and to watch how it pushed the shell around; what pleasure from cutting a hole in the desk, putting a fly in it, and then peeping down at it through a piece of paper! How entertaining sometimes to listen to the monotonous drip of water from the roof! How close an observer one becomes under such circumstances, when not the least noise nor movement escapes one's attention! Here we have the extreme application of the method which seeks to achieve results intensively, not extensively.

The more resourceful in changing the mode of cultivation one can be, the better; but every particular change will always come under the general categories of *remembering and forgetting*. Life in its entirety moves in these two currents, and hence it is essential to have them under control. It is impossible to live artistically before one has made up one's mind to abandon hope; for hope precludes self-limitation. It is a very beautiful sight to see a man put out to sea with the fair wind of hope, and one may even use the opportunity to be taken in tow; but one should never permit hope to be taken aboard one's own ship, least of all as a pilot; for hope is a faithless shipmaster. Hope was one of the dubious gifts of Prometheus; instead of giving men the foreknowledge of the immortals, he gave them hope.

To forget—all men wish to forget, and when something unpleasant happens, they always say: Oh, that one might forget! But forgetting is an art that must be practiced beforehand. The ability to forget is conditioned upon the method of remembering, but this again depends upon the mode of experiencing reality. Whoever plunges into his experiences with the momentum of hope will remember in such wise that he is unable to forget. *Nil admirari* is therefore the real philosophy. No moment must be permitted so great a significance that it cannot be forgotten when convenient; each moment ought, however, to have so much significance that it can be recollected at will. Childhood, which is the age which remembers best, is at the same time most forgetful. The more poetically one remembers, the more easily one forgets; for remembering poetically is really only another expression for forgetting. In a poetic memory the experience has undergone a transformation, by which it has lost all its painful aspects. To remember in this manner, one must be careful how one lives, how one enjoys. Enjoying an experience to its full intensity to the last minute will make it impossible either to remember or to forget. For there is then nothing to remember except a certain satiety, which one desires to forget, but which now comes back to plague the mind with an involuntary remembrance. Hence, when you begin to notice that a certain pleasure or experience is acquiring too strong a hold upon the mind, you stop a moment for the purpose of remembering. No other method can better create a distaste for continuing the experience too long. From the beginning one should keep the enjoyment under control, never spreading every sail to the wind in any resolve; one ought to devote oneself to pleasure with a certain suspicion, a certain wariness, if one desires to give the lie to the proverb which says that no one can have his cake and eat it too. The carrying of concealed weapons is usually forbidden, but no weapon is so dangerous as the art of remembering. It gives one a very peculiar feeling in the midst of one's enjoyment to look back upon it for the purpose of remembering it.

One who has perfected himself in the twin arts of remembering and forgetting is in a position to play at battledore and shuttlecock with the whole of existence.

The extent of one's power to forget is the final measure of one's elasticity of spirit. If a man cannot forget he will never amount to much. Whether there be somewhere a Lethe gushing forth, I do not know; but this I know, that the art of forgetting can be developed. However, this art does not consist in permitting the impressions to vanish completely; forgetfulness is one thing, and the art of forgetting is something quite different. It is easy to see that most people have a very meager understanding of this art, for they ordinarily wish to forget only what is unpleasant, not what is pleasant. This betrays a complete one-sidedness. Forgetting is the true expression for an ideal process of assimilation by which the experience is reduced to a sounding-board for the soul's own music. Nature is great because it has forgotten that it was chaos; but this thought is subject to revival at any time. As a result of attempting to forget only what is unpleasant, most people have a conception of oblivion as an untamable force which drowns out the past. But forgetting is really a tranquil and quiet occupation, and one which should be exercised quite as much in connection with the pleasant as with the unpleasant. A pleasant experience has as past something unpleasant about it, by which it stirs a sense of privation; this unpleasantness is taken away by an act of forgetfulness. The unpleasant has a sting, as all admit. This, too, can be removed by the art of forgetting. But if one attempts to dismiss the unpleasant absolutely from mind, as many do who dabble in the art of forgetting, one soon learns how little that helps. In an unguarded moment it pays a surprise visit, and it is then invested with all the forcibleness of the unexpected. This is absolutely contrary to every orderly arrangement in a reasonable mind. No misfortune or difficulty is so devoid of affability, so deaf to all appeals, but that it may be flattered a little; even Cerberus accepted bribes of honey-cakes, and it is not only the lassies who are beguiled. The art in dealing with such experiences consists in talking them over, thereby depriving them of their bitterness; not forgetting them absolutely, but forgetting them for the sake of remembering them. Even in the case of memories such that one might suppose an eternal oblivion to be the only safeguard, one need permit oneself only a little trickery, and the deception will succeed for the skillful. Forgetting is the shears with which you cut away what you cannot use, doing it under the supreme direction of memory. Forgetting and remembering are thus identical arts, and the artistic achievement of this identity is the Archimedean point from which one lifts the whole world. When we say that we *consign* something to oblivion, we suggest simultaneously that it is to be forgotten and yet also remembered.

The art of remembering and forgetting will also insure against sticking fast in some relationship of life, and make possible the realization of a complete freedom.

(*Either/Or,* Vol. 1, pp. 281–291)

4. THE ANGUISH OF THE TRAGIC: ANTIGONE

So draw nearer to me, dear brothers of Symparanekromenoi; close around me as I send my tragic heroine out into the world, as I give the daughter of sorrow a dowry of pain as a wedding gift. She is my creation, but still her outline is so vague, her form so nebulous, that each one of you is free to imagine her as you will, and each one of you can love her in your own way. She is my creation, her thoughts are my thoughts, and yet it is as if I had rested with her in a night of love, as if she had entrusted me with her deep secret, breathed it and her soul out in my embrace, and as if in the same moment she changed before me, vanished, so that her actuality could only be traced in the mood that remained, instead of the converse being true, that my mood brought her forth to a greater and greater actuality. I place the words in her mouth, and yet it is as if I abused her confidence; to me, it is as if she stood reproachfully behind me, and yet it is the other way around, in her mystery she becomes ever more and more visible. She is my possession, my lawful possession, and yet sometimes it is as if I had slyly insinuated myself into her confidence, as if I must constantly look behind me to find her; and yet, on the contrary, she lies constantly before me, she constantly comes into existence only as I bring her forth. She is called Antigone. This name I retain from the ancient tragedy, which for the most part I will follow, although, from another

point of view, everything will be modern. First, however,
a remark. I use a feminine figure because I firmly believe
that a feminine nature will be best adapted for showing the
difference. As woman she will have substantiality enough
for sorrow to show itself, but as belonging in a reflective
world, she will have reflection enough to mark the pain.
In order to experience sorrow, the tragic guilt must vacillate
between guilt and innocence; that whereby the guilt passes
over into her consciousness must always be a determination
of substantiality. But since in order to experience sorrow,
the tragic guilt must have this vagueness, so reflection must
not be present in its infinitude, for then it would reflect her
out of her guilt, because reflection in its infinite subjectivity
cannot let the element of inherited guilt remain, which
causes the sorrow. Since, however, her reflection is awake,
it will not reflect her out of her sorrow, but into it, each
moment transforming her sorrow into pain.

(Either/Or, Vol. 1, pp. 151–152)

Labdakos' family is, then, the object of the indignation
of the angry gods. Oedipus has slain the sphinx, liberated
Thebes; he has murdered his father, married his mother,
and Antigone is the daughter of this marriage. Thus goes
the Greek tragedy. Here I diverge from the Greek. All the
relationships are the same in mine, and yet everything is different. That he has slain the sphinx and liberated Thebes
is known to everyone, and Oedipus lives honored and
admired, happy in his marriage with Jocasta. The rest is
concealed from the eyes of men, and no suspicion has ever
called this horrible nightmare into actuality. Only Antigone knows it. How she has come to know it lies outside
the tragic interest, and everyone is free to work out his own
explanation in regard to it. At an early age, before she was
fully developed, dim suspicions of this horrible secret had
at times gripped her soul, until certainty with a single blow
cast her into the arms of anxiety. Right here I discover a

definition of the modern idea of the tragical. For anxiety is a reflection, and in this respect is essentially different from sorrow. Anxiety is the organ by which the subject appropriates sorrow and assimilates it. Anxiety is the energy of the movement by which sorrow bores its way into one's heart. But the movement is not swift like the thrust of a dart, it is successive; it is not once for all, but it is constantly continuing. As a passionate, erotic glance desires its object, so anxiety looks upon sorrow to desire it. As the quiet, incorruptible glance of love is preoccupied with the beloved object, so anxiety occupies itself with sorrow. But anxiety has another element in it which makes it cling even more strongly to its object, for it both loves and fears it. Anxiety has a two-fold function. Partly it is the detective instinct which constantly touches, and by means of this probing, discovers sorrow, as it goes round about the sorrow. Or anxiety is sudden, posits the whole sorrow in the present moment, yet so that this present moment instantly dissolves in succession. Anxiety is in this sense a truly tragic category, and the old saying: *quem deus vult perdere, primum dementat,* in truth rightfully applies here. That anxiety is determined by reflection is shown by our use of words; for I always say: to be anxious about something, by which I separate the anxiety from that about which I am anxious, and I can never use anxiety in an objective sense; whereas, on the contrary, when I say "my sorrow," it can just as well express that which I sorrow over, as my sorrow over it. In addition, anxiety always involves a reflection upon time, for I cannot be anxious about the present, but only about the past or the future; but the past and the future, so resisting one another that the present vanishes, are reflective determinations. Greek sorrow, on the other hand, like the whole of Greek life, is in the present tense, and therefore the sorrow is deeper but the pain less. Anxiety therefore belongs essentially to the tragic. Hence, Hamlet is deeply tragic because he suspects his mother's guilt.

5. JOB, EVIL AND SUFFERING

Job! Job! Job! Job! Didst thou indeed utter nothing but these beautiful words, "The Lord gave, the Lord hath taken away, blessed be the name of the Lord"? Didst thou say nothing more? In all thy distress didst thou merely continue to repeat these words? Why wast thou silent for seven days and nights? What went on in thy soul? When the whole world fell to pieces above thy head and lay in potsherds around thee, didst thou at once possess this superhuman composure, didst thou at once have love's interpretation and the frankheartedness of confidence and faith? Is thy door then closed against the afflicted man, can he expect from thee no other relief than that pitiable consolation which worldly wisdom offers by reciting a paragraph about the perfection of life? Hast thou nothing more to say? Dost thou not dare to say more than what the false comforters laconically mete out to the individual, what the false comforters, rigid as a master of ceremony, prescribe to the individual, that in the hour of distress it is seemly to say, "The Lord gave, the Lord hath taken away, blessed be the name of the Lord"—neither more nor less, just as one says "Prosit" when a person sneezes! No, thou who in the ripeness of thy days wast a sword for the oppressed, a cudgel to protect the old, a staff for the decrepit, thou didst not fail men when all was riven asunder—then thou wast a mouth for the afflicted, and a cry for the contrite, and a shriek for the anguished, and an assuagement for all who were rendered dumb by torments, a faithful witness to the distress and grief a heart can harbor, a trustworthy advocate who dared to complain "in anguish of spirit" and to contend with God. Why do people conceal this? Woe to him who devours the widow and the fatherless and defrauds them of their inheritance, but woe also to him who would slyly defraud the afflicted of the momentary consolation of relieving the oppression of his heart and "contending with God." Or in our time is godly fear so great that the afflicted man does not need what was customary in those old days? Does one perhaps not dare to complain before God? Is it now godly fear that has become greater, or fear and cowardice? Nowadays people are of the opinion that the natural expression of sorrow, the desperate language of passion, must be left to poets, who as attorneys in a lower court plead the sufferer's cause before the tribunal of human compassion. Further than this no one ventures to go. Speak therefore, O Job of imperishable memory! Rehearse everything thou didst say, thou mighty advocate who dost confront the highest tribunal, no more daunted than a roaring lion! There is pith in thy speech, in thy heart there is godly fear, even when thou dost complain, when thou wouldst justify thy despair against thy friends who rise up like robbers to assault thee with their speeches, and even when incited by thy friends thou dost tread their wisdom under foot and despise their defense of the Lord, accounting it the finite shrewdness of a veteran courtier or a worldly-wise minister of state. Thee I have need of, a man who knows how to complain aloud, so that his complaint echoes in heaven where God confers with Satan in devising schemes against a man.

Complain! The Lord is not afraid, He is well able to defend Himself, but how might He be able to speak in His defense if no one ventures to complain as it is seemly for a man to do? Speak, lift up thy voice, speak aloud, God surely can speak louder, he possesses the thunder—but that too is an answer, an explanation, reliable, trustworthy, genuine, an answer from God Himself, an answer which even if it crush a man is more glorious than gossip and rumor about the righteousness of providence which are invented by human wisdom and circulated by effeminate creatures and eunuchs.

My benefactor of imperishable memory, tormented Job, dare I join myself to thy company, may I listen to thee? Do not repell me, I am not standing here as an impostor beside thy ash heap, my tears are not false, although all I am able to do is to weep with thee. The joyful man seeks the company of gladness, although what gladdens him most intimately is the joy which dwells within him; and so the afflicted man seeks the company of sorrow. I have not been in possession of the world, have not had seven sons and three daughters, but he too may have lost all who possessed but little, he too may as it were have lost sons and daughters who lost his loved one, and he too was so to speak "smitten with sore boils" who has lost honor and pride, and along with that the will to live and the meaning of life.

(Repetition, pp. 110–113)

If I had not Job! It is impossible to describe and to *nuancer* what significance he has for me, and how manifold his significance is. I do not read him as one reads another book with the eye, but I read this book as it were with my heart, with the eye of the heart I read it, understanding as in a state of *clairvoyance* every particular passage in the most various ways. As the child puts his school-book under the pillow to make sure that he shall not have forgotten his lesson when he wakes up in the morning, so do I take the book with me to bed at night. Every word of his is food and gladness and medicine for my ailing soul. Now one word rouses me from my lethargy, so that I awaken to new disquietude; now it quiets the fruitless fury within me and puts an end to the horrible feeling of mute nausea produced by passion. You surely have read Job? Read him, read him over and over again. I cannot bring myself to quote a single outburst of his in a letter to you, although it is my joy to make transcripts again and again of all that he said, now in Danish characters, now in Latin script, now on a sheet of one size, now on that of another size. Every one of these transcripts is laid like a so-called "God's-hand-poultice" upon my sick heart. And upon whom indeed was God's hand laid as it was upon Job! But quote him—that I cannot do. That would be to wish to give his words my flavoring, to want to make his word mine in the presence of another man. When I am alone I do that, I appropriate every word; but so soon as anyone is present I know well what a young man has to do when old folks talk.

In the whole Old Testament there is no figure one approaches with so much confidence and frank-heartedness and trustfulness as Job, just because everything about him is so human, because he lies upon the confines of poetry. Nowhere in the world has the passion of pain found such an expression. What is Philoctetus with his complaints, which constantly remain on the earth and do not terrify the gods! What is his situation compared with that of Job, where the idea is always in movement!

Forgive me for telling you everything. You are my confident, and you are not able to reply. If anyone were to get to know this, it would distress me indescribably. At night I leave all the candles in my room lit, illuminating the whole apartment. Then I arise and read in a loud voice, almost shouting, one passage or another from Job. Or I open my window and shout out his words into the world. If Job is merely a poetical figure, if there never was any man who talked like this, then I make his words mine and assume the responsibility. More I cannot do, for who has such eloquence as Job, or is capable of improving anything that he said?

Although I have read the book again and again, every

word is new to me. When I come across a word it is at that instant born, primitively, or makes a primitive impression upon my soul. Like a drunkard I imbibe little by little all the intoxication of passion, until with these slow sippings I become almost dead-drunk. On the other hand, I hasten toward the book with indescribable impatience. A half word, and with that my soul plunges into his thought and into his outbursts. More swiftly than the plummet seeks the bottom of the sea, more swiftly than the lightning seeks the conductor, my soul slips into his thought and there remains.

At other times I am quieter. Then I do not read, I sit shrunken together like an ancient ruin and gaze at everything. Then it seems to be as though I were a little child who goes pottering about the room or sits in a corner with his toys. I have a strange sensation. I cannot understand what it is that makes the grown folks so passionate, I cannot understand what they are quarrelling about, and yet I cannot help listening. Then it seems to me that it was bad people gave Job all that affliction, that is was his friends who now sit and bark at him. Then I weep loudly, a nameless dread of the world and of life and of men and of everything wrings my heart.

Then I awake and begin again to read him aloud with all my might and with all my heart. Then suddenly I am struck dumb, I hear nothing more, see nothing, only in obscure outlines have I a presentiment of Job sitting upon his ash heap, and of his friends; but no one says a word, but this silence conceals within itself all that is horrible, as a secret which no one dare mention.

Then the silence is broken, and Job's tormented soul bursts out in a mighty shout. Him I understand, these words I make my own. The same instant I sense the contradiction in this, and then I smile at myself as one smiles at a little child who has put on his father's clothes. Or is it not something to smile at if anyone else but Job were to say, "O that a man might go to law with God, like a son of man with his fellow!" And yet dread comes over me as if I did not yet understand it, but as though I should some day come to understand, as though the terror about which I read was already lurking for me as I read about it, just as one becomes ill of the disease one reads about.

(*Repetition*, pp. 121–124)

The greatness of Job does not therefore consist solely in the fact that he said, "The Lord gave, the Lord hath taken away, blessed be the name of the Lord"—which he uttered, moreover, at the beginning and did not repeat later. But Job's significance is that the border conflicts incident to faith are fought out in him, and that the prodigious insurrection of the wild and bellicose powers of passion are here set forth.

Therefore Job does not tranquilize like a hero of faith, but he provided temporary relief. Job represents as it were the whole weighty plea presented on man's behalf in the great suit between God and man, the prolix and dreadful process of justice which had its ground in the fact that Satan raised a suspicion against Job, and which ends with the explanation that the whole thing is a trial of probation.

This category, "trial of probation," is neither aesthetic, nor ethical, nor dogmatic, it is entirely transcendent. Not until it is known to be a trial could a place be found for it in a dogmatic work. But so soon as this knowledge is at hand the elasticity of trial is weakened, and the category is really a different one. This category is absolutely transcendent and places man in a purely personal relationship of contradiction to God, in such a relationship that he cannot rest content with any explanation at second hand.

The fact that a great many people have this category ready at once on every occasion, the gruel needing only to be heated, merely proves that they have not comprehended it. The man who has a well developed consciousness of the world has a very long detour to make before he reaches this category. Such was the case with Job, who proves the breadth of his conception of the world by the firmness with which he is able to eschew all crafty ethical evasions and cunning wiles. Job is not a hero of faith, he gives birth with prodigious pains to the category of "trial"—precisely because he is so developed that he does not possess this category in childish immediacy.

I can see well that this category might have a tendency to erase and suspend reality as a whole by defining it as a trial with relation to eternity. Yet this objection has no force for me; for since a trial is *temporary* it is *eo ipso* qualified by relation to time and must be done away with in time.

(*Repetition,* pp. 129–131)

The tempests have raged themselves out—the thunderstorm is past—Job has been reproved before the eyes of men—the Lord and Job understand one another, they are reconciled, "the intimacy of the Lord dwells again in the tents of Job as in the former days"—men have learnt to understand Job, they come now to eat bread with him, to bemoan and comfort him, his brothers and sisters make each of them a present to him of a piece of money and a gold ring—Job is blessed and has received everything *double*. This is what is called a *repetition*. How much good a thunderstorm does after all! How blessed it must be after all to be reproved of God! Ordinarily a man is so likely to harden himself against reproof; when God passes judgment a man loses himself and forgets the pain in the love which is intent upon educating.

Who could have conceived this conclusion? And yet no other conclusion is conceivable—and neither is this. When everything has come to a standstill, when thought is brought to a halt, when speech becomes mute, when the explanation in bewilderment seeks the way home—then there must be a thunderstorm. Who can understand this? And yet who can find out any other conclusion?

Did Job lose his case? Yes, eternally; for he can appeal to no higher court than that which judged him. Did Job gain his case? Yes, eternally . . . for the fact that he lost his case *before God.*

So then there is such a thing as a repetition. When does it come about? Well, that's not so easy to say in any human language. When did it come about for Job? When all *conceivable* human certitude and probability pronounced it impossible. Little by little he loses everything; therewith hope vanishes gradually in proportion as reality, far from being mollified, makes heavier and heavier claims upon him. In the sense of immediacy all is lost. His friends, especially Bildad, know of only one way out, that by submitting to his chastisement he might hope to have a repetition in superabundance. For that Job is not willing. Thereupon the plot thickens, so that only by a thunderstorm can it be resolved.

(Repetition, pp. 132–133)

Within the sphere of religious suffering there lies the special type of religious conflict the Germans call *Anfechtung,* which category finds its determination only in this connection. Although I have in general to do with the religious address only as the organ of the religious view of life, I may incidentally have regard to its factual character in our time, here again in order to throw light upon the religiosity of the age with its pretensions of having advanced beyond medieval religiosity, in that I seek to assign its proper place to *Anfechtung,* incidentally recalling that nowadays we scarcely ever hear a word about it, or in so far as it is mentioned, we find it identified without further ado with temptation, aye, even with the ordinary troubles of life. As soon as we leave out the relationship to an absolute *telos* and let this exhaust itself in relative ends, *Anfechtung* ceases to exist. *Anfechtung* is in the sphere of the God-relationship what temptation is in the ethical sphere. When the ethical relationship to reality is the maximum for the individual, then temptation is his greatest danger. Hence it is quite in order that *Anfechtung* is left out, and it is only an instance of slovenliness that it is identified with temptation. But it is not only in the manner just described that *Anfechtung* differs from temptation, but the orientation of the individual is also different in the two cases. In temptation, it is the lower that tempts, in *Anfechtung* it is the higher; in temptation, it is the lower that allures the individual, in *Anfechtung* it is the higher that, as if jealous of the individual, tries to frighten him back. *Anfechtung* therefore originates first in the essentially religious sphere, and occurs there only in the final stage, increasing quite properly in proportion to the intensity of the religiosity, because the individual has discovered the limit, and *Anfechtung* expresses the reaction of the limit against the finite individual.

(*Postscript,* p. 410)

6. DESPAIR

The concept of the sickness unto death must be understood, however, in a peculiar sense. Literally it means a sickness the end and outcome of which is death. Thus one speaks of a mortal sickness as synonymous with a sickness unto death. In this sense despair cannot be called the sickness unto death. But in the Christian understanding of it death itself is a transition unto life. In view of this, there is from the Christian standpoint no earthly, bodily sickness unto death. For death is doubtless the last phase of the sickness, but death is not the last thing. If in the strictest sense we are to speak of a sickness unto death, it must be one in which the last thing is death, and death the last thing. And this precisely is despair.

Yet in another and still more definite sense despair is the sickness unto death. It is indeed very far from being true that, literally understood, one dies of this sickness, or that this sickness ends with bodily death. On the contrary, the torment of despair is precisely this, not to be able to die. So it has much in common with the situation of the moribund when he lies and struggles with death, and cannot die. So to be sick unto death is, not to be able to die—yet not as though there were hope of life; no, the hopelessness in this case is that even the last hope, death, is not available. When death is the greatest danger, one hopes for life; but when one becomes acquainted with an even more dreadful danger, one hopes for death. So when the danger is so great that death has become one's hope, despair is the disconsolateness of not being able to die.

It is in this last sense that despair is the sickness unto death, this agonizing contradiction, this sickness in the self, everlastingly to die, to die and yet not to die, to die the death. For dying means that it is all over, but dying the death means to live to experience death; and if for a single instant this experience is possible, it is tantamount to experiencing it forever. If one might die of despair as one dies of a sickness, then the eternal in him, the self, must be capable of dying in the same sense that the body dies of sickness. But this is an impossibility; the dying of despair transforms itself constantly into a living. The despairing man cannot die; no more than "the dagger can slay thoughts" can despair consume the eternal thing, the self, which is the ground of despair, whose worm dieth not, and whose fire is not quenched. Yet despair is precisely *self*-consuming, but it is an impotent self-consumption which is not able to do what it wills; and this impotence is a new form of self-consumption, in which again, however, the despairer is not able to do what he wills, namely, to consume himself. This is despair raised to a higher potency, or it is the law for the potentiation. This is the hot incitement, or the cold fire in despair, the gnawing canker whose movement is constantly inward, deeper and deeper, in impotent self-consumption. The fact that despair does not consume him is so far from being any comfort to the despairing man that it is precisely the opposite, this comfort is precisely the torment, it is precisely this that keeps the gnawing pain alive and keeps life in the pain. This precisely is the reason why he despairs—not to say despaired—because he cannot consume himself, cannot get rid of himself, cannot become nothing. This is the potentiated formula for despair, the rising of the fever in the sickness of the self.

A despairing man is in despair over *something*. So it seems for an instant, but only for an instant; that same instant the true despair manifests itself, or despair manifests itself in its true character. For in the fact that he despaired of *something,* he really despaired of himself, and now would be rid of himself. Thus when the ambitious man whose watchword was "Either Caesar or nothing" does not become Caesar, he is in despair thereat. But this signifies something else, namely, that precisely because he did not become Caesar he now cannot endure to be himself. So properly he is not in despair over the fact that he did not become Caesar, but he is in despair over himself for the fact that he did not become Caesar. This self which, had he become Caesar, would have been to him a sheer delight (though in another sense equally in despair), this self is now absolutely intolerable to him. In a profounder sense it is not the fact that he did not become Caesar which is intolerable to him, but the self which did not become Caesar is the thing that is intolerable; or, more correctly, what is intolerable to him is that he cannot get rid of himself. If he had become Caesar he would have been rid of himself in desperation, but now that he did not become Caesar he cannot in desperation get rid of himself. Essentially he is equally in despair in either case, for he does not possess himself, he is not himself. By becoming Caesar he would not after all have become himself but have got rid of himself, and by not becoming Caesar he falls into despair over the fact that he cannot get rid of himself. Hence it is a superficial view (which presumably has never seen a person in despair, not even one's own self) when it is said of a man in despair, "He is consuming himself." For precisely this it is he despairs of, and to his torment it is precisely this he cannot do, since by despair fire has entered into something that cannot burn, or cannot burn up, that is, into the self.

So to despair over something is not yet properly despair. It is the beginning, or it is as when the physician says of a sickness that it has not yet declared itself. The next step is the declared despair, despair over oneself. A young girl is in despair over love, and so she despairs over her lover, because he died, or because he was unfaithful to her. This is not a declared despair; no, she is in despair over herself. This self of hers, which, if it had become "his" beloved, she would have been rid of in the most blissful way, or would have lost, this self is now a torment to her when it has to be a self without "him"; this self which would have been to her her riches (though in another sense equally in despair) has now become to her a loathsome void, since "he" is dead or it has become to her an abhorrence, since it reminds her of the fact that she was betrayed. Try it now, say to such a girl, "Thou art consuming thyself," and thou shalt hear her reply, "Oh, no, the torment is precisely this, that I cannot do it."

To despair over oneself, in despair to will to be rid of oneself, is the formula for all despair, and hence the second form of despair (in despair at willing to be oneself) can be followed back to the first (in despair at not willing to be oneself), just as in the foregoing we resolved the first into the second. A despairing man wants despairingly to be himself. But if he despairingly wants to be himself, he will not want to get rid of himself. Yes, so it seems; but if one inspects more closely, one perceives that after all the contradiction is the same. That self which he despairingly wills to be is a self which he is not (for to will to be that self which one truly is, is indeed the opposite of despair); what he really wills is to tear his self away from the Power which constituted it. But notwithstanding all his despair, this he is unable to do, notwithstanding all the efforts of despair, that Power is the stronger, and it compels him to be the self he does not will to be. But for all that he wills to be rid of himself, to be rid of the self which he is, in order to be the self he himself has chanced to choose. To be *self* as he wills to be would be his delight (though in another sense it would be equally in despair), but to be compelled to be *self* as he does not will to be is his torment, namely, that he cannot get rid of himself.

Socrates proved the immortality of the soul from the fact that the sickness of the soul (sin) does not consume it as sickness of the body consumes the body. So also we can demonstrate the eternal in man from the fact that despair cannot consume his self, that this precisely is the torment of contradiction in despair. If there were nothing eternal in a man, he could not despair; but if despair could consume his self, there would still be no despair.

Thus it is that despair, this sickness in the self, is the sickness unto death. The despairing man is mortally ill. In an entirely different sense than can appropriately be said of any disease, we may say that the sickness has attacked the noblest part; and yet the man cannot die. Death is not the last phase of the sickness, but death is continually the last. To be delivered from this sickness by death is an impossibility, for the sickness and its torment . . . and death consist in not being able to die.

This is the situation in despair. And however thoroughly it eludes the attention of the despairer, and however thoroughly the despairer may succeed (as in the case of that kind of despair which is characterized by unawareness of being in despair, in losing himself entirely, and losing himself in such a way that it is not noticed in the least—eternity nevertheless will make it manifest his situation was despair, and it will so nail him to himself that the torment nevertheless remains that he cannot get rid of himself, and it becomes manifest that he was deluded in thinking that he succeeded. And thus it is eternity must act, because to have a self, to be a self, is the greatest concession made to man, but at the same time it is eternity's demand upon him.

(*Sickness,* pp. 150–154)

7. SOCRATES: PHILOSOPHY CONFRONTS DEATH

When one man investigates objectively the problem of immortality, and another embraces an uncertainty with the passion of the infinite: where is there most truth, and who has the greater certainty? The one has entered upon a never-ending approximation, for the certainty of immortality lies precisely in the subjectivity of the individual; the other is immortal, and fights for his immortality by struggling with the uncertainty. Let us consider Socrates. Nowadays everyone dabbles in a few proofs; some have several such proofs, others fewer. But Socrates! He puts the question objectively in a problematic manner: *if* there is an immortality. He must therefore be accounted a doubter in comparison with one of our modern thinkers with the three proofs? By no means. On this "if" he risks his entire life, he has the courage to meet death, and he has with the passion of the infinite so determined the pattern of his life that it must be found acceptable—*if* there is an immortality. Is any better proof capable of being given for the immortality of the soul? But those who have the three proofs do not at all determine their lives in conformity therewith; if there is an immortality it must feel disgust over their manner of life: can any better refutation be given of the three proofs? The bit of uncertainty that Socrates had, helped him because he himself contributed the passion of the infinite; the three proofs that the others have do not profit them at all, because they are dead to spirit and enthusiasm, and their three proofs, in lieu of proving anything else, prove just this.

(Postscript, p. 180)

A word read accidentally often teaches us more than anything. In his *Ethics,* Book III, chap. 2, where he explains the difference between wishing and choosing, Aristotle says: "One certainly cannot choose the impossible, but one can certainly wish it, thus one can, for example, wish to be immortal."

(Pap., X 5 A 31)

Right at the end of the second book of his *De Natura Deorum,* Cicero expresses in depth the spirit of paganism: there is a Providence which is concerned with everything, and with individuals; but, to be sure, with the elite among these. And he adds: the gods remember the important things, not the insignificant ones.

O the terrible desolation of the crime of treason against God! How is it possible even to dare believe that God is interested in me, if he is interested only in what is important? How dreadful that one could have the idea that God is interested in us for this reason, that we are somehow important to God.

No, Christianity turns things around. The more you are miserable, abandoned, insignificant, unhappy—be sure of it—the more God is interested in you.

Paganism is fellowship with God; God is but the superlative of human.

(Pap., X 4 A 442)

Scriver says that we always drive a good bargain with death; we get the best of it, "death brings something more." (Phil. 1, 21)

This manner of cheating death has more greatness than

the Epicurean way: death, says Epicurus, cannot lay its hand on me, because, when I am here, death is not, and when it is, I am no longer.

(Pap., X 4 A 60)

Cicero says (in *De Natura Deorum,* near the end of the second book) that the gods have no advantage over man other than immortality, but that this is not necessary for leading a happy life.

. . . .

In general, immortality came along only with Christianity, and why? Because Christianity requires us to die to the world. To have the strength to do this, immortality and eternity have to be firmly established. Immortality and dying to the world correspond to one another. With the suffering of dying to the world is born the hope of immortality.

(Pap., X 4 A 440)

8. TIME AND ETERNITY

In the sphere of historical freedom transition is a state. However, in order to understand this affirmation one must not forget that the new situation comes about by the leap. For if this is not kept in mind, transition acquires a quantitative preponderance over the elasticity of the leap.

So then, man was said to be a synthesis of soul and body; but he is at the same time *a synthesis of the temporal and the eternal*. I have no objection to recognizing that this has often been said; I have no wish to discover novelties, but rather it is my joy and my darling occupation to think upon things which seem perfectly simple.

As for the latter synthesis, it evidently is not fashioned in the same way as the former. In the former case the two factors were soul and body, and the spirit was a third term, but was a third term in such a sense that there could not properly be any question of a synthesis until the spirit was posited. The other synthesis has only two factors: the temporal and the eternal. Where is the third term? And if there be no third term, there is really no synthesis; for a synthesis of that which is a contradiction cannot be completed as a synthesis without a third term, for the recognition that the synthesis is a contradiction is precisely the assertion that it is not a synthesis. What then is the temporal?

When time is correctly defined as infinite succession, it seems plausible to define it also as the present, the past and the future. However this distinction is incorrect, if one means by it that this is implied in time itself; for it first emerges with the relation of time to eternity and the reflection of eternity in it. If in the infinite succession of time one could in fact find a foothold, i.e. a present, which would serve as a dividing point, then this division would be quite correct. But precisely because every moment, like the sum of the moments, is a process (a going-by) no moment is a present, and in the same sense there is neither past, present, nor future. If one thinks it possible to maintain this division, it is because we *spatialize* a moment, but thereby the infinite succession is brought to a standstill, and that is because one introduces a visual representation, visualizing time instead of thinking it. But even so it is not correctly thought, for even in this visual representation the infinite succession of time is a present infinitely void of content. (This is the parody of the eternal.) The Hindus speak of a line of kings which has reigned for 70,000 years. About the kings nothing is known, not even their names (as I assume). Taking this as an illustration of time, these 70,000 years are for thought an infinite vanishing; for visual representation they widen out spatially into an illusive view of a nothing infinitely void.* On the other hand, so soon as we let one moment succeed the other we posit the present.

The present, however, is not the concept of time, unless precisely as something infinitely void, which again is precisely the infinite vanishing. If one does not give heed to this, then, however swiftly one may let it pass, one has nevertheless posited the present, and having posited that, one lets it appear again in the definition of the past and the future.

---

* Moreover, this is space. Just here the practiced reader will see the proof that my representation is right, since for abstract thinking time and space are absolutely identical (*nacheinander* and *nebeneinander*), and they become so for visual representation, and so it is with the definition of God as omnipresent.

On the contrary, the eternal is the present. For thought, the eternal is the present as an annulled [*aufgehoben*] succession (time was succession, going by). For visual representation, eternity is a going-forth, yet it never budges from the spot, because for visual representation it is a present infinitely rich in content. Likewise in the eternal there is not to be found any division of the past and the future, because the present is posited as the annulled succession.

So time is infinite succession. The life which is in time and is merely that of time has no present. It is true that to characterize the sensuous life it is commonly said that it is "in the instant" and only in the instant. The instant is here understood as something abstracted from the eternal, and if this is to be accounted the present, it is a parody of it. The present is the eternal, or rather the eternal is the present, and the present is full. In this sense the Roman said of the Deity that He is *praesens* (*praesentes dii*), and in using this expression for the Deity His powerful aid was indicated at the same time.

The instant characterizes the present as having no past and no future, for in this precisely consists the imperfection of the sensuous life. The eternal also characterizes the present as having no past and no future, and this is the perfection of the eternal.

If one would now employ the instant to define time, and let the instant indicate the purely abstract exclusion of the past and the future, and by the same token of the present also, then the instant precisely is not the present, for that which in purely abstract thinking lies between the past and the future has no existence at all. But one sees from this that the instant is not a mere characterization of time, for what characterizes time is only that it goes by, and hence time, if it is to be defined by any of the characteristics revealed in time itself, is the passed time. On the other hand, if time and eternity are to touch one another, it must be in time—and with this we have reached the instant.

"The instant" [in Danish, *Øjeblikket*—"a glance of the eye"] is a figurative expression, and for that reason not so easy to deal with. Yet it is a pretty word to reflect upon. Nothing is so swift as a glance of the eye, and yet it is commensurable with the content and value of eternity. Thus when Ingeborg gazes out over the sea to descry Frithiof, this is a picture of what the figurative word signifies. An outburst of her emotion, a sigh, a word, has, as a sound, more the character of time, as a thing that vanishes it is more like the present, and has not so much the presence of the eternal in it, and for this reason a sigh, a word, etc. has power to help the soul to get rid of the weight which oppresses it, precisely because the oppression, if only it finds utterance, begins already to become a past. A glance is therefore a designation of time, but note that this means, of time in the fateful conflict when it is touched by eternity.* What we call "the instant," Plato calls "the sudden." However it may be explained etymologically, it is related at all events to the notion of invisibility, because by the Greeks time and eternity alike were conceived abstractly, since the Greeks lacked the concept of the temporal owing to the fact that they lacked the concept of spirit. In Latin it is called *momentum,* which by derivation (from *movere*) merely expresses the vanishing of time.**

---

* It is noteworthy that Greek art culminates in statuary, in which it is precisely the glance that is lacking. This, however, has its deep reason in the fact that the Greeks did not in the profounder sense comprehend the concept of spirit, and therefore did not in the profoundest sense comprehend the sensuous and the temporal. How striking is the contrast that in Christianity God is pictorially represented as an eye!

** In the New Testament there is a poetical paraphrase of the instant. Paul says that the world will pass away "in an instant, in the twinkling of an eye." By that he also expresses the thought that the instant is commensurable with eternity, because the instant of destruction expresses at the same instant eternity. Allow me to illustrate what I mean, and forgive me if there is found anything

Thus understood, the instant is not properly an atom of time but an atom of eternity. It is the first reflection of eternity in time, its first effort as it were to bring time to a stop. For this reason Hellenism did not understand the instant; for even if it comprehended the atom of eternity, it did not comprehend that it was the instant, did not define it with a forward orientation but with a backward, since for Hellenism the atom of eternity was essentially eternity, and so neither time nor eternity had true justice done it.

The synthesis of the eternal and the temporal is not a second synthesis but is the expression for the first synthesis in consequence of which man is a synthesis of soul and body sustained by spirit. No sooner is the spirit posited than the instant is there. For this reason it can be said reproachfully of man that he lives only in the instant, since this comes about by an arbitrary abstraction. Nature does not lie in the instant.

As it is with the sensuous, so it is also with the temporal; for the temporal seems even more imperfect, and the instant still more insignificant, than the apparently secure persistence of nature in time. And yet it is exactly the converse, for nature's security is due to the fact that time has no significance for it. Only in the instant does history begin. Man's

---

offensive in the parable I employ. Here in Copenhagen there once upon a time were two actors, who perhaps hardly reflected that a deeper significance might be found in their performance. They came on the stage, placed themselves opposite one another, and then began a pantomime representation of some passionate conflict. When the pantomimic play was in full swing, and the spectators were following the play with keen expectancy of what was to come after, the actors suddenly came to a stop and remained motionless, as though they were petrified in the pantomimic expression of the instant. This may produce a most comical effect, because the instant becomes accidentally commensurable with the eternal. The effect of sculpture is due to the fact that the eternal expression is expressed eternally; the comic effect, on the other hand, by the fact that the accidental expression was eternalized.

sensuousness is by sin posited as sinfulness, and therefore is lower than that of the beast, and yet this is because here the higher life begins, for now begins spirit.

The instant is that ambiguous moment in which time and eternity touch one another, thereby positing *the temporal,* where time is constantly intersecting eternity and eternity constantly permeating time. Only now does that division we talked about acquire significance: the present, the past, and the future.

In making this division, attention is at once drawn to the fact that in a certain sense the future signifies more than the present and the past; for the future is in a sense the whole of which the past is a part, and in a sense the future may signify the whole. This is due to the fact that the eternal means first of all the future, or that the future is the incognito in which the eternal, as incommensurable for time, would nevertheless maintain its relations with time. Thus we sometimes speak of the future as identical with eternity: the future life = eternal life. Since the Greeks did not have in a deeper sense the concept of the eternal, neither did they have the concept of the future. One cannot therefore reproach the Greek life for losing itself in the instant, or rather we cannot even say that it was lost; for by the Greeks the temporal was conceived just as naively as was the sensuous, because the category of spirit was lacking.

The instant and the future posit in turn the past. If the Greek life might be supposed to define time in any sense, it is as time past, yet without defining this by its relation to the present and the future, but defining it, like the definition of time in general, as a going-by. Here the significance of the Platonic recollection is evident. The Greek eternity lies behind, as the past into which one enters only backwards.* However, to say that eternity is the past is to present a per-

---

* Here again one must bear in mind the category I maintain, i.e. repetition, by which one enters eternity forwards.

fectly abstract concept of it, whether this be further defined philosophically (by the philosophical dying to the world) or historically.

In general, by seeing how the past, the future, the eternal are defined, one can see how the instant has been defined. If there is no instant, then the eternal appears to be behind, like the past. It is as though I were to picture a man walking along a road but do not assume that he takes a step, then the road behind him appears to be the distance traveled. If the instant is posited, but merely as a *discrimen*, then the future is the eternal. If the instant is posited, so is the eternal—but also the future, which comes again like the past. This appears clearly in the Greek, the Jewish, and the Christian conceptions. The concept around which everything turns in Christianity, the concept which makes all things new, is the fullness of time, is the instant as eternity, and yet this eternity is at once the future and the past. If one does not give heed to this, one cannot save any concept from heretical and treasonable admixtures which destroy the concept. One does not get the past as a thing for itself but in simple continuity with the future—and with that the concepts of conversion, atonement, redemption, are resolved in the significance of world-history, and resolved in the individual historical development. One does not get the future as a thing for itself but in simple continuity with the present—and with that the concepts of resurrection and judgment come to naught.

Let us now picture to ourselves Adam, and then remember that every subsequent individual begins exactly the same way, only within the quantitative difference which is the consequence of the fact of generation and of the historical situation. For Adam then, just as much as for every subsequent individual, there is the instant. The synthesis of the soulish and the bodily is to be posited by spirit, but the spirit is the eternal, and therefore this is accomplished only when the spirit posits at the same time along with this the second synthesis of the eternal and the temporal. So long as the eternal is not posited, the instant *is* not, or is only as a *discrimen*. Therefore, seeing that in the state of innocence the spirit is characterized merely as a dreaming spirit, the eternal manifests itself as the future, for this, as I have said, is the first expression of the eternal, is its incognito. Just as in the foregoing chapter the spirit when it was about to be posited in the synthesis or rather was about to posit the synthesis, as the spirit's (freedom's) possibility in the individual, expressed itself as dread, so here in turn the future, the possibility of the eternal (i.e. of freedom) in the individual is dread. When then the possibility of freedom manifests itself before freedom, freedom succumbs, and the temporal now emerges in the same way as did sensuousness with the significance of sinfulness. Here again I say that this is the last psychological approximation to the qualitative leap. The difference between Adam and the subsequent individual is that by the latter the future is conceived more reflectively than by Adam. Psychologically speaking, this "more" may have a terrible significance, but in relation to the qualitative leap its significance is unessential. The highest maximum of difference in comparison with Adam is that the future seems to be anticipated by the past, or, in other words, it is the dread that possibility has been lost before it has been lost.

The possible corresponds precisely to the future. For freedom the possible is the future; and for time the future is the possible. Corresponding to both of these in the individual life is dread. A precise and correct linguistic usage associates therefore dread and the future. It is true that one is sometimes said to be in dread of the past, and this seems to be a contradiction. Nevertheless, upon closer inspection it appears that this manner of speaking points in one way or another to the future. The past of which I am supposed to be in dread must stand in a relation of possibility to me. If I am in dread of a past misfortune, this is not in so far as it is past, but in so far as it may be repeated, i.e. become future. If I am in dread of a past fault, it is because I have not put it in an essential relation to myself as past, and have in some way or another prevented it from being past. For in case it is really past, I cannot be in dread but only repentant. If I do not repent, then I have first taken the liberty of making my relation to it dialectical, but thereby the fault itself has become a possibility and not something completely passed. If I am in dread of punishment, it is only when this is put in a dialectical relation with the fault (otherwise I bear my punishment), and then I am in dread of the possible and the future.

So again we have reached the point where we were in Chapter I. Dread is the psychological state which precedes sin, comes as near as possible to it, and is as provocative as possible of dread, but without explaining sin, which breaks forth first in the qualitative leap.

The instant sin is posited, the temporal is sin.* We do not

---

* From the characterization of the temporal as sinfulness death in turn follows as punishment. This is a progression, an analogy of which, *si placet,* may be found in the fact that, even in relation to the external phenomenon, death is more terrible in the degree that the organism is more perfect. Thus, whereas the death and decay of a plant diffuses an odor almost more delicious than its spicy breath, the decay of an animal, on the other hand, infects the air. It is true in a deeper sense that the more highly we value man, the more terrible death appears. The beast cannot properly be said to die; but when the spirit is posited as spirit, death appears terrible. The dread of death therefore corresponds to that of child-birth, though with this I do not subscribe to what in part is said truly, in part only wittily, in part enthusiastically, in part lightly, about death being a metamorphosis. At the instant of death man finds himself at the extremest point of the synthesis; the spirit cannot, as it were, be present, and yet it must wait, for the body must die. The pagan view of death—as the pagan's sensuousness was more naïve and his sense of time more carefree—was milder and more attractive, but it lacked the highest element. Let one read the beautiful essay by Lessing on the representation of death in classical art, and one cannot deny that one is put in a mood of pleasurable sadness by this picture of the sleeping genius, or by

say that the temporal is sinfulness, any more than that the sensuous is sinfulness; but for the fact that sin is posited the temporal signifies sinfulness. Therefore that man sins who lives merely in the instant abstracted from the eternal. If Adam (to speak again by way of "accommodation" and to speak foolishly) had not sinned, he would the same instant have passed over into eternity. On the other hand, so soon as sin is posited it does not avail to want to abstract oneself from the temporal, any more than it would from the sensuous.

(*Concept of Dread*, pp. 76–83)

observing the beautiful solemnity with which the genius of death bows his head and extinguishes the torch. There is, if one will, something indescribably persuasive and alluring in the thought of trusting oneself to such a guide, who is as tranquilizing as a recollection in which nothing is recollected. But on the other hand there is in turn something uncanny in following this mute guide; for he conceals nothing, his form is no incognito, as he is, so is death, and therewith all is over. There is an unfathomable sadness in seeing this guide with his friendly figure bend over the dying man and with the breath of his last kiss extinguish the last spark of life, while all he has experienced has already vanished little by little, and death only is left, which, itself unexplained, explains that the whole of life was a game in which all, the greatest and the least, went out like tapers, one by one, and at last the soul itself. But then there is implied by it also the muteness of annihilation, because the whole thing was only a childish game, and now the game is finished.

9. THE WORD OF GOD

1. First, it is necessary, up to a certain point, to know oneself. For he who does not know himself cannot recognize himself either, and we can never recognize ourselves except inasmuch as we know ourselves.

Thus there has to be some preparation. Materially also—when a man accidentally happens to see himself in a mirror, or when the mirror is so placed that he does not know that the image seen is a reflection of the mirror and that the reflection is himself—it happens that we do not recognize ourselves.

Paganism required: know yourself. Christianity answers: no, this "know yourself" is a preliminary. Then look at yourself in the mirror of the Word to really know yourself. There is no true knowledge of self without knowledge of God, or without being before God. To be in front of the mirror is to be in front of God.

2. You must not be afraid to see yourself. We know well enough man's physical fear of seeing himself, and that superstition believed that for a man to see himself was an omen of death.

And so also for the spiritual. To see ourselves is to die, to die to all illusion and to all hypocrisy. Great courage is required to dare to see ourselves, which can only happen in the mirror of the Word; otherwise, there is a rapid tumble into fraud, and recognizing ourselves is tantamount to Sancho's beating himself.

It is truth only that we must desire, and not, by vanity, want to see ourselves more beautiful, nor, by the folly of self-torture, want to see ourselves as pure devils.

3. We must bring to mind an implacable hatred for this "I" who has revealed himself in the mirror as that to which we must die, as the old man we have been.

(Pap., X 4 A 412)

Think of a couple in love. He has written his beloved a letter; and she begins wondering how others would understand the letter, or whether she will be the only one to read it.

Suppose now that this letter has the peculiarity that every isolated human being is the beloved, what then? What words can he use to express the fact that all these isolated persons are assembled together, and how can he take upon himself an entire package of erudition inherited from innumerable generations?

No, the intention of this letter is that it be read before God by each individual, alone, as an individual who has received the letter as his gift from God.

But the fact that this letter comes from God has been quickly forgotten. And the fact that it is for the individual has been completely forgotten. The human race has been substituted for the individual. That is why the sense of the Bible has been radically lost.

(Pap., X 3 A 348)

The strategy up to now has been to say: Holy Writ is a divine revelation, inspired, etc., so there must be perfect harmony in all it relates, even to the smallest detail, and it must be in impeccable Greek, etc.

Now, let us take things from another angle. Certainly God knows what it is to believe, what it is to require faith, and that this is precisely to deny direct communication and to put forward an ambiguity.

You see, now all the parts fit. It is precisely because God wants Holy Writ to be an object of faith and to be scandalous from every other point of view, that so much attention has been paid to these disagreements of detail, which, incidentally, could well be reconciled into agreements in eternity, and that the Bible is in a poor Greek. [etc.]

Take another example. God as pilot of the world evidently also wants to be the object of faith, wants us to believe that he is the loving father. [etc.] Now, a theory corresponding to the aforementioned theory of harmony ought to require that the world also be without ambiguity, to the point that we could directly put our finger on the fact that God is love. But that is a point that the world is far from reaching! And why isn't it? Because God wants to be believed.

(Pap., X 3 A 328)

The scene of the Last Judgment: Our Lord, a professor of theology.

Our Lord: "Did you seek first the kingdom of God?"

The professor: "No, that I cannot say. But "seek first the kingdom of God," that I know how to say in seven languages: (1) in Danish, (2) in German, (3) in French, (4) in Greek, (5) in Hebrew, (6) in Latin, (7) in Arabic, (8) in Aramaic, (9) in Phoenician . . . but I notice that I know it in nine languages, two more than I had promised." Our Lord turns his back on him while the professor goes on: "It is simply that I have put all my effort into investigation and research, day and night." It is here that the angel Gabriel interrupts him with a boot that knocks him for a million miles.

(Pap., X 3 A 398)

Previously, Holy Writ was imaginatively mirrored: this is what is behind allegorical interpretation. Fundamentally, it expresses the fact that we are unable to understand how this infinite thing has quite simply happened in history. The allegory, as a fundamental interpretation, is at bottom an indirect attack against Christianity, against the fact that Christ was an individual, and the apostle another individual who, in some enormous activity, threw onto a scrap of paper some words to a community.

Then came the Reformation, which made the most of that which had already been granted in principle, but not in definite opposition to the prevailing state of affairs; on the contrary, in accord with the Catholic Church, even though it was as little in accord as possible. But the persons concerned, an Erasmus for instance, did not dare to act decisively, having only the preoccupation that the thing be said. And it introduced a more realistically sound explanation.

But now we, in turn, by excessive sobriety, are drowning ourselves in scientific philology. It has almost been forgotten that the Bible is a Holy Writ, whereas before, in the case of excessive imagination, only a Holy Writ was seen in the Bible.

Above all, we omit this quite natural matter that the apostle is a being who, with unequalled agility, throws out some words to keep some community alerted.

(Pap., X 2 A 548)

If a childish orthodoxy has cast a comic light upon Christianity, so also has such Bible interpretation, which by its deferential timidity inverts the proper relationship without being aware of it, and is not so anxious to understand the Bible as to be understood by it, not so anxious to understand a Biblical text as to get a Biblical text to appeal to— just such a contradiction as when one who is engaged in affairs would ask counsel of a man (thus expressing the relationship of dependence), but asks it in such a way that he requires his counselor to answer thus and so, and ventures to use every means to get him to answer precisely thus. Deference to the authority of the counselor becomes a sly way of deriving advantage from his authority. But is that to seek counsel? It is in fact a cowardly way of shoving off all responsibility from oneself by never acting with independence—as though one had no responsibility for the way one gets a Bible text for one's support. Psychologically it is very remarkable how ingenious, how inventive, how sophistical, how persevering in learned investigations certain men may be, merely to get a Bible text to appeal to. On the other hand, they do not seem to observe that this precisely is to make a fool of God, to treat Him as a poor devil who has been foolish enough to commit something to writing and now must put up with what the lawyers will make of it. Thus it is a cunning little child will behave towards a severe father who has not known how to win the child's love. He reasons thus: If only I can get his permission, then it's all right, although I have to employ a little guile. But such a relation is not a tender and hearty one between father and son. And neither is it a hearty relationship between God and a human being when they are so remote from one another that there is place and use for all this anxiousness and sophistry and rumination of a dispirited deference. Examples of such behavior one finds most readily among talented men whose enthusiasm is not proportionate to their intellectuality. Whereas narrow and busy men fancy that they are acting and acting and acting, the mark of a certain type of intellectual is the virtuosity they display in avoiding action. It is pathetic that Cromwell, who indeed was a practised Bible-reader, had sophistry enough to find Biblical texts for his justification, or at least to find in a *vox populi* a *vox dei* to the effect that it was by an act or dispensation of providence he became Protector of England, not by any act of his, for indeed the people had elected him. As one rarely sees a real hypocrite, so, too, a man entirely without conscience is rare, but a sophistical conscience is not rare, whether it be the agonizing self-contradiction of having to explain away a responsibility and being at the same time unconscious of what one is doing, or morbidity in a man who is perhaps well meaning, a morbidity which involves great suffering and makes the unhappy man's breathing more straitened and painful than the most troubled conscience when it is able to breathe out in sincerity.

A childish orthodoxy, a pusillanimous Bible interpretation, a foolish and unchristian defense of Christianity, a bad conscience on the part of the defenders with respect to their own relation to it, all this has in our time its share in occasioning passionate and frantic attacks upon Christianity. One should not chaffer, should not want to alter Christianity.

(Postscript, pp. 534–535)

III An Existential Itinerary From Anguish to Love

1. ANGUISH AND SIN

One may liken dread to dizziness. He whose eye chances to look down into the yawning abyss becomes dizzy. But the reason for it is just as much his eye as it is the precipice. For suppose he had not looked down.

Thus dread is the dizziness of freedom which occurs when the spirit would posit the synthesis, and freedom then gazes down into its own possibility, grasping at finiteness to sustain itself. In this dizziness freedom succumbs. Further than this psychology cannot go and will not. That very instant everything is changed, and when freedom rises again it sees that it is guilty. Between these two instants lies the leap, which no science has explained or can explain. He who becomes guilty in dread becomes as ambiguously guilty as it is possible to be. Dread is a womanish debility in which freedom swoons. Psychologically speaking, the fall into sin always occurs in impotence. But dread is at the same time the most egoistic thing, and no concrete expression of freedom is so egoistic as is the possibility of every concretion. This again is the overwhelming experience which determines the individual's ambiguous relation, both sympathetic and antipathetic. In dread there is the egoistic infinity of possibility, which does not tempt like a definite choice, but alarms (*ængster*) and fascinates with its sweet anxiety (*Beængstelse*).

(*Concept of Dread,* p. 55)

187

Sin's worst punishment is to fall back into it. Of course that is what the hardened and confident sinner does not understand. But when a man shudders at the thought of his own sin, when he is ready to endure all to avoid falling back into his old error, then the new fault is the sin's most terrible punishment.

Now, there are, especially for sins of thought, certain collisions where the dread of sin is almost capable of provoking it.

When one is at that point, a wrong turn into despair can easily be taken. That is what Vigilius Haufniensis has described (*Concept of Dread,* p. 167) by saying that dread loses its mind. As long as it keeps its head, it remains well established. This must remain the rule from all eternity— that sin must be vanquished. But in his despair, such an unfortunate man can have the idea, since this new sin is certainly the worst punishment for sin, that perhaps now he must resign himself to it.

It is in this way undoubtedly that we must understand quietism when it teaches that a man could be saved while remaining in sin, but since sin is the worst punishment, despair takes hold of him as if there were no more to be done.

The difference in the tactics to be used in the fight against temptation and against scruples can be seen here. In the face of temptation, it may be correct to fight by fleeing. Temptation must be avoided; we must try not to see or hear what is tempting. If it is a question of scruples, it is necessary to march to the encounter, committing ourselves to God and to Christ.

Today, since we have absolutely no idea what scruples are, someone who would suffer from them would actually be considered, among other things, to be a matchless sinner.

(Pap., X 1 A 637)

That God tries, even tempts a man—lead us not into temptation—is a thought by which one must not be frightened. The difference is simply how one looks at it. Unbelief, melancholy, and so on, at once grow anxious and afraid and really impute that God does so in order that man shall succumb; for, however far a melancholy anxiety may be from thinking such a thing of God, yet in the deepest sense it really does think that, but without knowing it or being conscious of it, just as it is said of a man in a passion that he does not know what he is doing. The believer on the other hand, apprehends everything the other way round; he believes that God does so *in order* that he should stand the test. Alas, and in a certain sense, it follows from this that unbelief, melancholy, anxiety, and so on, usually succumb, because they weaken themselves beforehand, and as a punishment for thinking evil of God; whereas faith is readily victorious.

But it is a severe education, the education from inborn dread to faith. Dread is the most terrible kind of tribulation, and it is a long way until the point is reached where the same man is practiced in faith; i.e., in looking at everything the other way round, in remaining confident and hopeful when that happens which formerly almost made him faint and expire with dread; and to go freely forward to meet that against which he formerly knew only one means of preservation: flight and so on.

He in whose soul there is an inborn dread can therefore easily have even a visionary idea of God's love. But he cannot make his relation to God concrete. If his idea of God's love has a deeper root in him, and if he is piously concerned, before all else, to nourish and preserve it, his life can in many ways, and for a long time, continue in the agony of suffering. In the concrete he does not receive the impression that God is love for dread continues to overwhelm him and prevents him from seeing the danger, the trial, the temptation; [etc.] from the true point of view it only exists in order that man shall endure it; all the same he only holds and clings the more firmly to the thought: yes, in spite of all, God is love.

That is a sign that he is reared to faith. Thus to keep

firmly hold of the thought, God is love, is the most abstract form of faith. But then, in time, he will succeed in achieving a relation to God in the concrete.

(*Journals*, n. 1064)

2. THE KNIGHT OF FAITH

Let us consider a little more closely the distress and dread in the paradox of faith. The tragic hero renounces himself in order to express the universal, the knight of faith renounces the universal in order to become the individual. As has been said, everything depends upon how one is placed. He who believes that it is easy enough to be the individual can always be sure that he is not a knight of faith, for vagabonds and roving geniuses are not men of faith. The knight of faith knows, on the other hand, that it is glorious to belong to the universal. He knows that it is beautiful and salutary to be the individual who translates himself into the universal, who edits as it were a pure and elegant edition of himself, as free from errors as possible and which everyone can read. He knows that it is refreshing to become intelligible to oneself in the universal so that he understands it and so that every individual who understands him understands through him in turn the universal, and both rejoice in the security of the universal. He knows that it is beautiful to be born as the individual who has the universal as his home, his friendly abiding-place, which at once welcomes him with open arms when he would tarry in it. But he knows also that higher than this there winds a solitary path, narrow and steep; he knows that it is terrible to be born outside the universal, to walk without meeting a single traveller. He knows very well where he is and how he is related to men. Humanly speaking, he is crazy and cannot make himself intelligible to anyone. And yet it is the mildest expression, to say that he is crazy. If he is not supposed to be that, then he is a hypocrite, and the higher he climbs on this path, the more dreadful a hypocrite he is.

The knight of faith knows that to give up oneself for the universal inspires enthusiasm, and that it requires courage, but he also knows that security is to be found in this, precisely because it is for the universal. He knows that it is glorious to be understood by every noble mind, so glorious that the beholder is ennobled by it, and he feels as if he were bound; he could wish it were this task that had been allotted to him. Thus Abraham could surely have wished now and then that the task were to love Isaac as becomes a father, in a way intelligible to all, memorable throughout all ages; he could wish that the task were to sacrifice Isaac for the universal, that he might incite the fathers to illustrious deeds—and he is almost terrified by the thought that for him such wishes are only temptations and must be dealt with as such, for he knows that it is a solitary path he treads and that he accomplishes nothing for the universal but only himself is tried and examined. Or what did Abraham accomplish for the universal? Let me speak humanly about it, quite humanly. He spent seventy years in getting a son of his old age. What other men get quickly enough and enjoy for a long time he spent seventy years in accomplishing. And why? Because he was tried and put to the test. Is not that crazy? But Abraham believed, and Sarah wavered and got him to take Hagar as a concubine—but therefore he also had to drive her away. He gets Isaac, then he has to be tried again. He knew that it is glorious to express the universal, glorious to live with Isaac. But this not the task. He knew that it is a kingly thing to sacrifice such a son for the universal, he himself would have found repose in that, and all would have reposed in the commendation of his deed, as a vowel reposes in its consonant, but that is not the task

—he is tried. That Roman general who is celebrated by his name of Cunctator checked the foe by procrastination—but what a procrastinator Abraham is in comparison with him! . . . yet he did not save the state. This is the content of one hundred and thirty years. Who can bear it? Would not his contemporary age, if we can speak of such a thing, have said of him, "Abraham is eternally procrastinating. Finally he gets a son. That took long enough. Now he wants to sacrifice him. So is he not mad? And if at least he could explain why he wants to do it—but he alway says that it is a trial." Nor could Abraham explain more, for his life is like a book placed under a divine attachment and which never becomes *publici juris.*

This is the terrible thing. He who does not see it can always be sure that he is no knight of faith, but he who sees it will not deny that even the most tried of tragic heroes walks with a dancing step compared with the knight of faith, who comes slowly creeping forward. And if he has perceived this and assured himself that he has not courage to understand it, he will at least have a presentiment of the marvellous glory this knight attains in the fact that he becomes God's intimate acquaintance, the Lord's friend, and (to speak quite humanly) that he says "Thou" to God in heaven, whereas even the tragic hero only addresses Him in the third person.

The tragic hero is soon ready and has soon finished the fight, he makes the infinite movement and then is secure in the universal. The knight of faith, on the other hand, is kept sleepless, for he is constantly tried, and every instant there is the possibility of being able to return repentantly to the universal, and this possibility can just as well be a temptation as the truth. He can derive evidence from no man which it is, for with that query he is outside the paradox.

So the knight of faith has first and foremost the requisite passion to concentrate upon a single factor the whole of the ethical which he transgresses, so that he can give himself the assurance that he really loves Isaac with his whole soul.* If he cannot do that, he is in temptation (*Anfechtung*). In the next place, he has enough passion to make this assurance available in the twinkling of an eye and in such a way that it is as completely valid as it was in the first instance. If he is unable to do this, he can never budge from the spot, for he constantly has to begin all over again. The tragic hero also concentrated in one factor the ethical which he teleologically surpassed, but in this respect he had support in the universal. The knight of faith has only himself alone, and this constitutes the dreadfulness of the situation. Most men live in such a way under an ethical obligation that they can let the sorrow be sufficient for the day, but they never reach this passionate concentration, this energetic consciousness. The universal may in a certain sense help the tragic hero to attain this, but the knight of faith is left all to himself. The hero does the deed and finds repose in the universal, the knight of faith is kept in constant tension.

* I would elucidate yet once more the difference between the collisions which are encountered by the tragic hero and by the knight of faith. The tragic hero assures himself that the ethical obligation [i.e., the lower ethical obligation, which he puts aside for the higher; in the present case, accordingly, it is the obligation to spare his daughter's life] is totally present in him by the fact that he transforms it into a wish. Thus Agamemnon can say, "The proof that I do not offend against my parental duty is that my duty is my only wish." So here we have wish and duty face to face with one another. The fortunate chance in life is that the two correspond, that my wish is my duty and vice versa, and the task of most men in life is precisely to remain within their duty and by their enthusiasm to transform it into their wish. The tragic hero gives up his wish in order to accomplish his duty. For the knight of faith wish and duty are also identical, but he is required to give up both. Therefore when he would resign himself to giving up his wish he does not find repose, for that is after all his duty. If he would remain within his duty and his wish, he is not a knight of faith, for the absolute duty requires precisely that he should give them up. The tragic hero apprehended a higher expression of duty but not an absolute duty.

Agamemnon gives up Iphigenia and thereby has found repose in the universal, then he takes the step of sacrificing her. If Agamemnon does not make the infinite movement, if his soul at the decisive instant, instead of having passionate concentration, is absorbed by the common twaddle that he had several daughters and *vielleicht* [perhaps] the *Ausserordentliche* [extraordinary] might occur—then he is of course not a hero but a hospital-case. The hero's concentration Abraham also has, even though in his case it is far more difficult, since he has no support in the universal; but he makes one more movement by which he concentrates his soul upon the miracle. If Abraham did not do that, he is only an Agamemnon—if in any way it is possible to explain how he can be justified in sacrificing Isaac when thereby no profit accrues to the universal.

Whether the individual is in temptation (*Anfechtung*) or is a knight of faith only the individual can decide. Nevertheless it is possible to construct from the paradox several criteria which he too can understand who is not within the paradox. The true knight of faith is always absolute isolation, the false knight is sectarian. This sectarianism is an attempt to leap away from the narrow path of the paradox and become a tragic hero at a cheap price. The tragic hero expresses the universal and sacrifices himself for it. The sectarian punchinello, instead of that, has a private theatre, i.e. several good friends and comrades who represent the universal just about as well as the beadles in *The Golden Snuffbox* represent justice. The knight of faith, on the contrary, is the paradox, is the individual, absolutely nothing but the individual, without connections or pretensions. This is the terrible thing which the sectarian manikin cannot endure. For instead of learning from this terror that he is not capable of performing the great deed and then plainly admitting it (an act which I cannot but approve, because it is what I do) the manikin thinks that by uniting with several other manikins he will be able to do it. But that is

quite out of the question. In the world of spirit no swin-
dling is tolerated. A dozen sectaries join arms with one
another; they know nothing whatever of the lonely temptations which await the knight of faith and which he dares
not shun precisely because it would be still more dreadful
if he were to press forward presumptuously. The sectaries
deafen one another by their noise and racket, hold the
dread off by their shrieks, and such a hallooing company of
sportsmen think they are storming heaven and think they
are on the same path as the knight of faith who in the solitude of the universe never hears any human voice but walks
alone with his dreadful responsibility.

The knight of faith is obliged to rely upon himself alone,
he feels the pain of not being able to make himself intelligible to others, but he feels no vain desire to guide others.
The pain is his assurance that he is in the right way, this
vain desire he does not know; he is too serious for that. The
false knight of faith readily betrays himself by this proficiency in guiding which he has acquired in an instant. He
does not comprehend what it is all about, that if another
individual is to take the same path, he must become entirely
in the same way the individual and have no need of any
man's guidance, least of all the guidance of a man who
would obtrude himself. At this point men leap aside, they
cannot bear the martyrdom of being uncomprehended, and
instead of this they choose conveniently enough the worldly
admiration of their proficiency. The true knight of faith is
a witness, never a teacher, and therein lies his deep humanity, which is worth a good deal more than this silly partici-
pation in others' weal and woe which is honored by the
name of sympathy, whereas in fact it is nothing but vanity.
He who would only be a witness thereby avows that no
man, not even the lowliest, needs another man's sympathy
or should be abased that another may be exalted. But since
he did not win what he won at a cheap price, neither does

he sell it out at a cheap price, he is not petty enough to take men's admiration and give them in return his silent contempt, he knows that what is truly great is equally accessible to all.

(*Fear and Trembling*, pp. 86–91)

3. THE RISK OF FAITH

Look, here is an example: *pistis,* as the good Greek authors used it (Plato, Aristotle), is accepted as designating something very inferior to *episteme. Pistis,* as a matter of fact, concerns the probable. That is why *pistis,* to provoke faith, is also, according to the ancients, the task of the orators.

But along comes Christianity, which elevates the concept of faith to an entirely different level of meaning, that of the faith precisely applicable to the paradoxical, and thus to the probable, yet in return, characteristic of the highest degree of certitude (cf. Hebrews 3, 1), of the knowledge of eternity, of the most impassioned certitude that makes us sacrifice all, even life, for this faith.

But what happens? With time, Christianity's impetus slows down, and then, rightly so, the ancient paganism reappears, and now by sheer force of verbiage, Christianity has been included in that notion of the ancients whereby science (*episteme* is above faith (*pistis*), whereas the notion of Christian faith is really situated in a separate sphere, of a quality above the classical dualism (*pistis-episteme*).

No, in the Christian sense, faith is at the pinnacle. And it is because of this very fact that the paradoxical character of Christianity is logically recognized. Here also it inverts the entire human scale of values. For, humanly speaking, as paganism also thought, *episteme* is higher than *pistis,* but God has seen fit to make folly out of human wisdom,

198

(1 Cor. 1, 20) to overturn the situation—here also the possibility of scandal is the sign—and to make of faith the supreme element.

(Pap., X 4 A 635)

A true sentence of Hugo de St. Victor (Helfferich: *Mystik*, Vol. I, 368).

'In things which are above reason faith is not really supported by reason, because reason cannot grasp what faith believes; but there is also a something here as a result of which reason is determined, or which determines reason to honour faith which it cannot perfectly understand.'

That is what I explained (*e.g.* in the *Final Postscript*); not every absurdity is 'the absurd' or the paradox. The effect of reason is in fact to know the paradox negatively, but not more.

(Journals, n. 1033)

Perhaps you will say: "But after all, it is God himself who has created this world with all its joys and its beauty. Is it not a contradiction then for Christianity to come along and change everything into sin and hold out to us the requirement of dying to the world?"

To that, in one sense, I have nothing to answer. The point does not concern me. If it remains established that this is what Christianity teaches, I can do nothing with such objections. But, in the first place, is this not a contradiction on your part? You accept a sacred text as the word of God; you accept Christianity as a divine doctrine; then, when you run up against something which cannot be reconciled to your reason or your heart, you say: "It is God's contradiction," when it is really one of your own, for you must respect this divine doctrine or accommodate yourself to it such as it is.

(Pap., X 4 A 260)

Hamann appropriately says that as the law abolishes grace, so to understand abolishes to believe.

That is precisely my point. But for Hamann, it is merely an aphorism; while for me, it is through quite a struggle that I have extracted it from an entire philosophy and culture until I ended up with the phrase: to understand that the faith cannot be understood, or—this is the most ethical side of the man who fears God—to understand that faith must not be understood.

The condition to be met for our salvation is to believe that everywhere and at every hour there is absolute beginning. For the selfish man who has been his own servant while serving illusions, for him to undertake a purer task would be a matter of believing absolutely that he is beginning anew; if not, he bungles any passage into the new task by bogging down in the past. So also for conversation in the strict sense, it is necessary to believe that it is possible to begin radically anew; if not, the past is essentially never left behind. It is the infinite intensity of faith's anticipation which has the courage to dare to believe in it, to dare transform the past into an absolute forgetting and to believe henceforth in an absolute beginning.

Moreover, the criterion of this truth of the faith would nevertheless be the courage which, inversely, dares take hold of its former trouble in all its depth. Thus each corresponds to the other. If we do not have the profound feeling or the courage for it, neither then can we succeed in truly beginning anew, for the real reason that prevents us from feeling deeply is the idea maintained within us that, to look at the matter closely, would perhaps be not only frightening but also prohibitive for all beginning anew. This is why we sweeten the problem somewhat by not looking our past too directly in the face, so that we might more surely reach this new beginning, and it is this conduct itself that prevents us from reaching it.

Beginning always has a double impetus with respect to

the past and towards the new. With the same strength by which it pushes back the past, it tackles the new.

(*Pap.,* X 2 A 371)

(In what precedes this, Kierkegaard shows the endless intervention of reason in our resolutions to combat evil within ourselves. . . .)

. . . So also reason in the matter of belief in Christianity. Faith is interested in firm conclusions, it seeks an absolute decision; reason on the contrary is interested in leaving open any deliberations. Like the police who would be uneasy if there were no crime, so is reason when deliberation is concluded. Faith wants to accept the absolute; reason to continue the deliberation.

How difficult it is to believe now, in this nineteenth century where everything has become a chaos of reflections and deliberations!

It is also truly a great help to us when all evidence points to the absurd as the object of faith; it shortens things considerably. Yes, it could be said, among other things, that it is out of solicitude for men, so they might come to believe despite all, if God has destined the object of faith to be the absurd, and if he had it be said in advance what was, is, and must be the absurd.

(*Pap.,* X 2 A 624)

* That it is possible to fight thus, dazzled by the sun, and yet see to fight, the Romans demonstrated at Zama; that it is possible to fight thus dazzled, and yet see to conquer, the Romans demonstrated at Zama. And now the warfare of faith! Is this struggle perhaps a foolish little trick, a mock combat of gallantry, this strife that is more persistent than a thirty years' war, because the task is not merely to acquire but still more hotly to preserve, where every day the heat is

* Notes

as burning as the one day of the battle of Zama! While the understanding despairs, faith presses on to victory in the passion of its inwardness. But when the believer uses all his understanding, every last desperate resource of thought, merely to discover the difficulty that the paradox presents, then there is indeed no part of his understanding left with which to explain the paradox—but for all that, there may still be a rich faith-content in the passion of his inwardness. Sitting quietly in a ship while the weather is calm is not a picture of faith; but when the ship has sprung a leak, enthusiastically to keep the ship afloat by pumping while yet not seeking the harbor: this is the picture. And if the picture involves an impossibility in the long run, that is but the imperfection of the picture; faith persists. While the understanding, like a despairing passenger, stretches out its arms toward the shore, but in vain, faith works with all its energy in the depths of the soul: glad and victorious it saves the soul against the understanding. Has anyone done this, is there anyone who is engaged in doing it? What business is that of mine, provided this is what it means to believe. And though I am still far from having fully understood the difficulty of Christianity (and an explanation which renders the difficulty easy must be regarded as an evil temptation), I can none the less understand that the struggle of faith is not a subject for vaudeville poets, and that its strenuosity is not a diversion for *Privatdocents.*

(*Postscript,* pp. 201–202)

*Now if only I might escape the fate of having a facile thinker explain to a reading public how stupid my entire book is, as is more than sufficiently evident from my willingness to be responsible for such an assertion as that Christianity is not a doctrine. Let us try to understand one another. Surely it is one thing for something to be a philosophical doctrine which desires to be intellectually grasped and speculatively understood, and quite another thing to be a doctrine that proposes to be realized in existence. If the question of understanding is to be raised in connection with a doctrine of the latter sort, this must consist in understanding that the task is to exist in it, in understanding the difficulty of existing in it, and what a tremendous existential task such a doctrine posits for the learner. At a time when it has come to be generally assumed in connection with such a doctrine (an existential communication) that it is very easy to be what the doctrine requires, but very hard to understand this doctrine speculatively, one may be in harmony with the doctrine (the existential communication) when he seeks to show how difficult it is existentially to submit to the doctrine. In the case of such a doctrine, it is contrariwise a misunderstanding to speculate upon it. Christianity is a doctrine of this kind. To speculate upon it is a misunderstanding, and the farther one goes in this direction the greater is the misunderstanding. When one finally reaches the stage of not only speculating about it, but of understanding it speculatively, one has reached the highest pitch of misunderstanding. This stage is reached in the mediation of Christianity and speculation, and hence it is quite correct to say that modern speculation is the most extreme possible misunderstanding of Christianity. This being the case, and when it is furthermore admitted that the nineteenth century is so dreadfully speculative, it is to be apprehended that the word "doctrine" will at once be interpreted to mean a philosophical doctrine which demands to be understood, and ought to be understood. To avoid this danger I have chosen to call Christianity an existential communication, in order definitely to indicate its heterogeneity with speculation.

(Postscript, p. 339)

To a certain extent, a corrective often makes itself heard at the expense of what is corrected. If this is so, an apparently penetrating mind can in turn reproach the corrective of seeing but one side of things and he can easily persuade the public that things are so. Great God! Nothing is easier for him who, first, has given the corrective, to add also the complementary aspect. But then the corrective stops being a corrective and becomes itself something to be corrected.

(*Pap.,* X 1 A 640)

Without risk there is no faith. Faith is precisely the contradiction between the infinite passion of the individual's inwardness and the objective uncertainty. If I am capable of grasping God objectively, I do not believe, but precisely because I cannot do this I must believe. If I wish to preserve myself in faith I must constantly be intent upon holding fast the objective uncertainty, so as to remain out upon the deep, over seventy thousand fathoms of water, still preserving my faith.

In the principle that subjectivity, inwardness, is the truth, there is comprehended the Socratic wisdom, whose everlasting merit it was to have become aware of the essential significance of existence, of the fact that the knower is an existing individual. For this reason Socrates was in the truth by virtue of his ignorance, in the highest sense in which this was possible within paganism. To attain to an understanding of this, to comprehend that the misfortune of speculative philosophy is again and again to have forgotten that the knower is an existing individual, is in our objective age difficult enough. "But to have made an advance upon Socrates without even having understood what he understood, is at any rate not "Socratic." Compare the "Moral" of the *Fragments.*

Let us now start from this point, and as was attempted in the *Fragments,* seek a determination of thought which will really carry us further. I have nothing here to do with the question of whether this proposed thought-determination is true or not, since I am merely experimenting; but it must at any rate be clearly manifest that the Socratic thought is understood within the new proposal, so that at least I do not come out behind Socrates.

When subjectivity, inwardness, is the truth, the truth becomes objectively a paradox; and the fact that the truth is objectively a paradox shows in its turn that subjectivity is the truth. For the objective situation is repellent; and the expression for the objective repulsion constitutes the tension and the measure of the corresponding inwardness. The paradoxical character of the truth is its objective uncertainty; this uncertainty is an expression for the passionate inwardness, and this passion is precisely the truth. So far the Socratic principle. The eternal and essential truth, the truth which has an essential relationship to an existing individual because it pertains essentially to existence (all other knowledge being from the Socratic point of view accidental, its scope and degree a matter of indifference), is a paradox. But the eternal essential truth is by no means in itself a paradox; but it becomes paradoxical by virtue of its relationship to an existing individual. The Socratic ignorance gives expression to the objective uncertainty attaching to the truth, while his inwardness in existing is the truth. To anticipate here what will be developed later, let me make the following remark. The Socratic ignorance is an analogue to the category of the absurd, only that there is still less of objective certainty in the absurd, and in the repellent effect that the absurd exercises. It is certain only that it is absurd, and precisely on that account it incites to an infinitely greater tension in the corresponding inwardness. The Socratic inwardness in existing is an analogue to faith; only that the inwardness of faith, corresponding as it does, not to the repulsion of the Socratic ignorance, but to the repulsion exerted by the absurd, is infinitely more profound.

Socratically the eternal essential truth is by no means in its own nature paradoxical, but only in its relationship to an existing individual. This finds expression in another Socratic proposition, namely, that all knowledge is recollection. This proposition is not for Socrates a cue to the speculative enterprise, and hence he does not follow it up;

essentially it becomes a Platonic principle. Here the way swings off; Socrates concentrates essentially upon accentuating existence, while Plato forgets this and loses himself in speculation. Socrates' infinite merit is to have been an *existing* thinker, not a speculative philosopher who forgets what it means to exist. For Socrates therefore the principle that all knowledge is recollection has at the moment of his leave-taking and as the constantly rejected possibility of engaging in speculation, the following two-fold significance: (1) that the knower is essentially *integer,* and that with respect to the knowledge of the eternal truth he is confronted with no other difficulty than the circumstance that he exists; which difficulty, however, is so essential and decisive for him that it means that existing, the process of transformation to inwardness in and by existing, is the truth; (2) that existence in time does not have any decisive significance, because the possibility of taking oneself back into eternity through recollection is always there, though this possibility is constantly nullified by utilizing the time, not for speculation, but for the transformation to inwardness in existing.*

---

* This will perhaps be the proper place to offer an explanation with respect to a difficulty in the plan of the *Fragments,* which had its ground in the fact that I did not wish at once to make the case as difficult dialectically as it is, because in our age terminologies and the like are turned so topsy-turvy that it is almost impossible to secure oneself against confusion. In order if possible clearly to exhibit the difference between the Socratic position (which was supposed to be the philosophical, the pagan-philosophical position) and the experimentally evoked thought-determination which really makes an advance beyond the Socratic, I carried the Socratic back to the principle that all knowledge is recollection. This is, in a way, commonly assumed, and only one who with a specialized interest concerns himself with the Socratic, returning again and again to the sources, only for him would it be of importance on this point to distinguish between Socrates and Plato. The proposition does indeed belong to both, only that Socrates is always departing from it, in order to exist. By holding Socrates down to the proposition that all knowledge is recollection, he becomes a speculative

The infinite merit of the Socratic position was precisely to accentuate the fact that the knower is an existing individual, and that the task of existing is this essential task. Making an advance upon Socrates by failing to understand this is quite a mediocre achievement. This Socratic principle we must therefore bear in mind, and then inquire

philosopher instead of an existential thinker, for whom existence is the essential thing. The recollection-principle belongs to speculative philosophy, and recollection is immanence, and speculatively and eternally there is no paradox. But the difficulty is that no human being is speculative philosophy; the speculative philosopher himself is an existing individual, subject to the claims that existence makes upon him. There is no merit in forgetting this, but a great merit in holding it fast, and this is precisely what Socrates did. To accentuate existence, which also involves the qualification of inwardness, is the Socratic position; the Platonic tendency, on the other hand, is to pursue the lure of recollection and immanence. This puts Socrates fundamentally in advance of speculative philosophy; he does not have a fantastic beginning, in which the speculative philosopher first disguises himself, and then goes on and on to speculate, forgetting the most important thing of all, which is to exist. But precisely because Socrates is thus in advance of speculation, he presents, when properly delineated, a certain analogous resemblance to that which the experiment described as in truth going beyond the Socratic. The truth as paradox in the Socratic sense becomes analogous to the paradox *sensu eminentiori,* the passion of inwardness in existing becomes an analogue to faith *sensu eminentiori.* That the difference is none the less infinite, that the characterization which the *Fragments* made of that which in truth goes beyond the Socratic remains unchanged, it will be easy to show; but by using at once apparently the same determinations, or at any rate the same words, about these two different things, I feared to cause a misunderstanding. Now I think there can be no objection to speaking of the paradoxical and of faith in reference to Socrates, since it is quite correct to do so when properly understood. Besides, the old Greeks also used the word $\pi i\sigma\tau\iota\varsigma$, though not by any means in the sense of the experiment; and they used it in such a manner that, especially with reference to a work of Aristotle where the term is employed, it would be possible to set forth some very enlightening considerations bearing upon its difference from faith *sensu eminentiori.*

whether the formula may not be so altered as really to make an advance beyond the Socratic position.

Subjectivity, inwardness, has been posited as the truth; can any expression for the truth be found which has a still higher degree of inwardness? Aye, there is such an expression, provided the principle that subjectivity or inwardness is the truth begins by positing the opposite principle: that subjectivity is untruth. Let us not at this point succumb to such haste as to fail in making the necessary distinctions. Speculative philosophy also says that subjectivity is untruth, but says it in order to stimulate a movement in precisely the opposite direction, namely, in the direction of the principle that objectivity is the truth. Speculative philosophy determines subjectivity negatively as tending toward objectivity. This second determination of ours, however, places a hindrance in its own way while proposing to begin, which has the effect of making the inwardness far more intensive. Socratically speaking, subjectivity is untruth if it refuses to understand that subjectivity is truth, but, for example, desires to become objective. Here, on the other hand, subjectivity in beginning upon the task of becoming the truth through a subjectifying process, is in the difficulty that it is already untruth. Thus, the labor of the task is thrust backward, backward, that is, in inwardness. So far is it from being the case that the way tends in the direction of objectivity, that the beginning merely lies still deeper in subjectivity.

But the subject cannot be untruth eternally, or eternally be presupposed as having been untruth; it must have been brought to this condition in time, or here become untruth in time. The Socratic paradox consisted in the fact that the eternal was related to an existing individual, but now existence has stamped itself upon the existing individual a second time. There has taken place so essential an alteration in him that he cannot now possibly take himself back into the eternal by way of recollection. To do this is to speculate;

to be able to do this, but to reject the possibility by apprehending the task of life as a realization of inwardness in existing, is the Socratic position. But now the difficulty is that what followed Socrates on his way as a rejected possibility, has become an impossibility. If engaging in speculation was a dubious merit even from the point of view of the Socratic, it is now neither more nor less than confusion.

The paradox emerges when the eternal truth and existence are placed in juxtaposition with one another; each time the stamp of existence is brought to bear, the paradox becomes more clearly evident. Viewed Socratically the knower was simply an existing individual, but now the existing individual bears the stamp of having been essentially altered by existence.

Let us now call the untruth of the individual *Sin*. Viewed eternally he cannot be sin, nor can he be eternally presupposed as having been in sin. By coming into existence therefore (for the beginning was that subjectivity is untruth), he becomes a sinner. He is not born as a sinner in the sense that he is presupposed as being a sinner before he is born, but he is born in sin and as a sinner. This we might call *Original Sin*. But if existence has in this manner acquired a power over him, he is prevented from taking himself back into the eternal by way of recollection. If it was paradoxical to posit the eternal truth in relationship to an existing individual, it is now absolutely paradoxical to posit it in relationship to such an individual as we have here defined. But the more difficult it is made for him to take himself out of existence by way of recollection, the more profound is the inwardness that his existence may have in existence; and when it is made impossible for him, when he is held so fast in existence that the back door of recollection is forever closed to him, then his inwardness will be the most profound possible. But let us never forget that the Socratic merit was to stress the fact that the knower is an existing individual; for the more difficult the matter becomes, the greater the temptation to hasten along the easy road of speculation, away from fearful dangers and crucial decisions, to the winning of renown and honors and property, and so forth. If even Socrates understood the dubiety of taking himself speculatively out of existence back into the eternal, although no other difficulty confronted the existing individual except that he existed, and that existing was his essential task, now it is impossible. Forward he must, backward he cannot go.

Subjectivity is the truth. By virtue of the relationship subsisting between the eternal truth and the existing individual, the paradox came into being. Let us now go further, let us suppose that the eternal essential truth is itself a paradox. How does the paradox come into being? By putting the eternal essential truth into juxtaposition with existence. Hence when we posit such a conjunction within the truth itself, the truth becomes a paradox. The eternal truth has come into being in time: this is the paradox. If in accordance with the determinations just posited, the subject is prevented by sin from taking himself back into the eternal, now he need not trouble himself about this; for now the eternal essential truth is not behind him but in front of him, through its being in existence or having existed, so that if the individual does not existentially and in existence lay hold of the truth, he will never lay hold of it.

Existence can never be more sharply accentuated than by means of these determinations. The evasion by which speculative philosophy attempts to recollect itself out of existence has been made impossible. With reference to this, there is nothing for speculation to do except to arrive at an understanding of this impossibility; every speculative attempt which insists on being speculative shows *eo ipso* that it has not understood it. The individual may thrust all this away from him, and take refuge in speculation; but it is impossible first to accept it, and then to revoke it by means of speculation, since it is definitely calculated to prevent speculation.

When the eternal truth is related to an existing individual it becomes a paradox. The paradox repels in the inwardness of the existing individual, through the objective uncertainty and the corresponding Socratic ignorance. But since the paradox is not in the first instance itself paradoxical (but only in its relationship to the existing individual), it does not repel with a sufficient intensive inwardness. For without risk there is no faith, and the greater the risk the greater the faith; the more objective security the less inwardness (for inwardness is precisely subjectivity), and the less objective security the more profound the possible inwardness. When the paradox is paradoxical in itself, it repels the individual by virtue of its absurdity, and the corresponding passion of inwardness is faith. But subjectivity, inwardness, is the truth; for otherwise we have forgotten what the merit of the Socratic position is. But there can be no stronger expression for inwardness than when the retreat out of existence into the eternal by way of recollection is impossible; and when, with truth confronting the individual as a paradox, gripped in the anguish and pain of sin, facing the tremendous risk of the objective insecurity, the individual believes. But without risk no faith, not even the Socratic form of faith, much less the form of which we here speak.

When Socrates believed that there was a God, he held fast to the objective uncertainty with the whole passion of his inwardness, and it is precisely in this contradiction and in this risk that faith is rooted. Now it is otherwise. Instead of the objective uncertainty, there is here a certainty, namely, that objectively it is absurd; and this absurdity, held fast in the passion of inwardness, is faith. The Socratic ignorance is as a witty jest in comparison with the earnestness of facing the absurd; and the Socratic existential inwardness is as Greek light-mindedness in comparison with the grave strenuosity of faith.

(*Postscript,* pp. 182–188)

For a finite being—and that after all is what man is (cf. Balle's *Lesson Book*)—the negative infinity is the highest attainable, and the positive is a precarious assurance. Intellectual existence, especially for the religious man, is not easy, the believer lies constantly out upon the deep and with seventy thousand fathoms of water under him. However long he may lie out there, there is no assurance that little by little he will find himself lying upon land, stretched out at his ease. He may become calmer, more accustomed to his position, and find a sense of security which loves jest and the joyous mind—but up to the last minute he lies above a depth of seventy thousand fathoms. If immediacy is done away with, as in fact everybody loudly requires, then this situation comes about. There are to be enough difficulties in life for everybody. Let the poor feel the hard pressure of poverty and anxiety about a livelihood, he who elects a spiritual existence by virtue of the religious will have the comfort, which I well understand he needs, of knowing that he too suffers in life and that before God there is no respect of persons. For to become "positive" does not procure for any man personal respect in God's eyes, even though this has been accounted wisdom since the time Speculation took charge of religion by taking its life.

This I have understood well in spite of the fact that I myself am not religious, but at least I do not presume to take religion by force and merely try to understand with the cunning of an observer the object I experiment with. The religious seeks no support in the historic, still less than does the comic, and for a higher reason; it presupposes the unity of the tragic and the comic in passion, and with a new passion or with the same it chooses the tragic, and this situation again makes every historic support meaningless; it is never finished, at least not in time, and hence only as delusion can it be so represented. So then, in case a man who had been steadily listening to an orator who talked of things religious were to go to him and say, "Are you, sir, of the opinion that I now have faith, seeing that I have been listening to you so steadily?" Perhaps then the orator, in an excess of what is called good nature, sympathetic concern, for which one receives thanks in letters to the editor, might reply, "Why, certainly that is my opinion. Only do not fail to hear my addresses, and come to me freely if again you are assailed by doubt," etc. My experimental observation (devoid of all good nature and sympathetic concern) prompts me to the opinion that he would have done better to reply, "My dear man, would you make fun of me? I dare not even vouch for my wife, yea, not even for myself, for I lie constantly above a depth of seventy thousand fathoms of water."

If only now no one would tempt me, promise me perhaps gold and forests green, the favor of maidens and the applause of reviewers—but then require an answer to the question whether my experiment is a real history, whether at the bottom of it there is something real. Why, yes, certainly there is something real at the bottom of it—namely, the categories. However, for an unknown author the temptation is not so great, everyone will easily see that the whole thing is a prank—which nevertheless it is not, for it is an experiment. Tragedy has the interest of reality, comedy has the disinterestedness of metaphysics, but the experiment lies in the invisible unity of jest and earnest. The dialectic tension between form and content and between content and form prevents any immediate relationship to it, and in this tension the experiment avoids the honest handshake of earnestness and the rollicking fellowship of jest. The experiment constantly addresses the reader as "you," to indicate a ceremonious distance. The poetic hero would arouse enthusiasm by his triumph, would distress one by his sufferings (would have the interest of reality), the comic hero would awaken laughter, the *quidam* of the "experiment" desires nothing of the sort, without making any demands he is in every way "at your service," he cannot annoy you, for in this respect also he is "at your service," willing to be ignored without any risk whatsoever on your part, and that all the more because it is absolutely indeterminable whether one paid attention to him gained anything by it or suffered damage from it.

(*Stages,* pp. 402–404)

4. SIN AND ITS FORGIVENESS

To believe in the remission of his sins is the decisive crisis by which a man becomes spirit; he who does not believe in it is not spirit. That is where maturity of spirit is found; otherwise said, all immediacy is lost, a man is not only incapable of anything by himself, but also can only harm himself. But how few actually have the personal experience of understanding that in their own case, they are reduced to this extremity—here is the absurd, the scandalous, the paradoxical, the remission of sins.

Most men never become spirits, never live through the test of becoming so. They undergo this development: childhood, adolescence, maturity, old age. There is nothing to boast about; it is not their merit, they have nothing to do with it. It is only a vegetative, or, at most, animal process. But, as for becoming spirit, they will never live through the trial.

The remission of sins has no particular, individual thing in view, as if people were completely good. Here is the puerile: the child always asking forgiveness for a particular act, to have done that yesterday or to have forgotten this today; [etc.] he will never begin to think, no one will ever get him to understand that he is radically evil. No, on the contrary, remission has in view not so much particular acts as the totality. It looks at our entire ego which is sinful and which perverts everything at the slightest touch.

215

So the man who, in truth, has lived and lives the trial of the belief in the remission of sins, has certainly become another man. All is forgotten. But things don't go on for him as they do for the child who, once forgiveness is obtained, becomes again the same child. No, he has aged eternally. From here on in, he is spirit; all immediacy and his selfishness, all his selfish attachment to the world and to himself are lost. From here on in, speaking humanly, he is old, immensely old; but for eternity, he is young.

(Pap., VIII A 673)

As a true, a profound love is first expressed by the feeling of its own unworthiness, so the need for the remission of sin is the sign of our love for God. But on his own, no man can have the idea that God loves him. This has to be announced to man. That is the Gospel, revelation. But precisely because no one can, on his own, have the idea that God loves him, neither can man imagine to what extent he is a great sinner. Consequently, the Augsburg Confession teaches that it must be revealed to man how great a sinner he is. For without divine aid, no man knows it. He simply *is* a sinner before God.

But the two necessities go hand in hand. When a man does not grasp the extent to which he is a great sinner, he cannot love God; and when he does not love God, by the fact that he is told to what extent God loves him, he cannot understand what a great sinner he is. The interiority of the awareness of sin is precisely the passion of love. For certainly the law makes of man a sinner, but love makes of him a much greater sinner. Without doubt, he who fears God and trembles can feel that he is a sinner; but the man who truly loves feels he is an even greater sinner.

(Pap., VIII A 673)

It is to be remembered that the forgiveness of sin is the paradoxical satisfaction by virtue of the absurd. In order merely to observe how paradoxical it is, the eternal recollection of guilt as the highest expression must come in between, lest the spheres become confused and the Christian conception be prated into childish definitions of the forgiveness of sin which belong where the ethical is not present, still less the religious, and still less the Christian.

(Postscript, p. 479)

To keep thinking about one's sin and to refuse to believe that it is forgiven is also culpable, in the sense that it is to have a paltry opinion of Christ's merit.

(Pap., X 2 A 477)

ORIGINAL SIN IS GUILT

That is the real paradox. How paradoxical that it may best be seen thus. It is formed by compounding qualitatively different categories. To inherit is a natural category; guilt is an ethical and spiritual category. Now who would ever think, says reason, of putting them together, of saying that something is inherited which by definition cannot be inherited.

It must be believed. The paradox of Christian truth is invariably due to the fact that it is truth as it exists for God. The standard of measure and the end is superhuman; and there is only one relationship possible: faith.

(Journals, n. 1061)

To examine the matter more closely, it would seem that original sin, which is an article of faith, is not fundamentally an aggravation, but, to understand it well, a softening, which can be recognized from the fact that there is a redeemer having rendered satisfaction for the whole human race.

But it must remain established that the universality of the sin cannot be an object of knowledge, but only of faith;

it is a message of revelation. Outside of this, I have only to concentrate with all my seriousness on the idea that I am a sinner.

(Pap., X 2 A 483)

They all abandoned Christ, even the apostle renounced him. Only the thief on the cross stayed faithful, to the end and in the last moment; but binding him also were the awareness of sin and the nearness of death.

(Pap., X 3 A 180)

The situation in confession resembles that of death: one is alone before God.

The thought of death is pushed as far away as possible; people do not want to be troubled by it; and Christianity precisely wants to bring it as close to us as possible.

Admit it: that is how we live. Our relationship to Christianity is like a man who insures himself for his funeral expenses; we place ourselves in the hands of possibility, and count on being Christian at death; but as you live, so shall you die.

(Pap., X 3 A 710)

So you are immortal. Do not give yourself the trouble of doubting it or even of trying to prove it. You are immortal. You go on to the hereafter, and eternity is not the land of shadows, but of light, of transparence, where nothing is hidden, but held up to the light, and it is the same also in confession. Think of it closely. You are alone before God, and he is all light; he inhabits a light which none can penetrate, but he is a light that can penetrate everything. Oh! Take hold of that moment so that you might reveal yourself entirely. It will be too late afterwards, when in eternity you are obliged to reveal yourself entirely.

(Pap., X 3 A 711)

In the relationship to God, the most difficult cases are those where, on the human level, one is correct, or at least, not quite wrong. Before God, it is perhaps easiest to say: "I was a rascal, I acted like a rascal, forgive me." Repentance is, in short, the easiest and most natural relationship to God.

That is why, even in some situations where I humanly think I am right, before God, only to have peace, I prefer admitting that I must have been a rascal, but that God surely will forgive me.

(Pap., X 3 A 772)

To forgive sin is divine not only in the sense that only God can do so, but also in the sense that no one can forgive sin without God's assistance. Men, if they truly succeed in forgiving sins, are not up to it. No! What narrowness, what stinginess, what nastiness, and what reservations in their forgiving, so that a sinner would say: "Ah! No thanks! I would rather be convicted and suffer my punishment so that I might be spared their miserable and sordid forgiveness, which, even if I had perhaps been saved and had become something excellent, would come ringing at my door and, led by envy, present itself as my creditor."

What a difference there is between the human and the divine!

Man's basic tendency is to uncover sin, to succeed in learning evil about others. We are thus assured that they are no different from us! The only kind of pardon which can really stand up is that where everyone considers the debt settled. The joy of the divine is to forgive sin; just as He is almighty in creating from nothing, so God is almighty in transforming [our sins] to nothing. For to forget, to forget as an almighty can, is this not to transform to nothing?

(Pap., XI 2 A 3)

The difference between a pagan and a Christian is not that the latter is without sin, no, but in how he looks at his sin and how he is sustained in his effort. When a pagan sins, precisely as he is more profound and noble, a terrible halt occurs in his effort; he becomes melancholic, dreams again and again about his fault, and the sin perhaps gains a greater and greater hold on him, with the result that, out of desperation, he falls lower and lower. The Christian has a savior; he has recourse to grace. As in the case of a child, his sin transforms itself into fatherly chastisement, aiming to guide his progress and perhaps he does advance with steadier foot from this point on. Boldness is not lack of thought, but confidence in grace. The speed with which we put aside the thought of a sin may be weakness, may be lack of thought; but it can also be courage, by the very depth and confidence of our idea of grace.

(Pap., X 2 A 456)

5. THE CONTEMPORARY
OF CHRIST

The God has thus made his appearance as Teacher (for we now resume our story), and has assumed the form of a servant. To send another in his place, one high in his confidence, could not satisfy him; just as it could not satisfy the noble king to send in his stead even the most trusted man in his kingdom. But the God had also another reason; for between man and man the Socratic relationship is the highest and truest. If the God had not come himself, all the relations would have remained on the Socratic level; we would not have had the Moment, and we would have lost the Paradox. The God's servant-form however is not a mere disguise, but is actual; it is not a parastatic body but an actual body; and from the hour that in the omnipotent purpose of his omnipotent love the God become a servant, he has so to speak imprisoned himself in his resolve, and is now bound to go on (to speak foolishly) whether it pleases him or no. He cannot then betray himself. There exists for him no such possibility as that which is open to the noble king, suddenly to show that he is after all the king—which is no perfection in the king (that he has this possibility), but merely discloses his impotence, and the impotence of his resolve, that he cannot really become what he desires to be. But while the God will not be able to send anyone in his place, he can indeed send someone before him, to arouse the learner's attention. This forerunner can of course know nothing of what the God will teach. For the God's presence is not accidental in relation to his teaching, but essential. The God's presence in human form, aye in the humble form of a servant, is itself the teaching, and the God must give the condition along with it (Chapter I) or the learner will understand nothing. Such a forerunner may then serve to arouse the learner's attention, but nothing more.

But the God did not assume the form of a servant to make a mockery of men; hence it cannot be his intention to pass through the world in such manner that no single human being becomes aware of his presence. He will therefore doubtless give some sort of sign, though every understanding resting upon an accommodation is essentially without value for one who does not receive the condition; for which reason he yields to the necessity only unwillingly. Such a sign when given is as capable of repelling the learner as of drawing him nearer. He humbled himself and took upon him the form of a servant, but he did not come to spend his life as a servant in some private employment, attending to his tasks without in any manner making himself known, either to his master or to his fellow servants— such a measure of wrath we dare not ascribe to the God. That he was a servant means then only that he was a common man, humble and lowly, not to be distinguished from the multitude of men either by soft raiment or other earthly advantages, nor yet by the innumerable legions of angels he left behind him when he humbled himself. But though in these ways resembling common men, his thoughts and cares are not like those which fill the minds of men in general. He goes his way indifferent to the distribution and division of earthly goods, as one who has no possessions and desires none; he is not concerned for his daily bread, like the birds of the air; he does not trouble himself about house and home, as one who neither has nor seeks a shelter or a resting-place; he is not concerned to follow the dead to the grave; he does not turn his head to look at the things that usually claim the attention of men; he is not bound to any woman, so as to be charmed by her and desirous of pleasing her. He seeks one thing only, the love of the disciple. All this seems indeed beautiful, but is it also appropriate? Does he not by this manner of life lift himself above the plane of what is valid for a human life? Is it right for a man to be as care-free as a bird, and even to surpass these creatures in unconcern, since they fly hither and thither in search of food? Ought he not rather to take thought for the morrow? True, we cannot imagine the God otherwise, but what does the imagination prove? Is it permissible thus to become a foot-loose wanderer, stopping wherever evening overtakes him? The question is whether a human being may venture to express the same idea; for otherwise the God has not realized the essential elements of a human life. We answer in the affirmative; a man may so venture if he has the needed strength. If he can so lose himself in the service of the spirit that it never occurs to him to take care for meat and drink; if he is certain that want will not distract him, and that distress will not confound for him the structure of his life, and teach him to rue that he did not first master the simple things before he presumed to understand more —then he may indeed venture, and his greatness will be more glorious than the serene security of the lilies of the field.

This lofty absorption in his mission will of itself suffice to attract the attention of the multitude, among whom the learner will doubtless be found. The latter will in all probability come from the humbler walks of life; for the wise and the learned will presumably wish first to propose captious questions to the Teacher, invite him to *colloquia,* or subject him to an examination, upon which they will assure him a permanent position and a secure livelihood.

Let us now picture the God going about in the city of his appearance (which city this is, is indifferent). To make his teaching known is the sole necessity of his life; it is his meat and drink. Teaching is his labor, and caring for the learner is his rest from labor. He has no friends nor kindred, but the learner is his brother and sister. It may readily be understood that a web of rumor will soon be woven, catching the curious multitude in its snare. Wherever the Teacher appears the crowd gathers, curious to see, curious to hear, and eager to tell others that they have seen and heard him. Is this curious multitude the learner? By no means. Or if some one of the authorized teachers of that city sought him out secretly, in order to try his strength with him in argument—is he the learner? By no means. If this teacher or that multitude *learn* anything, the God serves merely as an occasion in the strict Socratic sense.

The God's appearance has now become the news of the day, in the market-place, in the homes of the people, in the council chamber, in the ruler's palace. It gives occasion for much foolish and idle talk, perhaps also for some earnest reflection. But for the learner the news of the day is not an occasion for something else, not even an occasion for the acquirement in Socratic sincerity of a deeper and fuller self-knowledge; for the learner it is the Eternal, the beginning of eternity. The news of the day the beginning of eternity! If the God had permitted himself to be born in an inn, wrapped in swaddling-clothes and laid in a manger, could the contradiction have been greater than that the news of the day should be the swaddling-clothes of the Eternal, aye, as in the supposed instance its actual form, so that the *Moment* is really decisive for eternity! Unless the God grants the condition which makes it possible to understand this, how is it to be supposed that the learner will be able to discover it! But that the God himself gives this condition has been shown above to be a consequence of the *Moment,* and it has also been shown that the Moment is the Paradox, and that without it we are unable to advance, but return to Socrates.

Here at the outset let us take care to make it clear that the question of an historical point of departure arises even for a contemporary disciple; for if we are not careful here, we shall meet with an insuperable difficulty later (in Chapter V), when we come to deal with the case of the disciple whom we call the disciple at second hand. The contemporary disciple gets an historical point of departure for his eternal consciousness as well as any later disciple; for he is contemporary with precisely that historical phenomenon which refuses to be reduced to a moment of merely occasional significance, but proposes to interest him in another sense than the merely historical, presenting itself to him as a condition for his eternal happiness. If this is not so, then (deducing the consequences conversely) the Teacher is not the God but only a Socrates, and if he does not conduct himself like a Socrates, he is not even a Socrates.

But how does the learner come to realize an understanding with this Paradox? We do not ask that he understand the Paradox but only understand that this is the Paradox. How this takes place we have already shown. It comes to pass when the Reason and the Paradox encounter one another happily in the Moment, when the Reason sets itself aside and the Paradox bestows itself. The third entity in which this union is realized (for it is not realized in the Reason, since it is set aside; nor in the Paradox, which bestows itself—hence it is realized *in* something) is that happy passion to which we will now assign a name, though it is not the name that so much matters. We shall call this passion: *Faith.* This then must be the condition of which we have spoken, which the Paradox contributes. Let us not forget that if the Paradox does not grant this condition the learner must be in possession of it. But if the learner is in possession of the condition he is *eo ipso* himself the

Truth, and the moment is merely the moment of occasion (Chapter I).

The contemporary learner finds it easy enough to acquire adequate historical information. But let us not forget that with respect to the Teacher's birth he will be in the same position as the disciple at second hand; if we wish to urge absolute historical precision there will be only one human being who is fully informed, namely the woman of whom he permitted himself to be born. But though a contemporary learner readily becomes an historical eye-witness, the difficulty is that the knowledge of some historical circumstance, or indeed a knowledge of all the circumstances with the reliability of an eye-witness, does not make such an eye-witness a disciple; which is apparent from the fact that this knowledge has merely historical significance for him. We see at once that the historical in the more concrete sense is a matter of indifference; we may suppose a degree of ignorance with respect to it, and permit this ignorance as if to annihilate one detail after the other, historically annihilating the historical; if only the Moment remains, as point of departure for the Eternal, the Paradox will be there. Suppose a contemporary who had reduced his hours of sleep to a minimum in order that he might follow this Teacher about, attending him more closely than the pilot-fish the shark; suppose him to keep a hundred spies in his service to watch over the Teacher everywhere, conferring with them each evening in order to obtain a description of the Teacher's movements exact to the minutest detail, accounting for what he had said and where he had been each hour of the day, because his zeal led him to attach importance even to the least trifle—would such a contemporary be the disciple? By no means. If he is accused of historical inaccuracy he can wash his hands of the accusation, but that is all. Suppose another contemporary who concerned himself solely with the doctrine which this Teacher was wont upon occasion to expound. If every word of instruction that fell from his lips seemed more important to him than his daily bread; if he kept a hundred assistants watching for every syllable, so that nothing should be lost; if he conferred with them carefully each evening, in order to obtain a presentation of the doctrine that should have the highest possible reliability—would he on this account be the disciple? By no means, no more than Plato was a disciple of Socrates. Suppose that a contemporary who had been living abroad returned at a time when the Teacher had only a day or two to live. If engagements had prevented him from going to see the Teacher, so that he was brought into touch with him only at the last moment, when he was about to yield his spirit—would this historical ignorance prevent him from becoming the disciple, provided the Moment became for him decisive for eternity? For the first contemporary, the life of the Teacher was merely an historical event; for the second, the Teacher served as an occasion by which he came to an understanding of himself, and he will be able to forget the Teacher (Chapter I). As over against an eternal understanding of oneself, any knowledge about the Teacher is accidental and historical only, a mere matter of memory. As long as the Eternal and the historical are external to one another, the historical is merely an occasion. If then such a zealous learner, though not carrying things so far as to become a disciple, were to discourse loudly and volubly of how much he owed the Teacher, so that his eulogy was almost endless and its gilding priceless; if he were to resent our explanation that the Teacher had been merely an occasion, neither his eulogy nor his resentment could further our inquiry, since both had the same ground, namely, that though lacking in the courage to understand he had nevertheless not lacked the audacity to go beyond. By romancing and trumpeting in his manner one only deceives oneself and others, in so far as one persuades oneself and others that one really has thoughts—since one owes them to another. Though politeness is ordinarily not supposed to cost anything, such politeness as his is dearly purchased. The enthusiastic outpouring of gratitude, perhaps itself not devoid of tears nor without a moving effect upon others, is a misunderstanding; for the thoughts that such a man has he certainly does not owe to another, and the nonsense he talks is all his own. Ah, how often has it not happened that someone has politely insisted upon owing Socrates a great debt, although he owed Socrates absolutely nothing! Whoever understands Socrates best understands precisely that he owes him nothing, which is as Socrates would have it, and which it is beautiful to have been able to will; whoever believes that he owes Socrates so great a debt may be tolerably certain that Socrates stands ready to acquit him of it without payment, since it will doubtless cause him regret to learn that he has unwittingly furnished anyone with capital for such usurious speculations. But if the entire situation is non-Socratic, as we have assumed, the disciple will owe *all* to the Teacher; which is quite impossible in relation to Socrates, since as he himself says, he was unable to *beget*. This relationship of owing all to the Teacher cannot be expressed in terms of romancing and trumpeting, but only in that happy passion we call Faith, whose object is the Paradox. But the Paradox unites the contradictories, and is the historical made eternal, and the Eternal made historical. Everyone who understands the Paradox differently may keep the honor of having explained it, which honor he won by not being content to understand it.

It is easy to see, though it scarcely needs to be pointed out, since it is involved in the fact that the Reason is set aside, that Faith is not a form of knowledge; for all knowledge is either a knowledge of the Eternal, excluding the temporal and historical as indifferent, or it is pure historical knowledge. No knowledge can have for its object the absurdity that the Eternal is the historical. If I know Spinoza's doctrine, then I am in so far not concerned with Spinoza but with his doctrine; at some other time I may be concerned historically with Spinoza himself. But the disciple is in Faith so related to his Teacher as to be eternally concerned with his historical existence.

Now if we assume that it is as we have supposed (and without this assumption we return to the Socratic order of things), that the Teacher himself contributes the condition to the learner, it will follow that the object of Faith is not the *teaching* but the *Teacher*. The Socratic principle is, that the learner being himself the Truth and in possession of the condition can thrust the teacher aside; the Socratic art and the Socratic heroism consisted precisely in helping men to do this. But Faith must steadily hold fast to the Teacher. In order that he may have the power to give the condition the Teacher must be the God; in order that he may be able to put the learner in possession of it he must be Man. This contradiction is again the object of Faith, and is the Paradox, the Moment. That the God has once for all given man the requisite condition is the eternal Socratic presupposition, which comes into no hostile collision with time, but is incommensurable with the temporal and its determinations. The contradiction of our hypothesis is that man receives the condition in the Moment, the same condition which, since it is requisite for the understanding of the eternal Truth, is *eo ipso* an eternal condition. If the case is otherwise we stand at the Socratic principle of Recollection.

It is easy to see, though it scarcely needs to be pointed out, since it is involved in the fact that the Reason is set aside, that Faith is not an act of will; for all human volition has its capacity within the scope of an underlying condition. Thus if I have the courage to will the understanding, I am able to understand the Socratic principle, i.e., to understand myself, because from the Socratic point of view I have the condition, and so have the power to will this understanding. But if I do not have the condition (and this is our assumption, in order not to be forced back on the Socratic order of things) all my willing is of no avail; although as soon as the condition is given, the Socratic principle will again apply.

The contemporary learner enjoys one advantage, which the learner of a later generation alas! will doubtless greatly envy him, if only for the sake of doing something. A contemporary may go where he can see the Teacher—and may he then believe his eyes? Why not? But may he also believe that this makes him a disciple? By no means. If he believes his eyes he is deceived, for the God is not immediately knowable. But then perhaps he may shut his eyes. Just so; but if he does, what profit does he have from his contemporaneity? And when he shuts his eyes he will presumably try to form some conception of the God. But if he is able to do this by himself, he is evidently in possession of the condition. What he conceives, moreover, will be a figure revealing itself to the inner eye of the soul; if he now beholds this, the figure of the servant will confuse him when he again opens his eyes. Let us go on. We have assumed that the Teacher dies; now that he is dead, what will the learner who had been his contemporary do? Perhaps he has sketched some portraits of him; he may even have in his possession an entire series of such portraits, depicting and accurately reflecting every change that by reason of age or state of mind may have taken place in the outward appearance of the Teacher. When he examines these portraits and assures himself that such and such was his appearance, may he then believe his eyes? Why not? But is he on that account a disciple? By no means. But then he may proceed to form some conception of the God. But the God cannot be conceived; it was for this very reason that he appeared in the form of a servant. And yet the servant-form is no deception; for if such were the case, this moment would not be the Moment, but an accidental circumstance, a mere appearance, which as an occasion infinitely vanishes in comparison with the Eternal. And if the learner had the power to form a conception of the God by himself, he must himself have had the condition. Thus he needed only a reminder to be enabled to form this conception, in a manner well within his capacity; though of this he may not previously have been aware. But if this is the case, the reminder will vanish instantly like a tiny atom in the eternal potentiality which was present in his soul, and which now becomes a reality, but again as reality eternally presupposes itself.

How does the learner then become a believer or disciple? When the Reason is set aside and he receives the condition. When does he receive the condition? In the Moment. What does this condition condition? The understanding of the Eternal. But such a condition must be an eternal condition.—He receives accordingly the eternal condition in the Moment, and is aware that he has so received it; for otherwise he merely comes to himself in the consciousness that he had it from eternity. It is in the Moment that he receives it, and from the Teacher himself. All romancing and trumpeting abroad about one's cleverness in penetrating the God's incognito, though without receiving the condition from the Teacher; that one took notice of him by the impression he made, such a strange feeling coming over one in his presence; that there was something in his voice and mien, etc., etc.—all this is but silly twaddle, by which one does not become a disciple but only makes a mockery of the God.[1] The servant-figure was no incognito. And when in the strength of his omnipotent resolve, which is like his love, the

---

[1] Every determination of his nature which makes the God immediately knowable is indeed a milestone on the way of approximation, but one which marks an increase instead of a decrease in the distance; it does not measure toward the Paradox but away from it, back past Socrates and the Socratic ignorance. This needs to be carefully noted, lest one experience in the world of the spirit what befell the traveller who asked if the road on which he was journeying went to London, and was told by the Englishman that it did; in spite of which he failed to reach London, because the Englishman had omitted to mention that he needed to turn about, since he was proceeding in the opposite direction.

God makes himself the equal of the humblest, let no inn-keeper or professor of philosophy imagine that he is a shrewd enough fellow to detect anything, unless the God gives the condition. And when the God in the form of a servant stretches forth the hand of omnipotence, let no astonished and open-mouthed beholder imagine that he is a disciple because he is astonished, and because he can gather others about him who in their turn are astonished over his story. If there is no necessity for the God to give the condition, the learner knew from the beginning how it is with the God, even if he did not know that he knew it; the other is not even the Socratic thought, but infinitely lower.

But the outward figure (we do not mean its detail) is not a matter of indifference to the disciple. It is what he has seen and his hands have handled. However, the out-ward figure is not important in the sense that he would cease to be a believer if he happened to meet the Teacher some day on the street and did not at once recognize him or even walked some distance with him on the way without realizing that it was he. The God gave to the disciple the condition that enables him to see him, opening for him the eyes of Faith. But it was a terrible thing to see this outward figure, to have converse with him as with one of us, and every moment that Faith was not present to see only the servant-form. When the Teacher is gone from the disciple in death, memory may bring his figure before him; but it is not on this account that the disciple believes, but because he received the condition from the God, and hence is enabled again to see, in memory's trustworthy image, the person of the God. So it is with the disciple, who knows that he would have seen nothing without the condition, since the first thing he learned to understand was that he was in Error.

But in that case is not Faith as paradoxical as the Para-dox? Precisely so; how else could it have the Paradox for its object, and be happy in its relation to the Paradox? Faith is itself a miracle, and all that holds true of the Paradox also holds true of Faith. But within the framework of this miracle everything is again Socratic, yet so that the miracle is never cancelled—the miracle namely, that the eternal condition is given in time. Everything is Socratic; the relation between one contemporary and another in so far as both are believers is entirely Socratic: the one owes the other nothing, but both owe everything to the God.

❊   ❊

I think I hear someone say: "Then it seems that the contemporary derives absolutely no advantage from his contemporaneity; and yet if we assume what you have assumed about God's appearance among men, it lies so near at hand to count the contemporary generation blessed, because it saw and heard."—"Aye, truly it lies near at hand; so near I think, that this generation has doubtless also counted itself blessed. Shall we assume that this was the case? For otherwise it was surely not happy, and our praise of this generation is merely an expression for the fact that by acting differently under the same circumstances, one might have become happy. But if this is the case, our praise may need to be qualified in a variety of ways, when we consider the matter more carefully, and may in the last analysis become altogether ambiguous. Suppose, as we sometimes read in old chronicles, that an emperor celebrated his marriage for an entire week with festivities the like of which had never before been seen, every breath of air being scented with perfume, while the ear found it constantly vibrant with music and song, so as to enhance the enjoyment of the costliest viands, set forth in richest abundance. Day and night the festivities continued, for the night was made as bright as the day by torches that illumined the scene—but whether seen by the light of day or by the illumination of the night, the queen was more beautiful and more gracious than any mortal woman; and the whole was an enchantment, wonderful as the most audacious desire in its still more audacious fulfilment. Let us assume that all this had happened in the past, and that we had to be content with the meager and fasting report of what had taken place—why should we not, humanly speaking, count the contemporaries happy? That is to say those contemporaries who saw and heard and grasped with their hands; for otherwise of what avail would it be to be contemporary? The splendors of the imperial marriage-feast and the rich abundance of its pleasures were directly accessible to sight and touch, so that anyone who was a contemporary in the stricter sense would presumably have feasted his eyes and made his heart to be glad. But suppose the splendor had been of a different kind, not immediately apparent to the senses, what profit would there then be in being a contemporary, since one would not on that account necessarily be contemporary with the splendor? Such a contemporary could scarcely be counted happy, nor could we bless his eyes and ears; for he was not contemporary with the splendor, neither hearing nor seeing anything of it. And this not because he lacked time and opportunity (in the immediate sense), but because of something else, which could be lacking even if he himself had been present, and favored with opportunities for seeing and hearing to the fullest extent, and had not permitted these opportunities (in the immediate sense) to go unused. But what does it mean thus to say that one can be a contemporary without being contemporary, that one may be a contemporary and though utilizing this advantage (in the immediate sense) yet be a non-contemporary—what does this mean except that it is quite impossible to be an immediate contemporary of such a Teacher and of such an event; so that the real contemporary is not the real contemporary by virtue of an immediate contemporaneity, but by virtue of something else? A contemporary may for all that be a non-contemporary; the real contemporary is such not by virtue of his immediate contemporaneity; *ergo,* it must also be possible for a non-contemporary (in the immediate sense) to be a contemporary, by virtue of that something which makes the contemporary a real contemporary. But the non-contemporary (in the immediate sense) is of course the member of a later generation, whence it must be possible for an individual so situated to be a real contemporary. Or what do we mean by being contemporary? Is it perhaps this kind of a contemporary that we praise, one who can speak as follows: 'I ate and drank in his presence, and he taught in our streets. I saw him often, and knew him for a common man of humble origin. Only a very few thought to find something extraordinary in him; as far as I am concerned, I could see nothing remarkable about him, and I was certainly as much of a contemporary as anybody.' Or is this what we mean by calling anyone a contemporary, and is he a contemporary to whom the God must say if they meet in another life, and he seeks to urge his contemporaneity: 'I do not know you'? And so it was in truth, just as it was equally true that such a contemporary could not have known the Teacher. Only the believer, i.e., the non-immediate contemporary, knows the Teacher, since he receives the condition from him, and therefore knows him even as he is known."—"Stop there a moment, I beg you; for if you keep on talking in this fashion I will not be able to get in a single word. You talk like a disputant for the doctorate, or better still, you talk like a book; and what is worse for you, you talk like a very particular book. For here again, whether wittingly or unwittingly, you have introduced some words into the discourse which are not your own, nor by you placed in the mouths of the speakers. The words are very well known, except that you have substituted the singular for the plural. Here are the scripture passages (for the words are taken from the Bible): 'We have eaten and drunk in thy presence, and thou hast taught in our streets'; 'I tell ye, I know not whence ye are.' However, let this pass without further comment for the present. But are you not drawing too sweeping a conclusion when you infer from the Teacher's reply to a given individual, 'I do not know you,' that this individual was not a contemporary and had not known the Teacher? If the emperor of whom you spoke had said to one who claimed contemporaneity with his splendid marriage-feast, 'I do not know you,' would the emperor thereby have proved that he was not a contemporary?"—"By no means would the emperor have proved such a thing; he would at the most have proved himself a fool, not content like Mithridates to know the name of every soldier in his army, but pretending to know every contemporary, and assuming to decide by this knowledge whether any given individual had been contemporary or not. The emperor was immediately knowable, and hence someone may very well have known the emperor, even if the emperor did not know him. But the Teacher of our hypothesis was not immediately knowable; he could be known only when he himself gave the condition. Whoever received the condition received it from the Teacher himself, and hence the Teacher must know everyone who knows him, and no one can know the Teacher except through being known by him. Are we not agreed on this point, and do you perhaps at once perceive the remoter consequences of what we have been saying? When the believer is the believer and knows the God through having received the condition from the God himself, every successor must receive the condition from the God himself in precisely the same sense, and cannot receive it at second hand; for if he did, this second hand would have to be the hand of the God himself, and in that case there is no question of a second hand. But a successor who receives the condition from the God himself is a contemporary, a real contemporary; a privilege enjoyed only by the believer, but also enjoyed by every believer."—"Indeed, now that you have pointed it out I clearly perceive the truth of this, and I already descry the far-reaching consequences. I am only surprised that I had not discovered it for myself, and I would give a great deal for the honor of having been the discoverer."—"And I would give still more if I could be sure that I had fully understood it; this concerns me far more than who discovered it. But I have not yet entirely understood it, as I shall show you presently in a later chapter, at which time I will rely on your assistance, you who have at once understood the whole. But with your permission I shall now submit what the lawyers call a brief, summarizing what I have expounded and understood up to the present time. And as I present this brief I ask you to look to your rights and to assert them; for I hereby summon you *sub poena praeclusi et perpetui silentii*. The immediate contemporaneity can serve only as an occasion. (a) It can serve as occasion for the acquirement of historical knowledge. In this respect a contemporary of the emperor's marriage-feast is far more fortunately situated than a contemporary of the Teacher; for the latter merely gets an opportunity to see the servant-form, and at most one or another mysterious deed, in relation to which he must remain uncertain whether to admire or to resent being made a fool of, since he will presumably not even wish to persuade the Teacher to do it over again, as a juggler does, in order to give the spectators a better opportunity to see how the trick is turned. (b) It may serve as an occasion for the contemporary to acquire a Socratic deepening of his self-knowledge, in which case the contemporaneity vanishes as nothing in comparison with the Eternal which he discovers within himself. (c) Finally (and this is our assumption, lest we be thrown back on Socrates), it may serve as an occasion by means of which the contemporary, as one who is in Error, receives the condition from the God, and so beholds his glory with the eyes of faith. Aye, happy such a contemporary! But such a contemporary is not in the immediate sense an eye-witness; he is contemporary as a believer, in the autopsy of Faith. But in this autopsy every non-contemporary (in the immediate sense) becomes a contemporary. If then some member of a later generation, perhaps even moved by his own romanticism, yearns to be a contemporary in the immediate sense, he only proves himself a pretender, recognizable like the false Smerdes by the absence of ears—the ears of Faith namely, though he may have asses' ears long enough to permit even a contemporary (in the immediate sense) to hear himself into being a non-contemporary. If such a man continues to romance about how splendid it is to be a contemporary (in the immediate sense), betraying a restless eagerness to be up and away, he must doubtless be allowed to go; but if you watch him you will readily see, both from the nature of his movements and the direction he takes, that he goes not to meet the Paradox with its awe and fear, but rather trips off like a dancing-master to be in time for the emperor's nuptials. And though he gives his expedition a sacred name, preaching fellowship for others so that they join the pilgrimage in crowds, he will none the less scarcely discover the holy land (in the immediate sense), since it is not to be found either on the map or on the earth; his journey is a jest, like the children's game of seeing somebody to 'grandmother's door.' And though he may give himself no rest, runs faster than a horse can trot or a man can lie, he runs only with the lime-rod, misunderstanding himself as birdcatcher; for if the birds do not come to him of their own accord, it will certainly not help to run after them.—In only one respect could I be tempted to count a contemporary (in the immediate sense) more fortunate than the member of some later generation. For if we assume that centuries intervene between this event and the period of a succeeding generation there will presumably have accumulated much gossip about this thing, so much foolish chatter that the untrue and confusing rumors with which the contemporary (in the immediate sense) had to contend, did not prove nearly so serious an obstacle to the realization of a right relationship. And that so much the more, since the echo of the centuries, like the echo in some of our churches, would not only have tended to surround Faith with noisy chatter, but might even have transformed Faith itself into chatter; which could not very well have happened in the first generation, when Faith must have revealed itself in all its pristine vigor, through the contrast easily distinguishable from everything else."

(Fragments, pp. 68–88)

CHRISTIANITY AS THE ABSOLUTE; THE CONTEMPORARY OF CHRIST

With this invitation to all them "that labor and are heavy laden" Christianity did not come into the world, as the parsons snivellingly and falsely introduce it, as an admirable example of the gentle art of consolation but as the absolute. It is out of love that God wills it so, but also it is God who wills it, and He wills what He will. He will not suffer Himself to be transformed by men and be a nice human God. He will transform men, and that He wills out of love. He will have nothing to do with man's pert inquiry about why and why did Christianity come into the world. It is and shall be the absolute. Therefore everything men have hit upon relatively to explain the why and the wherefore is falsehood. Perhaps they have hit upon an explanation out of a humane compassion of a sort, which thinks that one might chaffer about the price, for God presumably does not understand men. His requirements are exorbitant, and so the parsons must be on hand to chaffer. Perhaps they hit upon an explanation in order to stand well with men and get some advantage out of preaching Christianity; for when it is toned down to the merely human, to what has "entered into the heart of man," then naturally people will think well of it, and quite naturally also of the amiable orator who can make Christianity so gentle a thing. If the Apostles had been able to do that, people would also have thought well of the Apostles. But all this is falsehood; it is a misrepresentation of Christianity, which is the absolute. But what, then, is the use of Christianity? It is, then, merely a plague to us! Ah, yes, that too can be said. Relatively understood, the absolute is the greatest plague. In all moments of laxness, sluggishness, dullness, when the sensuous nature of man predominates, Christianity seems madness, since it is incommensurable with any finite wherefore. What is the use of it, then? The answer is "Hold thy peace! It is the absolute!" And so it *must* be represented, viz. in such a way as to make it appear madness in the eyes of the sensuous man. And hence it is true, so true, so true in another sense, when the wise and prudent man in the contemporary situation condemns Christ by saying, "He is literally nothing"—most certainly true, for He is the absolute. Christianity came into the world as the absolute, not for consolation, humanly understood; on the contrary, it speaks again and again of the sufferings which a Christian must endure, or which a man must endure to become and to be a Christian, sufferings he can well avoid merely by refraining from becoming a Christian.

There is an endless yawning difference between God and man, and hence, in the Contemporary situation to become a Christian, to be transformed into likeness with God, proved to be an even greater torment and misery and pain than the greatest human torment, and hence also a crime in the eyes of one's neighbors. And so it will always prove when becoming a Christian in truth comes to mean to become contemporary with Christ. And if becoming a Christian does not come to mean this, then all the talk about becoming a Christian is nonsense and self-deception and conceit, in part even blasphemy and sin against the second commandment of the law and sin against the Holy Ghost.

For in relation to the absolute there is only one tense, the present. For him who is not contemporary with the absolute there is only one tense, the present. For him who is not contemporary with the absolute, it has no existence. And as Christ is the absolute, it is easy to see that with respect to Him there is only one situation, that of the contemporary. The five, the seven, the fifteen, the eighteen hundred years are neither here nor there; they do not change Him, neither do they in any wise reveal who He was, for who He is is revealed only to faith.

Christ is, if I may express it so seriously, not a comedian, not at all a merely historical person. But this is the difference between poetry and reality: contemporaneity. The difference between poetry and history is clearly this, that history is what really occurred, whereas poetry is the possible, the imaginary, the poetized. But what really occurred, the past, is not the real, except in a special sense, i.e. in contrast with poetry. It lacks the determinant which is the determinant of truth as inwardness and of all religiousness, the "for thou." The past is not reality for me; only the contemporary is reality for me. What you live contemporaneously with is reality, for thee. And thus every man can be contemporary only with the age in which he lives, and then with one thing more: with Christ's life on earth; for Christ's life on earth, sacred history, stands for itself alone outside history.

History you can read and hear about as referring to the past. Here, if you like, you can form your judgments according to the upshot. But Christ's life on earth is not a past event; in its time eighteen hundred years ago it did not wait, nor does it wait now, for any assistance from the upshot. An historical Christianity is absurd and unchristian confusion; for what true Christians there are in each generation are contemporary with Christ, have nothing to do with Christians of former generations, but everything to do with the contemporary Christ. His earthly life accompanies the race and accompanies every generation in particular, as the eternal history; His earthly life possesses the eternal contemporaneousness. And all the professional lecturing on Christianity (which lecturing has its stalking-blind and stronghold in the notion that Christianity is something past, and in the history of the eighteen hundred years) transforms it into the most unchristian of heresies, a fact which everyone will perceive, and therefore give up lecturing, if only he will try to imagine the generation contemporary with Christ delivering lectures; but indeed every generation of believers is contemporary.

If you cannot prevail upon yourself to become a Christian in the contemporary situation, or if He in the contemporary situation cannot move you and draw you to Himself, then you will never become a Christian. You may honor, praise, thank, and reward with all worldly goods Him who made you believe that you nevertheless are a Christian, but he deceives you. You might count yourself fortunate if you were not contemporary with anyone who dared to say this; you may become exasperated to frenzy at the torture, like sting of the 'gadfly,' of being contemporary with one who says it. In the first case you are deceived; in the second, you have at least heard the truth.

If you cannot endure the contemporary situation, cannot endure the sight of reality; if you are unable to go out in the street and perceive that it is God in this horrible procession, of men in your same condition, if you do not fall to the ground worshiping Him, then you are not essentially a Christian. What you have to do then is unconditionally to admit this to yourself, so that above all you may preserve humility and fear and trembling with relation to what it means in truth to be a Christian. For that is the way you must take to learn and to get training in fleeing to grace in such a wise that you do not take it in vain. Do not, for God's sake, repair to anyone to be "set at ease." For sure enough it was said, "Blessed are the eyes which see the things that ye see," which saying the parsons make much ado about—strangely enough, it is sometimes perhaps

in order to preserve a worldly smartness which precisely
in the contemporary situation would be rather out of place
—just as if this was not said solely and only about the contemporaries who had become believers. If the glory had
been directly visible, so that everybody as a matter of course
could see it, then it is false that Christ humbled Himself
and took upon Him the form of a servant; it is a superfluous to give warning against being offended, for how in the
world could anybody be offended by glory attired in glory!
And how in the world can it be explained that with Christ
it fared as it did, that not everybody rushed up to see what
was directly to be seen! No, there was "nothing about Him
for the eye, no glamor that we should look upon Him,
no outward appearance that we should desire Him" (Isa.
53, 2); directly there was nothing to be seen but a lowly
man, who, by signs and wonders and by affirming that He
was God, continually posited the possibility of offence. A
lowly man who thus expressed (1) what God understands
by compassion, and the very fact of being the lowly and
poor man when a man will be the compassionate one is
included in this; and (2) what God understands by man's
misery, which in both cases is utterly different from what
man's understanding is, and which in every generation
until the end of time everyone for his own part must learn
from the beginning, beginning always at the same point as
every other man who is a contemporary with Christ, practicing it in the contemporary situation. Human hot-headed-
ness and unruliness naturally are of no help at all. In how
far a man may succeed essentially in becoming a Christian,
no one can tell him. But dread and fear and despair are of
no avail. Candor before God is the first and last. Candidly
to admit to oneself where one is, with candor before God,
holding the task in view however slowly it goes, though one
only creeps forward. Yet one thing a man has: he is in the
right position, facing forward, not misled and deceived by
the trick of poetizing Christ, so that instead of being God

He becomes that languishing compassion which men themselves have invented, so that Christianity instead of drawing
men to heavenly places is impeded on its way and becomes
the merely human.

(Training in Christianity, pp. 66–70)

FAITH AND HISTORY

The coming of Christ is and remains a paradox. To his
contemporaries the paradox lay in the fact that he, this
particular individual man who looked like other men,
spoke like them, followed their habits and customs, was
the son of God. To later generations the paradox is different; for as they do not see him with their physical eye it
is easier to imagine him as the son of God, and then that
which gives offence and scandal is that he adopted the habit
of mind of a particular age. And yet, had he acted differently it would have been a great injustice to his contemporaries; for then they would have been the only ones to
have had a paradox at which to be scandalized. It is, however, my opinion that his contemporaries had the more
difficult paradox: for the sentimental longing to have been
contemporary with Christ, which many people talk about,
does not mean much; to witness such a paradox is a very
serious matter.

(Journals, n. 417)

History has to be put aside. The state of our own times
has to be established. That has to be the standard: as I
judge things in and of my own times, so I am. Everything
tiresomely repeated afterwards is only illusion.

Fundamentally, that is where my entire literary production has aimed. And also the fact of my using experiences
instead of "real" stories.

Luther's error lies in his not having gone back far enough,

in not having made us contemporaries enough of Christ.

Then what would judge Christianity would be the possibility of scandal.

What a terrible calamity! For this way, Christianity was taken for vanity. How would one judge a country which claimed it had millions of lovers like Romeo and Juliet! Behold what the people of Christendom were led to believe: that they were all Christians!—when a Christian is more rare than Romeo and Juliet.

(Pap., IX A 95)

However, in connection with being a contemporary of Christ, one remark has to be noted when this is to be the criterion of being Christian.

What I have developed in various writings on contemporaneity, that it is the standard in the poetic, historical, and ethical orders, this is the absolute truth and thus in one sense remains valid as well in what concerns Christ as a real person in history.

But Christ is at the same time a dogmatic reality. That is the difference. His death in fact is indeed the redemption.

Here, the category takes a qualitative turn. The death of one witness of the truth must teach me to want to die for truth as he did, to want to resemble him. But how is one to have the same will in relation to Christ's death? His death, as a matter of fact, is not a task to be imitated, but redemption. Nor do I dare to imagine Christ as a purely historical figure. In meditating on his life and death, I meditate, or ought to meditate, on the fact that I am the sinner.

Yet it is equally necessary to say that, in one sense at least, it has become easier for men to make themselves into and to be Christians after Christ's death than during his lifetime. His redemptive death has to be valued as a means of attaining this. Furthermore, during his lifetime, he had the task of expressing a model and of pushing the price of truth to the point where he would be killed. But, again, he can be of help to Christians after his death.

Thus it is not quite so simple that Christ is the model and that we are but to imitate him. In the first place, I need his assistance to be able to resemble him; and in the second place, inasmuch as he is the Savior and Redeemer of humanity, I certainly cannot imitate him.

The medieval conception of Christ as model, that age's beautiful zeal to resemble him, are like the impatient dash of youth.

But, as a man grows older, so the qualitative difference between the ideal and the man who wants to resemble it grows deeper. That is fundamentally why Luther fought the pretension of too zealously and fervently wanting to make of Christ only the Model. All the more nowadays bursts forth the idea that the model is something else at the same time, that he alone can help us. Finally, this side of things has been so strongly emphasized that the fact of his being a model has almost ended by vanishing as something too elevated, which, however, must not happen.

(Pap., X 1 A 132)

Still, it must be remembered that in contemporaneity, the paradox is above human control as an object of faith, which is precisely why the apostles were endowed with superhuman strength in order to endure belief. For us, it is a bit easier, and besides, we have grace as the fruit of Christ's death. But we should never forget this point: if it can be fully proven by its consequences that Christ is who he said he was, then he is not an object of faith.

(Pap., X 2 A 447)

FAITH AND DEATH

Most men live continuously from cradle to grave without being stopped in the medium of this flux, temporality, the simple quantitative [etc.]. Finally, death comes to stop them, and at that moment they pay attention to Christianity, with regrets for not having taken it up before, and this regret helps them to gain a relationship to Christianity, and then they die.

While he lives, natural man does not fear death, no more than he fears coming to a stop. Now, death and stopping have much in common. Stopping is like when a fish is pulled from the water and must breath air. Natural man abhors this other element, this monstrous power which there is in stopping, and about which he well understands, from its slightest hold upon us, that the limitless extent of its hold is incalculable. And the unlimited, man, the infinite, the eternal immobility of stopping, are like dying for him whose element is the "up to a certain point."

Christianity transformed into doctrine can insert itself perfectly into the bustle and the quantitative of temporality and the "without stopping," but that does not lead to Christianity. On the other hand, stopping can become just one more paragraph in the doctrine of Christianity, and that does not do much good either.

In the account of the thief on the cross, there is a typical characteristic that is not brought out. All, all have deserted Christ, even the apostle has denied him; the crucified thief is the only Christian who was Christ's contemporary. Christianity is so very far above men, and if I dare say so infinitely far in the most extenuated of situations like contemporaneity with Christ, that while Christ lived, even the apostle could not stand with Christ. It was only to a thief, an agonizing thief, that the awareness of sin and the situation of death came as a help to link him to Christ.

What is it that makes death the "situation" for becoming Christian? It is the conclusion, the absolute conclusion, that now, it is all over. That is what helps in making an absolute offer to the absolute. For the dying man to whom we dare not say that the end is near, but who is led to believe that he will eventually recover, for him, death is not the "situation."

Even for the Christian who is the truest and the most serious in his existence, it would still not be, I think, till his death that he absolutely attests to the fact that he is a Christian. We all have some relation to Christianity; we have, so to speak, a stake in it. But the higher the stakes we have played for, the more our final offer in death will be true, and the more we will then be in a position to reach an altogether absolute offer. There is only one man who, during his lifetime, is known to have made an absolute offer and to have stood fast, while clinging to life, and to have upheld and expressed at every moment this absolute offer. That man was himself the absolute. We humans need support, and, at the moment of death, man is helped by the situation to become the truest that he could ever be.

(Pap., X 3 A 47)

FAITH AND GRACE

In contemporaneity, Christ cannot offer the slightest discount in the requirement; for then it is his life that would have been changed, and he really had to fulfill the law to the end.

That is why he does not get angry that no one can be his disciple.

Then he dies and his death is the birth of grace.

In dying, he also gave the thief a discount (Luke 23, 40), for here, there could be no question of "imitation." Still, just because it was out of the question, it cannot exactly be said that there was a discount involved. However, what is shown here is that imitation just as such is not the absolute condition. For in this case, Christ, by a miracle, ought to have made the thief come down from the cross, brought him to life to see then what would have become of his imitation.

In consenting to a reduction in the requirements during

his lifetime, Christ would not have been the Savior of the world; for being the fulfillment of the requirement, he is also the requirement. He has the obligation to express the requirements of the faith in the extreme; he must make existence explode.

But then he leaves the world with these words: "Believe in me." (John 14, 1) Here is faith—grace. In his lifetime, he had to set out the equation: faith = imitation; although he, best of all, understood that none of his contemporaries could express imitation, which, pushed to the limit, would have been equivalent to being one's own model.

(*Pap.*, X 3 A 712)

THE MATURITY OF FAITH

To be brought up from childhood in Christianity nevertheless does have its good side, if we must truly become Christians. It is to succeed in living an experience analogous to that of Christ's contemporaries. First of all, they cherished worldly illusions. Then everything turned around, and it became a matter of being earnest Christians in spirit and in truth. It's the same when, from childhood, we are brought up in Christianity. The child assimilates Christianity as an earthly gospel . . . and, at a later age, fear will come to this same man, when he will have to receive the spiritual impression of Christianity.

(*Pap.*, X 4 A 539)

6. THE CLOISTER

The cloister wishes to express inwardness by means of a specific outwardness which is supposed to be inwardness. But this is a contradiction, for being a monk is just as truly something external as being an alderman. Mediation abolishes the absolute *telos,* but an individual existing in true pathos will express for himself every moment that the absolute *telos* is the absolute *telos.* The profoundity of all this lies in the inviolate stillness of the inner life; but herein lies also the possibility of deception and the temptation to say that one has done it. Now if anyone wishes to lie about this it will be his affair, and I shall be quite content to believe everything he says. For if it is something great, I might perhaps be able to do the same; and whether he has really done it or not, does not interest me at all. I will merely suggest to him that it would be prudent to abstain from adding that he *also* mediates; for then he informs against himself. The existing individual who has once received the absolute direction toward the absolute *telos,* and understands it as his task to exercise himself in this relationship, is perhaps an alderman, perhaps like any one of the other aldermen; and yet he is not like them, though when you look at him he seems wholly like them. He may possibly gain the whole world, but he is not as one who desires it. He may be a king; but every time he holds his scepter in his outstretched hand, resignation looks first to see whether he expresses existentially the absolute respect for the absolute *telos*—and the glory of his crown fades, although he wears it royally. It fades as it once faded in the great moment of resignation, though he now wears it in the third decade of his reign; it fades as it will some time fade in the hour of death, before the eyes of the witnesses standing by, and for his own failing sight. But thus it fades for him also in the hour of the fullness of his power. What then became of mediation? And yet there was no one who entered a cloister.

The individual does not cease to be a human being, nor does he divest himself of the manifold composite garment of the finite in order to clothe himself in the abstract garment of the cloister. But he does not mediate between the absolute *telos* and finite ends. In his immediacy the individual is rooted in the finite. But when resignation has convinced itself that he has acquired the absolute direction toward the absolute *telos,* all is changed, and the roots have been severed. He still lives in the finite, but he does not have his life in the finite. His life has, like that of other human beings, the various predicates of a human existence, but he is in them as one who is clothed in the borrowed garments of a stranger. He is a stranger in the world of the finite, but does not manifest his heterogeneity, his separation from *worldliness,* by a foreign mode of dress. This would be a contradiction, since he would thereby qualify himself in a worldly manner. He is incognito but his incognito consists in having an appearance entirely like others. Just as the dentist has loosened the soft tissues about a tooth and cut the nerve, so the roots of his life in the finite have been severed. It is not his task to give the tooth an opportunity to grow fast again, which would be mediation. In the great moment of resignation he had no thought of mediation, but committed himself by a choice, and it is now similarly his task to acquire the requisite facility in the renewal of this choice, and in giving it existential expression. The individual does indeed remain in the finite, where he confronts the difficulty of maintaining himself in the absolute choice while still living in the finite, but just as he deprived the finite of its unchecked vitality in the moment of resignation, so it remains his task to reinstate repeatedly the determination by which this was first accomplished. Let the world give him everything, it is possible that he will see fit to accept it. But he says: "Oh, well," and this "Oh, well" means the absolute respect for the absolute *telos*. If the world takes everything from him, he suffers no doubt; but he says again: "Oh, well"—and this "Oh, well" means the absolute respect for the absolute *telos*. Men do not exist in this fashion when they live immediately in the finite.

Whether for the Eternal, the Omniscient, the Omnipresent, it is as important whether a man forfeits his eternal happiness or a sparrow falls to the ground, I shall make no attempt to decide. Nor shall I say whether, when all comes to rest in eternity, it will appear that the most insignificant circumstance was absolutely important. I can truly avow that *time* will not permit me, because, in fact, I live in time. In existence at any rate, or for an existing individual, it cannot be so. An existing individual is himself in process of becoming, and a grandiose mediation (not even as in the Greek manner toilsomely acquired throughout an entire life, but merely legitimating itself on paper in the German fashion) is for an existing individual merely monkeyshines. A mortal eye cannot endure the dizzy sight, and the ethical will absolutely forbid him to make the attempt to see the most insignificant thing as equally important with that which is absolutely decisive. An *existing* individual cannot find, and dare not give himself, the *calm* needed to become fantastic; for as long as he is in existence he will never become eternal. In existence the watchword is always *forward:* and so long as the watchword is forward, it is man's task to exercise himself in making the absolute distinction, in attaining facility in making the distinction more and more easily, and in cultivating a good consciousness with himself.

But it is not mediation when the greatly experienced individual confidently believes that he makes the absolute distinction with ease and joy. Or when the wife of graying years is happily convinced that her husband is absolutely loyal, of what is she convinced? Is it of his mediation, and of his mediating and divided heart? Or is it not of his steady and quiet maintenance of the absolute distinction of love; only that she is in glad confidence so convinced that he makes the distinction with ease and expertness that she needs no external proof. Only it must not be forgotten that marriage is not the absolute *telos,* and that the principle which holds true absolutely of the absolute can therefore only imperfectly apply to the relative.

If God were in the immediate sense the ideal for human beings, it would be right to endeavor to express a direct likeness. Thus when a distinguished man is an ideal for me, it is quite proper for me to attempt to express a direct resemblance to him, since we are both human beings and both within the same sphere. But as between God and a human being (for let speculative philosophy keep *humanity* to play tricks with) there is an absolute difference. In man's absolute relationship to God this absolute difference must therefore come to expression, and any attempt to express an immediate likeness becomes impertinence, frivolity, effrontery, and the like.* If God in His lofty majesty were

---

* It is something quite different when God, in a very childlike age and for the innocence of the naïve consciousness, becomes a reverend old man or the like, and lives on a friendly footing with the devout. Thus I remember having read in *"Biblische Legenden der Muselmänner"* as published by Weil, that God Himself personally attended the funeral of one of the saintly characters in the story, walking in front of the coffin, while the four angels walked behind. The innocent naïveté of this sort of thing is manifest among other things from the fact that when we now read it, it evokes a pure and innocent humorous effect. This childlike piety is of course free from any desire to affront God; it is on the contrary happy to invest Him with the best that its invention affords.

to say to a human being: "You are of no more importance to me than a sparrow"; and if it were proper for a human being to express a direct likeness with the divine majesty, it would then become meritorious to reply: "You and your existence are likewise no more important to me than a sparrow": whether this reply is to be positively interpreted, because everything had become equally important for this exalted man, or negatively, because nothing had any importance. But this would surely be a mad blasphemy. Precisely because there is an absolute difference between God and man, man will express his own nature most adequately when he expresses this difference absolutely. *Worship* is the maximum expression for the God-relationship of a human being, and hence also for his likeness with God, because the qualities are absolutely different. But the significance of worship is, that God is absolutely all for the worshipper; and the worshipper is again one who makes the absolute distinction.

One who distinguishes absolutely has a relationship to the absolute *telos,* and *ipso facto* also a relationship to God. The absolute distinction is just the thing to clear a space about the absolute end, so as to make room for it, just as a marshal clears the way for a procession. It keeps the mob of relative ends at a distance, in order that the absolutely distinguishing individual may effect a relationship to the absolute. There is nothing meritorious in the attempt of an existing individual to approximate the equilibrium which possibly exists for the Eternal; for one who exists, the passionate decisiveness is precisely the maximum. Existing is in this respect something like walking. When everything is, and is at rest, it seems plausible enough to say that everything is equally important, provided I can acquire a view of it which is equally calm. But as soon as movement is introduced, and I am myself also in motion, my program in walking consists in constantly making distinctions. Only that this comparison cannot indicate the nature of the absolute distinction, since walking is a finite process.

But it does not follow from the fact that the task is to exercise the absolute distinction, that the existing individual becomes indifferent to the finite. This was an exaggeration characteristic of the Middle Ages; the medieval spirit did not have complete confidence in its inwardness until this became an outwardness. But the less outwardness, the more inwardness, and an inwardness expressed through its opposite (the outwardness of being wholly like all others, and that there is outwardly nothing to see) is the highest inwardness—provided it is there. This qualification must always be added, and also the warning that the less outwardness the easier the deception. An adult may very well whole-heartedly share in the play of children, and may even be responsible for really bringing life into the game; but he does not play as a child. One who understands it as his task to exercise himself in making the absolute distinction sustains just such a relationship to the finite. But he does not mediate. The inwardness of the Middle Ages was not sure of itself, and therefore wanted to see the external expression. It was in so far an unhappy inwardness, resembling a love-relationship in which the lovers are in sickly fashion jealous to see the outward expression of their love. In the same way the Middle Ages believed of God that He was jealously eager to see the outward expression. True inwardness demands absolutely no outward sign. The passion of the infinite pervades the exercise of the absolute distinction, but it desires to remain an inwardness, free from jealousy, envy, or suspicion. It does not wish contentiously to attract attention to itself as something outwardly remarkable, which would only be a loss instead of a gain, as when God's invisible image is made visible. It does not wish to create a disturbance in the finite, but neither does it mediate. In the midst of the finite and its manifold temptations, in order to forget the absolute distinction, it proposes to be for the individual his absolute inwardness; and as for other things, he may be an alderman, and so forth. But the maximum of attainment is simultaneously to sustain an absolute relationship to the absolute end, and a relative relationship to relative ends.

If this cannot be done, or if one is not willing to accept this as the task, analogies to the monastic movement are unconditionally to be preferred, whether this assertion provokes hissing or singing, is met with tears or with laughter in the speculative nineteenth century. The monastic movement had at any rate passion, and a respect for the absolute *telos*. But entering the cloister must not be regarded as something meritorious. On the contrary, this step must be taken in humility before God, and not without a certain self-deprecation. Just as a sick child does not regard it as any merit of its own that it is permitted to stay at home with the parents; just as a woman in love does not regard it as meritorious not to be able for a single minute to be out of sight of her beloved, and unable to win sufficient strength to have the thought of her lover with her while attending to her ordinary tasks; just as she does not regard it as meritorious to be permitted to sit with him at his work and be constantly at his side: so also must the candidate for the cloister look upon his relationship to God. And if he so understands it, there will be nothing more to say against his choice, whatever people may think of this in the nineteenth century.

But the sick child will soon discover the difficulty, not because the parents are not tender and loving, but because the constant association gives so many opportunities for conflict. And the woman in love will soon discover the difficulty, not because her lover is not a fine fellow, but because the constant sight of him, day after day and every hour of the day, brings in its train a tendency to languidness and debility. The candidate for the cloister will also soon discover the same sort of thing. For here again the clergy-man often deceives us. He says on Sunday that the hallowed place breathes such an air of quiet and solemnity, and that if we could only remain there always, we should doubtless soon become holy men and women; but the trouble is that we must go out into the world's confusion. Shame on the clergyman, so to delude us into thinking that the fault is in the world and not in ourselves; teaching us pride, as if we had chosen the more difficult task, especially if out there in the world we do not have the absolute *telos* with us every moment. I thought it was the clergyman's duty to teach us humility, and that he ought therefore to say to us: "Now go to your homes, and give thanks to God, who knows all human weaknesses, that it is not required of you to stay here and to occupy yourselves solely in prayer and singing psalms and praising God, in which case you would perhaps discover trials and temptations of which God now permits you to remain ignorant." Going to church once a week, when otherwise immersed in the manifold business of life, readily produces an illusion by means of the aesthetically foreshortened perspective. But just for this reason the clergyman ought to know how to call our attention to this danger of illusion, rather than repeatedly to misuse the Middle Ages in order to insinuate seductive misconceptions into the minds of his hearers.

In our time there is really no very great reason for warning people against the cloister, and in the Middle Ages the reason was not what might perhaps first come to mind. Had I lived in the Middle Ages, I could never have chosen to enter a cloister. And why not? Because anyone who entered a cloister was in the Middle Ages accounted a saint, and that in all seriousness. Hence when I walked about the streets and met a poor fellow mortal who was perhaps a much better man than I,* he would bow in submission and

---

* And this perhaps is not so hypothetical after all, even if I were a quite different man than I am; for the human being who in sincerity and earnestness considers another as a holy man, shows *eo ipso* by this humility that he is better than the other.

regard me pathetically and in earnest as a holy man. But this seems to me the most terrible of all misunderstandings, a profanation of the holy, a betrayal of the absolute relationship to the absolute *telos*. If a cloister were set up in a modern environment the entrants would be regarded as mad. When we read nowadays a physician's program for a new asylum, it has a certain resemblance to an invitation to a cloister. This I regard as an extraordinary advantage. To be considered mad is something like; it is encouraging, it protects the inwardness of the absolute relationship. But to be considered in real earnest a holy man must make one anxious unto death. To give the cloister the color of a lunatic asylum I regard as the nearest thing to an outward appearance like that of all other men. For in that case the outwardness does not directly assume to express the inwardness, which was precisely the fault of the Middle Ages. I at least think as follows: Let me come to be whatever the world has in store for me, it will scarcely be anything that could be called greatness; and if the lot be ever so insignificant, I shall strive to put up with it. But there is one thing I pray that I may escape: to be regarded in earnest as a holy man; for if anyone were to dub me saint in a spirit of mockery that would be something quite different, not inappropriate, and rather encouraging.

But let due respect be shown for the monastic movement of the Middle Ages. The clergyman says indeed that the life of the cloister was an evasion of the danger, and that it is a greater thing to remain among the perils of life—but surely not with the assistance of mediation? Let us at any rate try to understand one another, and seek to agree as to what we mean by the danger. The candidate for the cloister saw his greatest danger in the failure to sustain each moment an absolute relationship to the absolute *telos*. The mediation principle knows nothing of any such danger.

(*Postscript,* pp. 366–373)

The Middle Ages made an energetic attempt existentially to think God and the finite together, but came to the conclusion it could not be done, and the expression for this is the cloister. The religiosity of our age is more advanced. But if the God-relationship and the finite world in all its smallest detail (where the difficulty becomes greatest) are to be held together existentially, the assent to the finite must find expression within the sphere of religiosity itself; and it must be of such a character that the individual does not here again make the transition from the God-relationship to a mode of existence in entirely different categories.

Lower forms of religiosity than that of the medieval monastic movement will at once be recognizable by the existence in them of the above division, whereby the God-relationship becomes something for itself, and the rest of life something separate and different. There are therefore three lower forms: (1) that in which the individual goes home from the Sunday God-relationship to exist quite immediately in the dialectic of the pleasant and the unpleasant; (2) that in which the individual turns from the Sunday God-relationship to exist in a finite ethic, and quite fails to notice the persistent claim of the God-relationship, while he attends to his business, earns money, and so forth; (3) that in which he goes home from the Sunday God-relationship to have his life in a speculative-ethical view, which permits the God-relationship to exhaust itself without further ado in relative ends, a view of life whose formula is: an efficient performance of vocational duties, as king, as carpenter, as tight-rope walker, etc., is the highest expression of the God-relationship, so that in so far one does not really need to go to church. For every such form of religiosity absolves itself, by going to church once a week, from the necessity of having the God-relationship present with it every day in everything; on Sunday it obtains, not precisely like the child, permission to enjoy itself the week through, but it obtains absolution from further thinking about God throughout the week.

The religiosity which is to be an advance upon the medieval must find an expression in its devout reflections for the principle that the religious individual exists on Monday in the same categories, and will on Monday actually so exist. The Middle Ages were praiseworthy in that they were earnestly concerned about this problem; but then they arrived at the conclusion that it could be done only in the cloister. The religiosity of our age goes further; on Sunday the clergyman says that we must always bear in mind the fact that we can do nothing of ourselves; but for the rest we must be as other men, we must not enter the cloister; we can take our outings in the Deer Park—but surely we must first consider the relationship to God through the religious intermediary principle that a man can do absolutely nothing of himself. And it is this that makes life so tremendously strenuous, and it is this that makes it possible that perhaps all men are in truth genuinely religious individuals; because true religiosity is the religiosity of the secret inwardness, the secret inwardness in the religious individual, who even employs all his art in order that no one shall notice anything special in his demeanor. For just as the criterion of God's omnipresence consists in His being invisible, so the criterion of true religiosity is its invisibility, i.e. there is nothing outwardly to be seen. The god that can be pointed out is an idol, and the religiosity that makes an outward show is an imperfect form of religiosity.

(*Postscript,* pp. 423–424)

THE DUTY OF ADORATION

We left the religious individual in the crisis of his sickness, but this sickness is not unto death. We shall now permit him to be strengthened by precisely the same concept that annihilated him, the conception of God. I use again a foreshortened perspective, because the chief interest of my task has not yet begun; and I do not dwell upon how the ethical (which is always somewhat distant from the absolute God-relationship) must enter in regulatively, and take command. Nevertheless, I shall ask the reader to pause at this point for one or two remarks. First and foremost, that in each generation there are doubtless not many who even get so far as to exhaust the suffering connected with the beginning of the absolute God-relationship; and next, that a beginning in the medium of existence is far from being something that is decided once for all; for it is only on paper that one finishes the first state, and then has nothing further to do with it. The absolute exertion in the medium of existence is and remains merely an approximation, though this must not be understood comparatively, in relation to the more or less of others, for then the individual will have lost his ideality. This is because the eternal aims from above at the existing individual, who by existing is in process of movement, and thus at the moment when the eternal strikes, he is already a little moment away. The beginning of an absolute decision in the medium of existence is the last thing in the world that can be characterized once for all, as something left behind; for the existing individual is not an abstract X, who passes through something and then goes on further, if I may so express myself, undigested through life. The existing individual becomes concrete in his experience, and in going on he still has his experience with him, and may in each moment be threatened with the loss of it; he has it with him not as something one has in a pocket, but his having it constitutes a definite something by which he is himself specifically determined, so that by losing it he loses his own specific determination. As a consequence of having made a decision in existence, the existing individual has attained a more specific determination of what he is; if he lays it aside, then it is not he who has lost something; he does not have himself while happening to have lost something, but he has lost himself and must now begin from the beginning.

The religious individual has thus got over his illness,* though tomorrow perhaps it may return as the result of a little carelessness. He strengthens himself perhaps by means of the edifying consideration that God who made man must Himself know best all the many things that may seem impossible to bring into connection with the thought of God, all this earthly distress, all the confusion in which he may be involved, and the necessity of diversion, of rest, even of sleep.

It follows of itself that we do not here have reference to

---

* In general there is nothing so faithfully guarded by the comical as the religious, and its nemesis is nowhere so instantly at hand as it is in the religious sphere. When one listens to an aestheticising religious discourse in church, it is of course one's duty to be edified, even if his reverence rattles on ever so topsy-turvily; but when one calls it to mind again at a different time, the comic effect is not uninteresting, and the law for it is that where the speaker spreads every sail of eloquence to express the highest, there he satirizes without knowing it! "The praying individual arises from his prayer so strengthened, so very much strengthened, so extraordinarily strengthened." But religiously a man's true strengthening consists in being prepared to find that the struggle may begin again the next moment. "The individual binds himself to God by a promise, a sacred pledge, that he will ever and always, and so forth; and now he rises from his prayer in such peace of mind, in such great peace of mind." But religiously one is very careful about making vows (cf. Ecclesiastes), and religiously the measure of the inwardness of the vow is the brevity of the posited term, and the distrust of oneself. No, the whole-souled inwardness of the individual and the consent of a heart purified from all doublemindedness to a promise for the present day, or for the forenoon—such a vow has religiously a greater degree of inwardness than this aestheticising clinking the glasses with Providence. The one procedure signifies that the maker of the vow has his life every day in the religious sphere, the other betrays satirically enough that he is a travelling member introduced by the clergyman.

that indulgence which is proclaimed in the world, where one man comforts himself by appealing to another, where men console themselves mutually, and leave God out of account. Every human being is gloriously constituted, but what ruins so many is, among other things, also this wretched tittle-tattle between man and man about that which should be suffered and matured in silence, this confession before men instead of before God, this hearty communication between this man and that about what ought to be secret and exist only before God in secrecy, this impatient craving for intermediary consolation. No, in suffering the pain of his annihilation, the religious individual has learned that human indulgence profits nothing, and therefore refuses to listen to anything from that side; but he exists before God and exhausts the suffering of being human and at the same time existing before God. Therefore it cannot comfort him to know what the human crowd knows, man with man, what men know who have a shopkeeper's notion of what it means to be a man, and a facile gossipy notion at seventeenth hand of what it means to exist before God. From God he must derive his consolation, lest his entire religiosity be reduced to a rumor. That is not to say that he is to discover new truths, etc.; no, he is merely to keep a watch over himself lest the craving for gossip and the lust for preaching should prevent him from experiencing what thousands upon thousands have experienced before him. If it be true even of love, that only then does a love experience become ennobling when it teaches a man to keep his feeling within himself, how much more is this true about the religious!

Let us think about what paganism dreamed of in myths, that a god fell in love with an earthly woman. If she remained in ignorance of the fact that he was a god, this relationship would constitute the greatest possible unhappiness; for in consequence of the belief that the same standard was applicable to both, she would plunge herself into despair by requiring of herself an impossible likeness. If, on the other hand, she came to know that he was a god, she would at first be annihilated in all her lowliness, so that she would hardly dare face her inferiority; she would make one desperate attempt after the other to raise herself to his level; she would suffer the pangs of anxiety every time her lowliness made it necessary for them to be separated; she would be tortured agonizingly by the question whether it was her lack of will or lack of ability.

Let us now make the application to the religious. Where is the limit for the particular individual in his concrete existence between what is lack of will and lack of power, between what is slackness and earthly selfishness, and what is the limitation of his finitude; when is, for an existing individual, the period of preparation over, when this question cannot return with all its first anxious strenuousness, when does this moment come in existence, which in its entirety is a period of preparation? Let all the dialecticians in the world combine their exertions, they cannot decide the question for a particular existing individual *in concreto*. For dialectics is in its truth a benevolent helper, which discovers and assists in finding where the absolute object of faith and worship is—there, namely, where the difference between knowledge and ignorance collapses in absolute worship with a consciousness of ignorance, there where the resistance of an objective uncertainty tortures forth the passionate certainty of faith, there where the conflict of right and wrong collapses in absolute worship with absolute subjection. Dialectics itself does not see the absolute, but it leads, as it were, the individual up to it, and says: "Here it must be, that I guarantee; when you worship here, you worship God." But worship itself is not dialectics. A dialectic that mediates is a derelict genius.

The earthly woman who was loved by the god would then first be annihilated in her lowliness; but then she would doubtless learn to stand erect in the consciousness that he must know all this better than she. She would be annihilated through thinking divinely about him, but would stand erect again through the conception that he thought humanly about her. Aye, even when a maiden of lowly station is united with king ruling over a foreign people, what suffering would she not endure in attempting to find assurance with respect to everything that reminded her of her lowliness, with respect to what seemed to constitute a hindrance to the relationship, striving to find peace of mind in that border warfare between being over-indulgent toward herself and requiring too much of herself!

But one ingredient in the lowliness of a human being is that he is temporal, and cannot endure to lead uninterruptedly the life of the eternal in time. And if his life is in time, then it is *eo ipso* piecemeal; and if it is piecemeal, it is sprinkled with diversions and distractions; and in the diversion the human being is absent from his God-relationship, or present in it, yet not as in the strong moment.

Men say it is a hardship when lovers are separated; should not then such separation be a heavy thing for the religious individual to bear, and is it less heavy because it is a diversion rather than a toilsome task that separates them, when the necessity for diversion is precisely the most unequivocal indication of his lowliness? For our religious individual is not so situated that the clergyman needs to admonish him to seek God; rather he is so strongly stirred that there must be diversion for him if he is not to perish. Here is the place where the monastic movement becomes tempting. Would it not become possible through superhuman exertion to approach nearer to God, to preserve the relationship without interruption, without sleep if possible! We say in another connection that love has power to make the lovers equal. Aye, and this is quite true with reference to a love-relationship between human beings, because they stand essentially on the same level, and the differences between them are accidental. Between God and man, however, there exists an absolute difference, and hence this direct equality is a presumptuous and dizzy thought, though this constitutes no comparative human indulgence from the utmost exertion. But since there is this absolute difference between God and man, how does the principle of equality in love express itself? By means of the absolute difference. And what is the form of this absolute difference? Humility. What sort of humility? The humility that frankly admits its human lowliness with humble cheerfulness before God, trusting that God knows all this better than man himself. The monastic movement is an attempt to be superhuman, an enthusiastic, perhaps even a devout attempt to resemble God. But herein lies the profound suffering of true religiosity, the deepest thinkable, namely, to stand related to God in an absolutely decisive manner, and to be unable to find any decisive external expression for this (for a happy love between human beings expresses itself externally in the union of the lovers). This inability is rooted in the necessary relativity of the most decisive external expression, in its being both too much and too little; it is too much because it involves a certain presumptuousness over against other men, and it is too little because it is after all a worldly expression.

(*Postscript,* pp. 436–440)

THE DUTY OF MODESTY

The error of the Middle Ages, and it has since been repeated, lies in our actions of often setting up a particular case as a rule for others. Not marrying is evidently a personal act. For the one who is involved, it can be that this is quite pleasing to God.

But it is another thing to set this up as a rule, even only to introduce others to it. Individual cases are the exception, and they ought to be aware of it; and for the reason that, far from recommending the same thing to others, on the contrary, the exception should recommend the general practice to them. The individual case is true, in fact, only if one is in an original relationship to God. The relationship to God can be defended only over against the general. Everything that does not have this originality is by that very fact unjustified when it wants to be the exception.

To stay with the example of not marrying, it is easy to show the steps to be followed. The resolution stays rigorously mute within the individual. So he lives as a bachelor, it is very true, but, if he stays silent, no other person can have any control over it.

This fact of not marrying can be explained in so many ways. For some time, no one will pay any attention to it, because there is no regulation age for marrying. People think, then, that like others, he is looking for a girl to marry. And as time passes, he is still a bachelor. This *non-factum* can be explained countless ways. The error of the Middle Ages was to make this noteworthy, and worse still, to make this a perfection or excellence.

I went through this struggle myself. In her distress and pain—she has suffered so much!—my fiancee asked me, when it was all over, "Tell me only one thing. Will you ever want to marry?" That was my struggle. I saw in her agitation that she was only a step away from turning decisively towards the religious life. In good conscience, I could have answered no. And then? Aware as I was of being a specific, individual case, was I then to interfere and sow confusion in her life? That is why I answered with a lie. If she had to take such a step, otherwise said, if this was to be true in her, and thus admissible, it ought to spring out of her own originality.

Now the truth is that she married afterwards, which I completely approved of, and for which I thanked God. If the opposite had been her truth, her conduct should have been otherwise. She would not have breathed a word of it to me, but in her originality and in her relationship to God, she would have decided not to marry and perhaps would have been right. But since she might have been thinking about it, she would not have had a simple and pure relationship to God, but a second-hand relationship. And when there is no first-hand relationship, nothing justifies our being an exception. With all her heart, she wanted to marry me. Afterwards, she had the idea that we should agree not to marry, that we stay single. Now, with regard to me, it was perhaps perfectly in order, for in me it was original; but in her it was derived. She would not have had a relationship to God, but would have found peace in a Platonic, loving relationship to me. But this kind of relationship is not religious, and hence, inadmissible. Only the original relationship to God justifies the exception.

(*Pap.*, X 1 A 485)

7. CATHOLICISM AND PROTESTANTISM

THE WORD OF GOD OUGHT TO BE PREACHED TO ONE PEOPLE; THE MEANS: THE CLERGY

The "common people" always represent a form of soundness from which something good can spring; that which amounts to something in the world and which comes from it is generally already weakened and corrupted, for all that is human is fragile, and generations are easily corrupted.

That is why, and for many other reasons, the word of God is and ought to be preached to the people.

But to preach it, men are still necessary, consequently forming the *medium* through which the word of God reaches the people. This medium is the clergy.

Now, it is easy to see that if this medium were free of all selfishness, then things would be perfect, the word of God arriving, so to speak, immediately to the people, the medium being free of all confusing elements.

But evil has always been fond of this medium, and still is.

Catholicism has correctly seen that it was good for this medium to belong as little as possible to this world; hence, celibacy, poverty, asceticism. [etc.] It is perfectly correct, calculated to remove selfishness from the medium. For all that, what happens? Satan throws himself into the ranks of the clergy, and through spiritual pride these men strain their wits to become something other than the medium: a court of appeal between God and man, as a reward to themselves for all their material renunciations.

And then, Protestantism did not overlook this error. And to guard against this spiritual pride, Protestantism contrived the notion that the clergy should be exactly like other men. So there is a completely laicized clergy: officials, dignitaries, married men with wives and children, more than ever entangled in all the airs of the temporal. And that is the medium through which God's word must resound! Yes, if this medium is only made to propagate sound, why not use mattresses just as well! No, such a clergy as this blocks the word of God, or if the word of God does pass through, it becomes something else entirely.

(Pap., XI 1 A 532)

LUTHER: THE REFORM

Luther is the exact opposite of the apostle.

The apostle expresses Christianity for the sake of God. He comes with authority from God and for his sake.

As for Luther, he expresses Christianity for the sake of man. He is fundamentally the reaction of the human against the Christian acting for the sake of God. From this follow also Luther's words: "I cannot do otherwise"—which are not at all the apostle's.

From this alone, you see, what confusion in having made an apostle of Luther.

In general, what Christianity has always lacked is a diagnostician to track down illness, and a dialectician.

(Pap., XI 2 A 266)

CATHOLICISM—PROTESTANTISM

Are not Catholicism and Protestantism related to each other like—it may seem extraordinary but it is really so physically—like a building which cannot stand, to a buttress which cannot stand alone, whereas the whole is even very firm and secure, so long as they keep together, the building and the buttress which supports it. In other words, surely Protestantism, Lutheranism is really a corrective; and the result of having made Protestantism into the regulative has been to produce great confusion.

As long as Luther lived it could not be seen clearly, for he was continuously in the tense atmosphere of battle, and straining every nerve as polemicist, as well as in the smoke and steam of the battle; and as long as the fight continues there is something which corresponds to steam and smoke and which prevents one having either the time, the peace, or the clarity to see whether the point can be carried and the transposition made. Luther fought, it is always said, polemically against Catholicism, but it cannot be achieved in this way; it becomes clear how it ought to be done, but there is no time to stop, we must go on to the next point. We are fighting, but it cannot be achieved in this way [etc.] and that is as far as it gets.

Then comes peace. Now we shall see whether Protestantism can stand by itself. Whether or not cannot perhaps be seen distinctly in a country where Catholicism exists side by side with Protestantism, for although they do not fight and each look to their own affairs there will be a reciprocal relationship at many points. In order to be able to see clearly whether and to what extent Protestantism can stand alone it is desirable to have a country where there is no Catholicism. There one would see whether Protestantism would not, presuming that it degenerated, lead to a form of corruption to which Catholicism, presuming it degenerated, did not lead, and whether that does not show that Protestantism is not fit to stand alone.

Let us try and realise this more clearly. It was after a heavy yoke had been upon men's shoulders for a long long time, after they had been frightened with death, judgment, and hell from generation to generation, with fasting and scourging, it was then that the bow broke. Out of a monastery cell broke the man Luther. Now let us be careful not to separate what belongs together, the background and the foreground, not to get a landscape without background, not to get something quite meaningless.

Now, what Luther dared to do was, under the circumstances, the truth; for the opposite had been falsely exaggerated.

Luther then, broke out of the monastery. But that was not really the best opportunity of seeing with sweet reasonableness how much truth there was in the opposite, when it was not exaggerated. Luther knew he was hardly safe, and it was therefore rather a question of making use of the advantage he had won, by having broken out, in order to wound the opposite as deeply as possible.

Now take the order of things, just as they were when Luther broke out. They were in error: take away the assumption necessary for Luther, and Lutheranism is perfectly meaningless. Try and imagine that what Luther in extreme tension attacked as being the extreme, that it had become a sort of result, in such a way that the extreme tension was omitted, and Lutheranism is absolute nonsense. Imagine a country, cut off from Catholic influence, to which this Lutheran result has been brought and there the generation now living has never heard a single word about the aspect of the question which is expressed by the monastery, asceticism and which the Middle Ages exaggerated; on the contrary, it is brought up from childhood, softened from childhood with the Lutheran notion of calming an anxious conscience, though it is important to note that there is not a soul who has made his conscience anxious, however distantly. What then is Lutheranism? Is there any sense in calming the anxious conscience, when the assumption, 'anxious consciences,' simply to not exist? Does not Lutheranism become meaningless, and what is worse, does it not become a refinement, which will denote the difference between degenerated Protestantism and the corruption of degenerated Catholicism.

And that is exactly what I wanted to show, together with the fact that it indicates that Protestantism is not fit to stand alone.

When Catholicism degenerates, what form will the corruption take? The answer is easy: hypocritical sanctimoniousness. When Protestantism degenerates, what form of corruption shall we find? The answer is not difficult: shallow worldliness. But in Protestantism this will show itself with a refinement which cannot occur in Catholicism.

Set them off one against the other, hypocritical sanctimoniousness and shallow worldliness; but I maintain that into the bargain there is a certain refinement which does not appear in Catholicism, and that is the result of Protestantism being calculated upon an assumption. That is the refinement I want to show.

Let us take a perfectly simple instance. Imagine a Catholic prelate who is completely worldly, naturally not to such an extreme that the law can punish him, or that nature itself will take its revenge; no, he is altogether too worldly to be so stupid; no, the whole thing is shrewdly calculated, and this is the worldliest thing about it for shrewd enjoyment, and then in turn for the enjoyment of this very shrewdness; and thus his whole life is the enjoyment of all possible pleasure such as no worldly-wise Epicurean could exceed. How then will the Catholic judge him? Well, I assume that he says quite becomingly, "It is not my business to pass judgment upon the higher clergy." But none the less the Catholic will readily see that it is worldliness. And why will he readily see this? Because the Catholic sees at the same time an entirely different side of Christianity expressed, fact which the prelate must put up with, for side by side with him there walks one who lives in poverty, and the Catholic thus has a profound sense that this is truer than the prelate's way of life, which, alas, is mere worldliness.

Now imagine on the other hand a Protestant country, where there is no trace of Catholicism, where for a long, long time people have accepted the Lutheran view, but without its original premise, where for a long, long time they have been rid of asceticism and fasting, of monks and of those who preach Christianity in poverty; and not only that, but have got rid of it thoroughly, as of something ridiculous and foolish, so that if any such figure were to turn up now, people would burst with laughter as at an outlandish beast; they have got rid of it as of a lower, an imperfect conception of Christianity. Imagine now in this Protestant country a Protestant prelate who is the exact counterpart of the Catholic. What then? Why, in this case the Protestant prelate possesses a refinement of pleasure, a refinement for which the Catholic prelate's mouth may water in vain, inasmuch as in the whole Protestant environment there is not a living soul that has a profound sense of the significance of renouncing the world, the sort of godliness which had its share of truth, even if it was exaggerated in the Middle Ages, because the religion of the land is built upon the result of Lutheranism, without its original premise that godliness is nothing but a frank-hearted enjoyment of life, which is indeed wonderful when one has witnessed Luther's fear and trembling and tribulation. Thus the Protestant prelate possesses a refinement of pleasure. The luck of it, the Catholic prelate might exclaim, the deuce take him! The refinement, namely, that his contemporaries look upon his worldliness and worldly enjoyment as godliness! Look, say the contemporaries one to another—and remember that in Catholicism the situation was that one said to the other, let us not look upon it or dwell upon it; it is just simply worldliness— behold frank-hearted Lutheranism, watch him over the turtle soup, there is no connoisseur like him, watch him at the oyster-feast, see how he can suck enjoyment from every situation, and how shrewdly he looks after his own affairs; so let us admire his frank-hearted Lutheranism! High he soars, in frank-hearted Lutheranism, high above the lower and imperfect ideal of entering a monastery, of fasting, of preaching Christianity in poverty. High he soars above it all in freedom of spirit and frank-hearted Lutheranism! The noble thing is not to wander away from the world, to flee from it. No, genuine Lutheranism is like the prelate, for this is godliness. His contemporaries do not merely put up with this or take pains to ignore it; no, they regard it with admiration, as godliness. . . .

Luther set up the highest spiritual principle, pure inwardness. It may become so dangerous that we can sink to the lowest of lowest paganism—however, the highest and the lowest are like one another—where sensual debauchery is celebrated as divine worship; and so in Protestantism a point may be reached at which worldliness is honoured and highly valued as piety. And this, as I maintain, cannot happen in Catholicism.

But why can it not happen in Catholicism? Because Catholicism has the universal premise that we men are pretty well rascals. And why can it happen in Protestantism? Because the Protestant principle is related to a particular premise: a man who sits in the anguish of death, in fear and trembling and much tribulation—and of those there are not many in any one generation.

*

It is not my intention herewith to introduce monasticism, even if I were able to; my endeavour is only directed towards contributing to our coming to an understanding with truth, with the help of a few admissions.

(Journals, n. 1327)

TEMERITY OF DESPAIR AND HUMILITY
WHICH DESPAIRS

It is quite true, undoubtedly, that there always have been frequent examples, in Catholicism, of a frenzied rashness seeking the desire to resemble Christ, to imitate the model, to be perfect. [etc.] But there is something good that always lives on in Catholicism: that nothing changes in the requirement of imitating Christ, nor in what must be understood by this.

On the other hand, what has Protestantism invented? It has invented a pure invention of the world. This humility which despairs, this humility which, once and for all, declares that it is too elevated for us, and then adapts itself to what the world wants, all the while earning two comforts. First being free of the effort of imitation, and then, that this surrender is honored, esteemed, thought of as humility.

Which of the two attitudes is worse? Oh Luther, no one has been so exploited as you by his partisans, doing exactly the opposite of what you wanted!

(Pap., X 5 A 139)

THE MAJESTY OF GOD: A SIDE OF
LUTHERAN DOCTRINE

Luther explains all the sufferings, all the scruples, all the persecutions and troubles as coming from the devil; without the latter, being a Christian would be an easy life.

From a Christian point of view, this conception is not valid. First of all, it comes from the fact that Luther considers Christianity to be fundamentally optimism. Misfortune and suffering have only a fortuitous relation to Christian existence. They spring from an exterior power, so that without this power, Christian existence would be but a closely woven system of joy; for, in itself and by itself, being a Christian does not have any relation to suffering.

Secondly, the problem is due to the fact that Luther does not raise the majesty of God to a high enough level in the order of the majestic. When, in fact, the majesty of God has opposite it a majesty of Satan's nature, a majesty so powerful over and against God that with the best will God cannot divert the suffering of his faithful, then, all things considered, we come to the conclusion that, humanly speaking, God has a cause, and that he is degraded by having it.

But men very much like to think that God has a cause; for immediately, then, we get busy and figure we can get a reduction in the price of being Christian. When someone, however great his majesty, has a cause, what happens? He necessarily needs men. He must have recourse to them. Let us consider some analogies. At the stockmarket, if we have to buy, the broker knows immediately that there is a profit in sight, because the customer is obliged to buy. When someone comes to sell at a second-hand bookstore, the shopkeeper immediately sniffs out a chance for profit, because the other is obliged to sell. And likewise also for someone who needs men.

It is this idea that has guided Christendom, but above all Protestantism, in its conduct. God, with an infinite majesty and having no cause in human terms, has become a majesty in need of men. In the end, to find one for God, we very nearly followed Vespasian's principle for money: don't get near enough to smell it. Perfect! Christianity came into this world to raise man to the highest ideal; but mankind gave the whole affair a new look . . . the requirement for being a Christian was so reduced as to have been dropped to nothing, for God needs men.

Compare this to Christ's answer to those who wanted to be his disciples (Luke 14, 26–33). It signifies, you see, that God, on the human scale, does not have a cause. Taking the form of a humble servant (Philippians 2, 7), without a place to rest his head (Matt. 8, 20), knowing what an enormous plot had been initiated against him, one would believe that this man needed men, that men could serve him, especially when so much was offered to him here. But no, Christ maintains the price of the absolute without making any changes. As he said before Pilate and the assembled crowd: "Yes, I am a king" (John 18, 37). His answer here is all majesty. It is as if he had said: "My friend, I am a majesty who does not need men." A miracle is far from having the majesty of such an answer, if one accepts the spirit of what is said.

Protestantism since Luther has completely abandoned the explanation of Satan as a supernumery power. In this way, the amount of pessimism nevertheless contained in Luther's Christianity has disappeared, and Christianity has entirely become a kind of nauseating candy, an idyll of procreators. [etc.]

The infamy of all subsequent Protestantism has been to drop this aspect, so conclusive for Luther, without bothering to replace it by another explanation of what Luther maintained in accordance with Scripture, that to be Christian is impossible without suffering. The infamy has been to drop an entire aspect which was so important, not seeming to notice and continuing to claim to be Lutheran. And yet, quite briefly, a pastor nowadays, especially in Denmark, is a private individual who is paid a salary to spout off on Sunday just about everything that happens to go through his head.

For a Christian, the necessity of suffering does not come from the devil. And it is precisely there that begin the loftiest spiritual tribulations of our relationship to Christianity, to think that suffering comes from God! When one must imagine a being who is all love, it is the worst strain on the mind and soul that this love be in one sense like an act of cruelty. Look! Man could not stand this strain, so he divided things up: God is love, from him comes all the good and nothing but the good. All the evil and all plagues, [etc.,] come from the devil. Otherwise one could not maintain that God is love. What is at most possible is that punishment for our sins comes from him.

But the contradiction that love causes the human misfortune of the beloved, through love certainly, but still, its human misfortune, this whole notion is almost murderous to the basis of our humanity. So we solved the difficulty with the story about the devil, as we do to help a child by telling him a story about the bad man who has done what God himself has done. We cannot tell the child the truth, because we want to cultivate in him the belief that only thoughts of joy and goodness are to be linked to God.

However, suffering does proceed from God. And it is no longer fortuitously related to Christian existence. No, suffering is inseparable from it.

The necessity of suffering depends on God's majesty. This majesty is so infinite that its only characteristic or form of expression is paradox. And the paradoxical for God is to be majestic to the point of having to be the beloved's misfortune. (Marginal note: the minor majesties recognize one another in the fact that they are the joy of the beloved—direct relationship) Infinite Majesty! Yet let us never forget that this majesty is love.

Suffering is the result of the fact that God and man differ qualitatively, and that the bumping together of the temporal and the eternal in time must produce suffering.

Suffering is due to the fact that God is the examiner. But if the examination is not to be mere acting, it has to be pursued in depth. Thus God, who examines to see if we have faith and if we love him, suffering more in his love than the person examined, has to pursue the examination in depth. What man would want so very much is some direct sign that he is loved by God. Rare, so very rare, is he who is so fervent not to have this desire. But, in truth, such cannot and must not be our relationship to God, if God is spirit. When God examines, it is necessary to push matters to the opposite extreme where it seems precisely that God abandons the beloved. This mode of examination can have differences of degree; but the essential characteristic is always present.

God is the examiner. This is a highly significant term. An examiner, in short, really has nothing in common with someone who, humanly speaking, has a cause. But, to be sure, in this era of phraseology, all concepts have been turned inside out, and we finally have no word to designate what elevation is. Nowadays, school teacher means someone who needs children, doctor someone who needs the sick, and professor someone who needs disciples. So undoubtedly also, examiner means someone who needs candidates for examination.

(Pap., XI 2 A 130)

TAKING GRACE SERIOUSLY

Christ was naturally the model in his lifetime: the task of faith consisted in not being scandalized by this individual who is God, but in believing, then in imitating Christ, by becoming his disciple.

Then Christ dies. And now behold, through Paul the apostle, the essential change. He puts infinite stress on the death of Christ as redemption: the object of faith becomes the redemptive death of Christ.

Thus the model as model becomes more and more distant. While Christ lived and the model was seen coming and going here on earth, existence was shattered; the absolute always shatters existence.

Then the change occurs: the model is apparently turned around, so that it is his death itself, his redemptive death, which is set off.

During all that time in which the apostle is preaching this doctrine, his existence never ceases to be its imitation. But so as not to be liable for sacrilege, as if the apostle thought to reach Christ's level by his imitation, he diverts all attention from the model and fixes it imperiously on the redemptive death of Christ.

Therein lies Christianity for us men. The life of Christ on earth is a Christianity which no man can endure.

Next, in time, imitation was again stressed in the wrong way.

Luther then reestablished the true relationship.

But Luther was misused. Imitation was completely left out, and grace became an object of pride.

Imitation is necessary, but not to the point of making us seem important in our own eyes, or of thus wanting to merit salvation. No, grace is the decisive element.

For the proper relationship, grace, and exactly that, must be preached by someone whose life, even the most rigorous, expresses imitation. If he who preaches grace is a man whose life expresses the opposite of imitation, then that is to make grace an object of pride. No. But when grace is preached by someone whose life, even a rigorous life, expresses imitation, then there is the true relationship. Here grace is truly valued. In this case, the more a man has seemed humanly near to merit . . . the truer then will be his preaching that our salvation is pure grace.

We see here again that Christianity is to the extent that its preacher is. So also is it as far from being a doctrine as possible.

(Pap., X 3 A 409)

8. THE PREACHING
OF THE GOSPEL

THE GENIUS AND THE APOSTLE

Finally it became clear to me that the misdirection of speculative philosophy, and its consequent assumed justification for reducing faith to the status of a relative moment, could not be anything accidental, but must be rooted deeply in the entire tendency of the age. It must, in short, doubtless be rooted in the fact that on account of our vastly increased knowledge, men had forgotten what it means to EXIST, and what INWARDNESS signifies.

When I understood this, it also became clear to me that if I desired to communicate anything on this point, it would first of all be necessary to give my exposition an indirect form. For if inwardness is the truth, results are only rubbish with which we should not trouble each other. The communication of results is an unnatural form of intercourse between man and man, in so far as every man is a spiritual being, for whom the truth consists in nothing else than the self-activity of personal appropriation, which the communication of a result tends to prevent. Let a teacher in relation to the essential truth—for otherwise a direct relationship between teacher and pupil is quite in order—have, as we say, much inwardness of feeling, and be willing to publish his doctrines day in and day out; if he assumes the existence of a direct relationship between the learner and himself, his inwardness is not inwardness, but a direct outpouring of feeling; the respect for the learner which recognizes that he is in himself the inwardness of truth, is precisely the teacher's inwardness. Let a learner be enthusiastic, and publish his teacher's praises abroad in the strongest expressions, thus, as we say, giving evidence of his inwardness; this inwardness is not inwardness, but an immediate devotedness; the devout and silent accord, in which the learner by himself assimilates what he has learned, keeping the teacher at a distance because he turns his attention within himself; this is precisely inwardness. Pathos is indeed inwardness, but it is an immediate inwardness, when it is expressed; but pathos in a contrary form is an inwardness which remains with the maker of the communication in spite of being expressed, and cannot be directly appropriated by another except through that other's self-activity; the contrast of the form is the measure of the inwardness. The more complete the contrast of the form, the greater the inwardness, and the less contrast, up to the point of direct communication, the less the inwardness. It may be difficult enough for an enthusiastic genius, who would so gladly make all men happy and bring them to a knowledge of the truth, to learn in this manner to restrain himself, and to give heed to the *nota bene* of reduplication, the truth not being a circular with signatures affixed, but the *valore intrinseco* of inwardness; for an idler and frivolous person this understanding comes more easily. As soon as the truth, the essential truth, may be assumed to be known by everyone, the objective becomes appropriation and inwardness, and here only an indirect form is applicable. The position of an apostle is different, for he has to preach an unknown truth, whence a direct form of communication may in his case have provisional validity.

(*Postscript,* pp. 216–217)

GOD ALONE IS JUDGE

Witness is a form of message exactly equidistant from the direct message and the indirect message. Witness is really direct communication, but without making a motive of the witness' contemporaries. For while he is addressing his *message* to his contemporaries, the witness addresses himself to God and makes of him the motive.

(Pap., X 1 A 235)

BEARING WITNESS

The communication of Christianity must ultimately end in bearing witness, the maieutic form can never be final. For truth, from the Christian point of view, does not lie in the subject, as Socrates understood it, but in a revelation which must be proclaimed.

In Christendom the maieutic form can certainly be used, simply because the majority in fact live under the impression that they are Christians. But since Christianity is Christianity the maieuticer must become the witness.

In the end the maieuticer will not be able to bear the responsibility because the indirect method is ultimately rooted in human intelligence, however much it may be sanctified and consecrated by fear and trembling. God becomes too powerful for the maieuticer and so he is the witness, though different from the direct witness in that he has been through the process of becoming one.

(Journals, n. 809)

A PENITENT CAN PREACH TRUTH BETTER

It can also be seen in the case of Peter. His denial of Christ gave him the impetus for what followed, for he had infinitely much to recapture by his repentance. To have persecuted the faithful gave Paul the impetus, because then he had infinitely much for which to atone.

(Pap., X 3 A 271)

It is existence that preaches, not the tongue. Take three churchmen of different material condition: a prelate, a well-to-do pastor, and a mendicant monk who is a real ascetic. All three preach about the "daily bread" which is requested in the Lord's Prayer; perhaps they say the same things; but is it not the orator, his face, his everyday life that furnishes the interpretation here! And so it is everywhere. That is also what a wicked world takes advantage of out of malice, in the same way that Christianity knows how to instill the necessity of preaching with one's existence so that everything not turn into trickery.

(Pap., X 3 A 307)

When it is Christ who preaches Christianity, what man could tolerate being Christian: Christ is betrayed by everyone.

When it is an apostle, we can, we others, really begin to get down to it.

And then comes the downfall . . . when it is a driveling idiot who preaches, then we are all Christians by the millions.

(Pap., X 3 A 407)

We have been as stingy as possible in making God's word really heard. We read a small slice of it, but the sermon abandons it almost immediately.

So I propose the following:

1. That we take the trouble of reading the entire New Testament, except perhaps the Apocalypse, during the course of the liturgical year.

2. That we read the sermons of orthodox masters of the Church from different periods. . . .

Let Martensen be obliged to read aloud one of Luther's sermons, and even one where Luther talks about speculation. That way no one would have to write against Martensen. . . .

(*Pap.,* X 3 A 534)

CHRISTIAN ELOQUENCE

Chateaubriand, in his *Génie du Christianisme,* speaks of it as something which distinguishes Christianity from paganism, as if it were something that paganism did not have. Tzschirner agrees to this in his letter to Chateaubriand, Leipzig, 1828.

Notice that there is a mistake in that. For in the Christian sense, this whole notion of Christian eloquence is in innumerable ways a piece of misleading information, an indirect proof thrust into the existential order; for then eloquence rises to the same level as the notion, and all political analogies also prove that a flourishing of eloquence has been seen with the decadence of states. Rather, the fact of not having known ecclesiastical eloquence might be the proof of the superior existential capability of paganism. And besides, the pagans had a match for Christian eloquence, that of the sophists. Eloquence is in great part and by its own nature, sophistry; this consists in substituting eloquence for necessary action.

(*Pap.,* X 3 A 648)

CAUSING SCANDAL—BEING SCANDALIZED

Christ cries out: "Woe to those who cause scandal, to those who bring scandal into the world" (Matt. 18, 7)— and yet the possibility of scandal is inseparable from any definition of Christianity. And Christ repeats often enough:

"Happy is the man who is not scandalized by me" (Matt. 11, 6).

Here is the difference. Divine truth is "Truth," but in such a way as to scandalize the world. It cannot be otherwise. But for all that, it cannot be said to cause scandal.

To cause scandal is entirely different. It is, for example, intentionally wanting to deprive a believer of his faith. For when the possibility of scandal is emphasized to strengthen us in the faith, then it is the true preaching of Christianity.

(*Pap.*, X 3 A 333)

THE DIFFERENCE BETWEEN THE ACTOR AND THE PREACHER

One day, Spang told me that he had had some of his most magnificent moments in the pulpit. Ah, yes! Alas! Such an intensification of imagination and emotion is also quite something from an esthetic viewpoint. But who knows if an actor would not say the same things about the silences he provokes in his audience, where you could hear a pin dropped and then suddenly the thunder of applause. [etc.] Who knows if an actor would not also say that he had some of his most magnificient moments on stage through that current which electrifies both actor and audience. And the pastor lays claim to more than that, he who is the same as the "I" speaking as an author.

And then it comes to be said fondly that a pastor feels the need to preach; that after a month or two of not preaching, he feels an emptiness, a regret. [etc.] No, thank you! What is so surprising that the man who has been spoiled by weekly esthetic raptures of the kind where, in an exalted enthusiasm, he rouses and is himself roused by describing faith, hope, love, the highest virtues, the blessedness of suffering [etc.]—what is so surprising in the fact that he should have regrets! When one has fallen into a barrel of liquor, is it so easy not to drink at all?

But where does one find room for the humble existence and action of morality in all of this?

For Mynster, no more than he can walk on his head, it is impossible, against any sort of dialectitian, to show the difference between a preacher and an actor. For the difference between pastor and player is precisely this existential trait of the pastor, that he is poor when he preaches about poverty; outraged, as he preaches about submitting to outrages [etc., etc.,] while the actor's task is to deceive by thrusting aside his own existence, whereas the preacher's task in the deepest sense is to preach through his life. A bit paradoxically, it could be said that preaching is almost the same as being silent; but existentially, it is to express with actions, with one's life, to express, I say, what usually requires words. A fine tone of voice, magnificent gestures [etc.,]—these are all fundamentally superfluous: a dumb man can preach, and so can a completely armless one.

(*Pap.,* X 2 A 149)

THE TORMENTS OF THE PREACHER

It is not wrong to say that we learn by teaching; but it is not always harmless. Thus when a young theologian begins to preach too soon, then it often turns easily against him! For instance, he gets used to portraying the splendor of the faith with all the fire and images he has in his arsenal. His actions, however, are not on a par with his preaching, for lack, up to then, of opportunity, life having hardly tested him yet. Let him realize that he will not at once be what is called an apostle, [etc.,] and it is not rare that he loses all his courage.

(*Pap.,* V A 12)

There is still the question of knowing whether monastic orders will not become necessary again, in order to have pastors or people living only for preaching. It is after all an error, through the Reformation and its political deviation, that Luther's marriage, in opposition to celibacy, should have brought the fact of marriage to be seen as a quasi-perfection. Provided celibacy is correctly understood, religion always needs celibates, especially nowadays.

(*Pap.*, X 3 A 114)

THE GOSPEL IS PREACHED FOR THE POOR

It is not one of Christ's historical remarks: I preach the Gospel for the poor, not—and even the order of the words stresses it—the Gospel is for the poor, where the stress is on the Gospel, that it is preached for the poor.

And by poor is understood not only poverty, but all who suffer, the miserable, the unfortunate, the victims of injustice, the lame, the crippled, lepers, and those possessed by the devil.

It is for them that the Gospel is preached. In other words, it is for them.

For them, the Gospel is the good news.

What good news? Not the kind that says, "here is money, health, recovery, [etc.]." No, no, that would not be Christianity.

No, the Gospel is the following good news for the poor: that to be unhappy in this world—as when human compassion passes you by, and people's instinct for life pushes cruelty into turning your misfortune into a fault—is the sign of the relationship to God, that these poor whom humanity eliminates even more cruelly by calling them guilty, that the Gospel is precisely for these men, for the poor.

It was this way in the beginning. That is the Gospel of the New Testament. It is preached for the poor and by poor men who, if they were not suffering, among other things, would become so in preaching it, for suffering is inseparable from Christianity. It is a matter of course for the audience, the Gospel is for the poor, and suffering always follows and accompanies preaching; the preacher must suffer for the doctrine.

But all that soon changed, and we have never stopped moving towards a greater and greater worldly assurance that this deformity is the Gospel.

For, when preaching Christianity is a livelihood, if possible, a profitable livelihood, well! That is the best way of preaching it . . . for the rich. There is nothing more simple. When preaching Christianity consists in climbing some ladder of rank and position to get as high as possible, to grab medals and decorations, then, yes, then—and that is what not only the preachers but also I myself see—it is the best way of preaching Christianity to the powerful. [etc.]

(*Pap.,* X 4 A 578)

THE SERVICE OF THE TRUTH

But then again, reason, reflection, is certainly also a gift of God. What are we to do with it, or where are we to put it, if we are not supposed to use it? And now if we use it in fear and trembling, not for our own benefit but to serve truth, when we use it thus in fear and trembling, and when, in addition, we believe that it is God in his infinite intensity who tips the scales, when we take risks, putting our trust in God and submitting to his will with an unconditional obedience, then is this not fearing God and serving him as can a man armed with reflection? This is not the same as what the direct man can do, yet it is perhaps serving God with more tenderness than the direct man. But in the case of reflection, a relationship to others, or to a good many others, would still take a maieutic form, a form which expresses fundamentally only a superiority among men. The reality of this superiority cannot be denied; but precisely because the experience proceeds maieutically, existence puts far stronger pressure on the superior man, for he is the stronger, than on the other.

In my case there has been no lack of evidence. All of my edifying discourses are really direct messages. It can only be a question of what—already in my journal of earlier years—has been going on within me for a long time: that is, to explain myself with precision as an author, what I say that I am, and how I understood myself from the start as a religious author.

(Pap., IX A 222)

9. THE VICTORY OF RECONCILIATION IN LOVE

Now what is the situation in this struggle? On one side stood the lover (or we could also call him the good, the noble, for in the first struggle it is not yet entirely clear that he is the lover), and he had the good on his side. On the other side stood the unloving one, fighting with the help of evil. Thus they strove. The lover had the task of maintaining himself in the good so that the evil should not gain power over him. Therefore he had to do not so much with the unloving person as with himself; it was not for the sake of the unloving person but for the sake of the good, also in the noble sense for his own sake, that he strove to win in this struggle. Therefore the two are related combatively yet externally to one another, in a certain sense irreconcilably striving, since the strife is between good and evil; the one strives with the help of the good and the other in league with the evil, and the latter becomes the vanquished.

Now the relationship is altered; it now becomes clearly apparent that it is the lover who is in the struggle, for he battles not only so that the good may come to be in him, but he battles *reconcilingly* in order that the good might be victorious in the unloving one, or he battles *in order to win the vanquished*. Consequently the relationship between the two is no longer an out-and-out relationship of combat, because the lover works on the side of the opponent for his advantage; he wills to battle the cause of the unloving one through to victory.

This is *reconciliation in love*. When the enemy or someone who has done you wrong comes to you and seeks restoration—and you are then willing to forgive: this is truly beautiful and laudable, and also loving. But, O, how slow! Do not say, "I did it *immediately, as soon as* he asked for it"—consider rather in what haste for reconciliation the true lover is compared with this, compared with this haste which by being dependent upon another's haste or slowness in asking for forgiveness is thereby *essentially* slowness, even though on occasion it comes very quickly. Long, long before the enemy thinks of seeking reconciliation, the lover is already reconciled with him; not only this, no, he has gone over to the enemy's side, battles for his cause, even though the enemy does not or does not want to understand it, and works to bring about reconciliation. Indeed, one can call this a battle of love or a battle in love! To battle with the help of the good *against* the enemy—this is laudable and noble; but to battle *for* the enemy—and against whom? —against oneself, if you will: this is, yes, this is loving or this is reconciliation in love! This is the way reconciliation is presented in Holy Scriptures. The words read, "So if you are offering your gift at the altar, and there remember"— yes, now what should one expect would and must follow, most likely that you have something against someone? But it does not continue this way. It reads, and if you "there remember that your brother has something against you, leave your gift there before the altar and go: first to be reconciled to your brother, and then come and offer your gift." But is this not too much to demand? Who is it, then, who needs forgiveness, the one who did wrong or the one who suffered wrong? Certainly he who did wrong is the one who needs forgiveness. But, O, the lover who suffered wrong needs to forgive or needs restoration, reconciliation, words which do not like *forgiveness* make a distinction by remembering right or wrong but in love note that both stand in need. In the perfect sense forgiveness is not reconciliation when forgiveness is asked for; but it is reconciliation to need to forgive beforehand long before the other person is perhaps thinking of seeking forgiveness. Therefore the Scriptures say, "Make friends quickly with your accuser," but one cannot ever be more agreeable than when one himself is the one in need; and one cannot be *quicker* to forgive than when one does it before it is asked for, yes, battles for the opportunity even when it meets resistance—not against the giving but against the receiving of forgiveness. Note well what the relationship is, for the truly Christian is always just the opposite of what the natural man most easily and naturally understands. "To battle for forgiveness"—who does not immediately understand this as battling to get forgiveness?—alas, for humanly speaking this is often difficult enough. And yet this is not at all what we are talking about; we speak here about battling in love so that the other will accept forgiveness, will permit himself to be reconciled. Is not this Christianity? It is indeed God in heaven who through the apostle says, "Be reconciled"; it is not man who says to God: "Forgive us." No, God loved us first; and again it was God who came first a second time, since it had to do with reconciliation—although from the standpoint of justice he certainly was the one who could well have waited. It is the same in relationship between man and man: there is true reconciliation when a person who does not, this is important to note, does not need the forgiveness is the one who offers reconciliation.

And so the lover battles in reconciliation in order to win the vanquished. *To win one vanquished!* What a beautiful linguistic use of the word *win*. Listen, now. When we say *win* a victory, one immediately hears the intensity of the strife. But when we speak of winning someone, to win one for oneself, what infinite mildness there is in it! What is quite so ingratiating as the thought and the expression "to win someone"; how could there now be any thought of strife! Two are required in every strife, and now there is only one: the unloving one, for the lover is in reconciliation his best friend, who wishes to win the vanquished. To win the vanquished. What a wonderful reversal there is in the whole thing! One would think that to win is less than to *over*come, because *over* suggests something which surpasses winning, and yet the discourse here is really on the ascent, is about the higher, although it is about winning one who is overcome. Perhaps in the understanding of pride it is greater to overcome, but in the understanding of love the lesser is the greater, "to win the one overcome." Beautiful strife, more beautiful than a lover's struggle, when the lover must be alone, and therefore all the more loving when he must be alone in battling through to reconciliation! Beautiful victory, most beautiful of all victories, when the lover succeeds in winning the vanquished.

To win one vanquished. Now you see the double victory the discussion is about! For when the lover wills to wage only one battle to overcome evil with good and has finally conquered, then he looks sharp to it that he stands after having conquered all. O, his downfall is only too close at hand if he does not permit love and godly consideration to lead him straightway into the next strife, to win the vanquished. If this is done, he is rightly guided past the dangerous reefs where one becomes proud of having held out in repaying evil with good, where one becomes self-important by having repaid evil with good. For when you go immediately into the next strife, who then becomes the more important one? The very one you strive to win? But then you are not the more important. Precisely this is the humbling which only love can endure, that everything goes backwards, as it were, while one goes forward, that things are reversed: when one himself has overcome all, the vanquished becomes the more important one. Let us suppose that the prodigal son's brother had been willing to do everything for his brother—one thing he still could never have gotten into his head: that the prodigal brother should be the more important one. It is really difficult to get it into one's head; it does not occur to a human being that way.

But to win one vanquished is always difficult and in the relationship we are discussing it involves a special difficulty. It is humiliating to be vanquished; therefore the vanquished person avoids particularly the one who vanquished him, because his downfall becomes greater by contrast and no one makes his downfall more clear than the one who vanquished him. And yet here it is the victor who is to win the vanquished, and consequently they must be brought together. Furthermore, the relationship involves a special difficulty. In less important matters it could be done something like this: in the presence of the vanquished the victor could hide the fact that he was the vanquished, piously deceive him as if it were he who was right, reconcilingly yield even by affirming him to be right where he nevertheless was wrong. We shall not decide to what extent this is ever permissible, but in the relationship under discussion the lover least of all dares to do this. It would be weakness, not love, to delude the unloving person into thinking that he was right in the evil which he did; it would not be reconciliation but treachery which would strengthen him in the evil. No, it is of special importance, and implicit in the work of love, that through the help of love the unloving person becomes clearly aware of how irresponsibly he has acted so that he deeply feels his wrong doing. This the lover has to do, and then he will also win the vanquished—but, no, it is not *also,* for it is one and the same since he truly desires only to win him to himself or to win him to truth and to himself, not to win him to himself by deceiving him. But the more deeply the vanquished comes to feel his wrong and to that extent his downfall, the more he feels himself thrust away from him who—in love deals him this *coup de grâce.* What a difficult task: simultaneously to thrust away from oneself and to win to oneself, simultaneously to be rigorous as the truth requires and yet be mild in such a way as love desires in order to win the one against whom rigour is employed! Truly it is a miracle if it succeeds, because it is, like everything Christian, directly opposite to the proverb: One cannot do two things at the same time. That the vanquished looks for the place where he falsely gets the easiest examination is easy to understand; but to win him to oneself with the help of truth's rigorous examination—this is difficult.

The deliberation now pauses in the task. Consider what would happen if the unloving person were pitted against another unloving one who had nourished and excited all his evil passions. Consider this *while you pause in order to see rightly how the lover conducts himself.*

The unloving one is vanquished. But what is the significance here of his being overcome? It means that he is vanquished by the good, the true. And what is it the lover wants? He wants to win him for the good and the true. But to be overcome, if this means to be won for the good and the true—is this so humiliating? Pay attention now to love and reconciliation. The lover gives no indication at all, nor does it even occur to him, that he is the one who has conquered, that he is the victorious master—no, it is the good which has conquered. In order to remove the humiliation and mortification, the lover interpolates something higher between the unloving one and himself and thereby gets himself out of the way. When there is no third in the relationship between man and man, and every such relationship becomes unsound, either too ardent or embittered. The third, which thinkers would call the idea, is the true, the good, or more accurately, the God-relationship; this third is a cooling factor in certain phases of a relationship and in others a soothing agent. In truth, the lover is too loving to take a posture over against the vanquished and himself be the victor who revels in the victory—while the other is the vanquished; it is simply unloving to want to be master of another person in this way. With the help of the third, which the lover gets placed between them, both are humbled: for the lover humbles himself before the good, whose needy servant he is, and, as he himself admits, in frailty; and the vanquished one humbles himself not before the lover but before the good. But when both are humbled in a relationship, there is no humiliation for either one of them alone. How resourceful love can be, what a handyman it is! Would you rather, as you say, that I should speak more seriously? O, you can be sure that the lover thinks it best for me to speak in this way, for there is a joy, even over the success of a concern rooted in the earnestness of the eternal, which makes one prefer to speak in this way. Furthermore, there is in this way of speaking a kind of shyness and to that extent again a concern for the one who is in the wrong. Often, perhaps, a reconciliation in love does not succeed, alas, because one goes at it too earnestly; this is because one has not learned from God (and this one learns from God) to be earnest enough himself to be able to go about it as lightly as the truth actually permits. Do not ever believe that earnestness is surliness; do not ever believe that earnestness is the grim countenance which spreads evil on sight: no one was ever earnest who has not learned from earnestness that one can also seem too earnest. If it has really become second nature to you to will to win your enemy, you will become so familiar with this kind of task that they will concern you as technical problems. When a fresh influx of love is continuously in you, when this supply is in order, then there is also time enough for being resourceful. But when there is resistance within the person himself, when in observing the rigorous commandment of love one has to force himself to go out to reconcile himself with his enemy, the matter easily becomes too serious and fails precisely because of—great earnestness. But this "great earnestness," however estimable it may be, particularly in contrast to irreconcilability, is not something we should strive for. No, the true lover is indeed resourceful.

(*Works of Love,* pp. 309–314)

10. GOD IS LOVE

Deep down in my soul you implanted the blessed assurance that you are love. You treated me paternally, like a child, and impressed the same thing upon me a second time, and proved to me that you were love. Then you were silent for a moment; you wished me to try my strength a little without the proof, to see whether I could do as much without the proof. Then all grew confused for me. I grew so frightened and afraid, imagining too that it was infinitely above me, and I was afraid I had gone too far, had been too forward, that I had tried you too long and that it was therefore a punishment that this should happen to me. . . .

(Journals, n. 1117)

GOD AS FATHER—A HUMAN FATHER

God is pure spirit. If you will not be such that God can be your father, then neither is he your father, he neither can be, nor desires to be so.

But then there is another distinction. It is not unknown that when a son returns repentant to his father, the father hardens his heart and will not forgive him. With God that

never happens; the moment you honestly desire it, God is
your father.

(Journals, n. 1181)

"He who sees his brother in need and closes his heart"
(1 John 3, 17)

Yes, he immediately closes the door to God also.

Love of God and love of neighbor are like two doors
that open at the same time; it is impossible to open one without also opening the other, and impossible to close one
without closing the other.

(Pap., X 3 A 739)

*The most blessed consolation, the eternally certain proof
that I am loved by God.*

This is the syllogism. Love (true love, not self-love which
only loves the remarkable, the brilliant and consequently
really loves itself) stands in inverse ratio to the greatness
and excellence of the object. And so if I am of infinitely,
infinitely little importance, if in my wretchedness I feel
myself to be the most miserable of all: then it is eternally,
eternally certain that God loves me.

Christ says: not a sparrow shall fall to earth unless it be
at his will. Oh, I bid lower still, to God I am less than a
sparrow—that God loves me becomes more certain still,
the syllogism more solid still in its conclusion.

It might seem to the Emperor of Russia that God could
overlook him, God has so much to attend to and the Emperor of Russia is so great. But not a sparrow—for God is
love, and love is in inverse ratio to the greatness and excellence of the object.

You feel lost in the world in your suffering, no one cares
for you, alas, and you conclude, neither does God care for
me. You fool! you traducer, to speak thus of God. No, if

there were anyone of whom it were literally true that he was of all the most neglected—he is the one whom God loves. Or if he were not quite the most neglected, if he still had a little human consolation—and that were taken from him: in the very same moment it would be more certain still that God loves him.

(*Journals,* n. 1213)

11. PRAYERS

The most important thing in life is to be in the correct position. This the Christian assumes in relation to the next day; for to him it is non-existent.—It is well known that in front of the actor, blinded as he is by the footlights, there is the deepest darkness, the blackest night. One might think that this would discompose him, render him uneasy. But no, ask him, and thou shalt hear him admit that this is precisely what gives him support, makes him calm, keeps him in the enchantment of deception. On the other hand, it would discompose him if he could see any single individual, catch a glimpse of an auditor. So it is with the next day. One sometimes complains and finds it tragic that the future is so dark before one. Ah, the misfortune is just this, that it is not dark enough when fear and presentiment and expectation and earthly impatience glimpse the next day! One who rows a boat turns his back to the goal towards which he labours. So it is with the next day. When by the help of eternity a man lives absorbed in today, he turns his back to the next day. The more he is eternally absorbed in today, the more decisively does he turn his back upon the next day, so that he does not see it at all. If he turns around, eternity is confused before his eyes, it becomes the next day. But if for the sake of labouring more effectually towards the goal (eternity) he turns his back, he does not see the next day at all, whereas by the help of eternity he sees quite clearly today and its task. But if a man is to labour effectually today, he must be in this position. It always involves delay and distraction to want to look impatiently every instant towards the goal, to see if one is coming a little nearer, and now a little nearer. No, be eternally and seriously resolved, then thou dost turn completely to the labour . . . and turn the back to the goal. Such is one's position in rowing a boat, but such is also the position when one believes. One might think that the believer would be very far from the eternal when he turns his back to it and lives today, while the glimpser stands and looks towards it. And yet it is the believer who is nearest the eternal, while the apocalyptic visionary is farthest from the eternal. Faith turns its back to the eternal in order precisely to have this with him today. But if a man turns, especially with earthly passion, towards the future, then he is farthest from the eternal, and then the next day becomes a prodigious confused figure such as fairy-tales describe. Just as those demons of whom we read in the Book of Genesis begat children by earthly women, so is the future the monstrous demon which of men's womanish imagination begets the next day.

But the Christian believes, therefore he is quit of the next day. The Christian assumes exactly the opposite position to that of the self-tormentors; for these forget today entirely by reason of their anxiety and preoccupation with the next day. The believer is present, and at the same time is, as this word also denotes in Latin, mighty. The self-tormentor is an absentee, and an enfeebled person. The wish is often heard in the world to be contemporary with one or another great event or great man, with the notion that contemporaneousness might develop a man and make him something great. Perhaps! But might it not be worth more than a wish to be contemporary with oneself? For how rare it is for a man to be contemporary with himself. Most men, in feeling, in imagination, in purpose, in resolution, in wish, in longing, in apocalyptic vision, in theatrical make-

believe, are a hundred thousand miles in advance of themselves, or several human generations in advance of themselves. But the believer (being present) is in the highest
sense contemporary with himself. And to be by the help of
eternity entirely contemporary with oneself is at the same
time the thing that most educates and develops, it is the
'great gain' of eternity. Therefore the Christian extols a
saying of Sirach (xxx. 23), as one of the severest of the
Church Fathers does, not as a rule of shrewdness but as an
expression of godliness: 'Love thy soul, and comfort thy
heart, and drive care far from thee.' Who indeed is so cruel
as the self-tormentor is towards himself! But all his pangs,
all these cruelly invented and cruelly employed instruments
of agonizing torture are comprised in this one word: the
next day. And now for the cure of it! It is related that in a
library in Spain there was found a book bearing this inscrip-
tion on the cover: 'The Best Cure for Heretics'. One opened
it, or rather tried to; and, lo, it was not a book, it was a
case containing a scourge. If one were to write a book
entitled 'The Best Cure for Self-Torment,' it could be written briefly: 'Let every day have enough in its own worries.'
Hence when the Christian works, or when he prays, he
talks only of today: he prays for the daily bread 'today', for
a blessing upon his work 'today', that he may avoid the
snares of the evil one 'today', that he may come nearer to
God's kingdom 'today'. For if a man who had become
acquainted with this terror were to pray thus in the passion
of his soul, 'Save me, O God, from myself and from the
next day', he would not be praying Christianly, and the
next day would already have acquired too much power
over him. For the Christian prays, 'Save me today from the
evil.' This is the surest salvation from the next day, with
the understanding that one will pray thus every day; if for
one day this is forgotten, the next day comes at once into
view. But the Christian does not forget to pray every day,
hence he saves himself throughout his life, faith saves his

courage, his joy, his hope. The dreadful enemy is on hand the next day, but the Christian does not paint the devil on the wall, does not conjure up evil and temptation, he does not talk at all of the next day, but only of today, and of this he talks with God.

(*Christian Discourses,* pp. 76–78)

O Lord Jesus Christ, fill my thoughts that it might be seen on me that I am thinking of you! And how can this be seen? . . . in my face turned up toward heaven? But that could just as well mean that I was looking for stars or dreams or visions. No! Let your image convince me, poor, despised, mocked, to preach your doctrine . . . then people would be able to see, not in my upturned gaze, but in my everyday, banal countenance, that I am thinking of you.

Oh heavenly powers! You who uphold the good, heavenly legions, help me to lift my voice so that, were it possible, it might be heard throughout the world—I have but one word, a single word to say. But if the power of saying nothing save one word or one phrase were granted me, the power of saying something that would be so firmly implanted as to be never forgotten, I have made my choice. Here is what I would say: do not forget, Christendom, Our Lord Jesus Christ was nothing!

(*Pap.,* X 3 A 11)

How rare it is to be able to say an unreserved *Amen* to a prayer! How rarely, if ever, has this happened even to someone who habitually prays with zeal and perseverance! It is even more rare than that moment of love where the lovers are absolutely one another's ideal. To say *Amen* so that there is not a word, not a single word to add; when *Amen* is that unique word which satisfies and fulfills! To have prayed so that every need is satisfied in the outpouring of prayer, so that we have said all that was in our hearts, to have said it completely, that is, to have become transparent to ourselves before God, in all our weakness, but also in all our hope! Oh! There are moments, and you have perhaps felt them often enough. There are moments when the treasures of language seem insufficient to give form to your torments, insufficient to express what you feel in your heart of hearts. But now this would be the opposite of such a moment; all the words of our language would be superfluous. What if they have all been forgotten? They are no longer needed. There is nothing to add but the *Amen!*

(Pap., IX A 24)

Here is an excellent remark which I read in Scriver, and for which he credits another author without naming him: Prayer is the daughter of the faith, but the daughter must support her mother.

(Pap., X 3 A 531)

"Every man who is preoccupied, afflicted, suffering, can find consolation only in prayer." Yes, it is true, quite true; but notice the following. Our prayer to God, we ordinary humans, is for an end to suffering, for the granting of better times, and thus do we find consolation in prayer. But the prayer of the witness of truth is for God to strengthen him that he might stand fast in suffering. His prayer sinks him deeper and deeper into suffering. The more fervent it is and the closer he is to God, the more he engages himself in suffering. Do you have the courage to pray like that?

(Pap., X 4 A 565)

Luke 24, 28. "And he made as if to go on, and they pressed him to stay with them, saying, 'stay with us for it is almost evening and the day is almost over'; so he went in to stay with them."

This is an imaginative expression of the relationship of the believer to Christ as his model. In one step, the model draws so far away that the believer feels himself reduced to nothing. Yet it is still necessary for the believer to go on trying. That is why the model must give in a bit. Then, despite their infinite imperfection, they still draw near. But then, often enough, it seems for a moment that the model would want "to go on," and so far that the believer following behind feels lost . . . and then begs him, "stay with me." This delay is a need for man, although it is a passion for patience in the model.

(Pap., X 2 A 347)

You who take care of the sparrow without requiring of him that he be like you; you who tenderly care for the sparrow by putting yourself in his place with the concern of father; you also take good care of man. And even if you demand of man an effort with respect to your image which you cannot demand of the sparrow, it is still without cruelty that you demand it of him. No, but with a father's concern, you put yourself in his place, and it is you who give him the strength to make the effort.

(Pap., X 2 A 342)

PRAYER

Lord Jesus Christ! A whole life long didst thou suffer that I too might be saved: and yet thy suffering is not yet at an end; but this too wilt thou endure, saving and redeeming me, this patient suffering of having to do with me, I who so often go astray from the right path, or even when I remained on the straight path stumbled along it or crept so slowly along the right path. Infinite patience, suffering of infinite patience. How many times have I not been impatient, wished to give up and forsake everything, wished to take the terribly easy way out, despair: but thou didst not lose patience. Oh, I cannot say what thy chosen servant says: that he filled up that which is behind of the afflictions of Christ in his flesh; no, I can only say that I increased thy sufferings, added new ones to those which thou didst once suffer in order to save me.

(Journals, n. 1030)

It is in a frail clay vase that we men carry the Most Holy. But you, Oh Holy Spirit, when you live in a man, then you live in what is infinitely inferior! You, spirit of holiness, you live in impurity and stain; you, spirit of wisdom, you inhabit folly; you, spirit of truth, you inhabit deceit! Oh live in me as a dwelling place! And you who seek not the comforts of a desirable home, which you would surely seek in vain, you who create and regenerate and make yourself a home, live in me as a dwelling place, so that one day you may finally be pleased with this home which you have prepared yourself in the stains, the malice, and the deceptions of my heart!

(Pap., X 2 A 344)

INDEX